$4.00

THE Baseball ◇ Research JOURNAL

As usual, we have many fascinating articles—statistical, historical, and a mixture of both—in this issue of *BRJ*. Tom Shieber's lead piece is a wonderful example of basic SABR research, which deserves a place on the required-reading list of anyone who wants a complete picture of the game. One special article, by Eddie Gold, is about John Tattersall, an early SABR member and creator of the Tattersall Homerun Log, which we hope will soon be made public in updated form.

We've also got Al Kermisch (what would a *Research Journal* be without his researcher's notebook?), David Voigt, and a sprinkling of the usual suspects I seem to round up every year as SABR's Claude Raines. Thankfully, we also have lots of first-time authors, whose work is so vital to the health of our Society. Geographically, we stretch from North Dakota to the Dominican Republic, and chronologically from 1845 to the late, lamented 1994 season.

—M.A.

Editor: Mark Alvarez
Designated Reader: Dick Thompson

THE BASEBALL RESEARCH JOURNAL (ISSN 0734-6891, ISBN 0-910137-57-9) Number 23. Published by The Society for Am... nd, OH, 44101. Postage paid at Birmingha... ...search, Inc. All rights reserved. Reprodu... ...hibited. Printed by EBSCO Media, Birmi...

The Society for American Baseball Research

History

The Society for American Baseball Research (SABR) was founded on August 10, 1971, by L. Robert "Bob" Davids and fifteen other baseball researchers at Cooperstown, New York, and now boasts more than 6,500 members worldwide. The Society's objectives are to foster the study of baseball as a significant American institution, to establish an accurate historical account of baseball through the years, to facilitate the dissemination of baseball research information, to stimulate the best interest of baseball as our national pastime, and to cooperate in safeguarding proprietary interests of individual research efforts of members of the Society.

Baseball Research Journal

The Society published its first annual *Baseball Research Journal* in January 1972. The present volume is the twenty-third. Most of the previous volumes are still available for purchase (see page 112). The editorial policy is to publish a cross section of research articles by our members which reflect their interest in history, biography, statistics and other aspects of baseball not previously published.

Interested in Joining the Society?

SABR membership is open to all those interested in baseball research, statistics or history. The 1995 membership dues are $35 US, $45 Canada & Mexico and $50 overseas (US funds only) and are based on the calendar year. Members receive the *Baseball Research Journal*, *The National Pastime*, *The SABR Bulletin*, and other special publications. To join SABR, use the form found on the bottom of the publication order form found on page 112. For further information, contact the SABR office at the address or phone below:

SABR
Dept. BRJ
PO Box 93183
Cleveland OH 44101
216-575-0500

The Evolution of the Baseball Diamond

Perfection came slowly

Tom Shieber

Red Smith once wrote: "Ninety feet between bases is the nearest to perfection that man has yet achieved."[1] Technically, this statement is incorrect: there has never been 90 feet between bases. In fact, in the nineteenth century, the distance between bases often varied from season to season as changes in the rules altered the placement of the bases on the infield diamond.[2] This "perfection" of the baseball diamond did not occur spontaneously, but evolved through more than 50 years of tinkering with the rules of baseball.

The modern baseball diamond is a square with sides 90 feet in length, and is used as an aid in the positioning of the bases and base lines. The term "diamond" was used early in the history of the game to differentiate the infield configuration of the "New York" game of baseball from that used in the "Massachusetts" game. In the New York game the batter, or striker, stood at the bottom corner of the infield, thus viewing a diamond-like positioning of the bases. However, the batter in the Massachusetts game would view the infield as a rectangle.

The positioning, orientation, size and make-up of the bases on the infield diamond were not always explicitly stated in the rules of the game. This lack of definition is not unusual, as much of the game itself was not detailed in the early rules. Rather than defining the game of baseball and how it was to be played,

Plate A

these early rules were used to differentiate the particular version of baseball being played from other similar baseball-like games of the era. Nevertheless, it is possible to trace the basic evolution of the baseball diamond.

The Amateur Era—The New York Knickerbocker Base Ball Club, formally organized in 1845, established the first written rules of baseball.[3] Of the original 20 rules, only 14 actually pertained to the game of baseball, and the remaining six concerned club matters. Of the 14 game rules, only the first re-

Tom Shieber operates a solar telescope at mt. Wilson Observatory in Southern California. He currently chairs the SABR Pictorial History Committee.

lated to the layout of the playing field: "1. The bases shall be from 'home' to second base, 42 paces; from first to third base, 42 paces, equidistant." Simple application of the Pythagorean theorem shows that a square whose diagonal is 42 paces has sides of slightly less than 30 paces. The Knickerbocker rules made no mention of the exact placement or size of the bases in the infield.

In 1856, an article in the December 13 issue of the *New York Clipper* listed the rules of baseball. These rules were essentially identical to the original Knickerbocker rules and were published along with a rudimentary diagram of the baseball infield. Unfortunately, the inaccuracies of the diagram render it useless in determining the exact orientation and positions of the bases of the era. In fact, the diagram shows the distance from home to second base to be noticeably longer than the distance from first to third base, though the rules clearly specify equal distances.[4] (see plate A.)

The first convention of baseball players was held in 1857, and a new set of rules, 35 in number, was adopted.[5] Sections 3 and 4 of these rules relate to the layout of the baseball diamond:

> 3. The bases must be four in number, placed at equal distances from each other, and securely fastened upon the four corners of a square, whose sides are respectively thirty yards. They must be so constructed as to be distinctly seen by the umpires and referee, and must cover a space equal to one square foot of surface; the first, second, and third bases shall be canvas bags, painted white, and filled with sand or saw-dust; the home base and pitcher's point to be each marked by a flat circular iron plate, painted or enameled white.

> 4. The base from which the ball is struck shall be designated the home base, and must be directly opposite to the second base; the first base must always be that upon the right hand, and the third base that upon the left hand side of the striker, when occupying his position at the home base.[6]

Rule 3, defining the size of the infield square, was carefully constructed so as to avoid the use of the word "pace." According to Daniel Adams, Knickerbocker club member and 1857 president of what would later be known as the National Associa-

tion of Base Ball Players, this rule was rewritten to simply clarify the distances on the ball field, the word "pace" being "rather vague."[7]

Adams' statement implies that the wording of the new rule did not change the size of the infield. Thus, the "pace" was meant to be understood as a measurement approximately equal to three feet. Yet, even today the meaning of the Knickerbocker "pace" is the subject of debate. Some baseball scholars believe the word "pace" should be interpreted as an exact measurement, which, during the 1840s, was defined as 2-1/2 feet.[8] Given a pace of 2-1/2 feet and again employing the Pythagorean theorem, each side of the infield diamond would be roughly 74-1/2 feet in length. Other historians take the point of view that a pace, being a unit of measurement defined solely by the individual doing the pacing, allowed for a scalable diamond dependent on the size of the players. Therefore, since a child's pace is smaller than that of an adult, the diamond as laid out by a child would be proportionally smaller than the adult's diamond.[9]

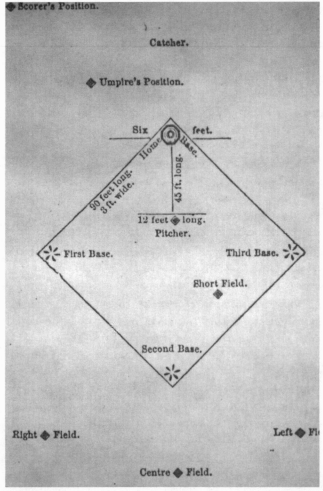

Plate B

Plate C

With the question of the true meaning of the pace yet unanswered, the exact size of the Knickerbocker infield square remains uncertain. The first baseball annual, *Beadle's Dime Base-Ball Player*, was published in 1860. In this guide, the rules regarding the baseball diamond remained unchanged from those adopted at the 1857 convention, but an accompanying diagram was new. The first, second, and third bases are represented by asterisks (certainly not representative of their actual shape), and home base is represented by the curious figure of an octagon inscribed within a slightly larger octagon (see plate B). Whereas home base was clearly stipulated to be circular, early drawings of baseball games often showed home base as having a smaller circle inscribed upon the plate (see plate C).

Following the official rules section of the 1860 *Beadle's* guide is an explanatory section in which editor Henry Chadwick reviewed and elaborated upon some of the rules of the game. With regard to home base, Chadwick stated that it should be "not less than nine inches in diameter."[10] Though there are numerous drawings, there is only one known photograph showing the circular home base (see plate D).

With regard to the first, second, and third bases, Chadwick stated that: "The proper size of a base is about fourteen inches by seventeen; but as long as it covers one square foot of ground ... the requirements of the rules will be fulfilled."[11] Note that the official rule required the base to "cover," not necessarily "be," one square foot of surface. Thus, by Chadwick's interpretation of the rule, any base that covers an area greater

than or equal to 12 square inches is legal.[12] Unfortunately, there are no known photographs or drawings clearly showing the bases of the era to be rectangular. The drawings and photographs that do exist show bases that appear to be square, or quite close to square.[13] Nevertheless, the explanatory section in every *Beadle's* guide up to and including that of 1871 states that the proper size of a base was 14 by 17 inches.

The rules as published in the 1861 *Beadle's* guide contained an addition to section 4:

> And in all match games, a line connecting the home and first base and the home and third base, shall be marked by the use of chalk, or other suitable material, so as to be distinctly seen by the umpire.[14]

The purpose of this rule was to aid the umpire in determining whether a hit ball was fair or foul.[15]

There were no further rule changes with regard to the layout of the baseball diamond until 1868. However, the 1867 *Beadle's* guide featured a departure from the old diagram of the baseball field to a more accurate representation of the infield. The bases are shown with their correct shapes, and, presumably, in their correct positions on the infield square (see plate E). Though the rules still did not explicitly state how the bases were to be oriented in the infield, the diagram implied that all four bases were to be centered on their respective corners of the infield square and that the first, second, and third bases were to be positioned such that two corners of each base touched the base lines. In other words, the bases were rotated

Plate D

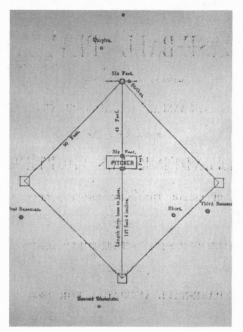

Plate E

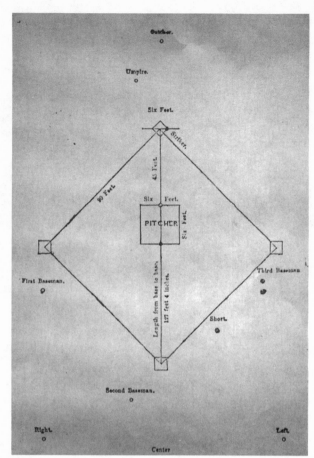

Plate G

45 degrees from their more familiar, modern orientation. This strange orientation of the bases is clearly seen in a number of drawings of ball games of the era (see plate F).

A major change in the rules regarding the layout of the baseball diamond occurred for the 1868 season, the first such change since the Knickerbocker rules had been written down more than 20 years before: The words "circular iron" were stricken from section 3 of the official rules. With this change, the rule regarding the size of the other bases was applied to home base as well: home base to "cover a space equal to one square foot of surface."[16] The official rules as published in the 1868 *Beadle's* guide noted this change in the shape of home base, but the same guide's infield diagram and explanatory section failed to reflect this change.[17] By the following year these mistakes were rectified. Interestingly, while the official rules still failed to stipulate the exact positioning of the bases on the infield square, the 1869 *Beadle's* diagram implied that, unlike the first, second, and third bases, home base was to be oriented with its sides parallel to the base lines (see plate G).

For most of its life, *DeWitt's Base Ball Guide* was, like *Beadle's*, edited by Henry Chadwick. It, too, contained an explanatory section elaborating upon the rules and play of the game. In the explanatory section of the 1869 *DeWitt's* guide, Chadwick stated that all four bases "should be at least eighteen inches square, although the rules prescribe that they shall cover one square foot of surface."[18] Meanwhile, the explanatory section in the 1869 *Beadle's* guide still stated that the bases should be "about fourteen inches by seventeen." Chadwick's contradictory statements as published in the two guides were repeated for three years. In 1872, the discrepancy was resolved when both guides simply dropped the sections that included the suggested base sizes.

An additional change to the official rules of 1868 occurred with the following amendment to section 4: "The base bag shall be considered the base, and not the post to which it is, or should be, fastened."[19] No doubt, the previous season (or seasons) saw occurrences of bases becoming dislodged from their original position, leaving both runner and fielder dumbfounded as to which one was the true base. The post was a block of wood or stone, sunk into the infield ground and level with the playing surface, to which the bases were attached by stakes (see plate D).

Plate F

The Openly Professional Era—With the exception of one minor alteration to the rules, the layout of the infield diamond remained unchanged as the era of openly professional teams dawned. Starting with the season of 1872, home base was no longer to be made of iron, but of "white marble or stone, so fixed in the ground as to be even with the surface."[20]

Whereas diagrams of the baseball infield had long since shown first, second, and third bases centered on their respective corners of the diamond, not until 1874 did the rules officially require this placement. The exact positioning of home, first, and third (but technically not second) base was implied in a new foul line rule (rule 5, section 8) stating:

> The foul ball lines shall be unlimited in length, and shall run from the center of the home base through the center of the first and the third base to the foul ball posts....[21]

A change in the exact positioning of home base occurred for the season of 1874. An addition to rule 1, section 6, required home to be "with one corner of it facing the pitcher's position."[22] This orientation had been implied in diagrams of the baseball infield since 1869. Furthermore, since 1869, Chadwick's explanatory section of the *Beadle's* guide mentioned this orientation of home base.[23] The reason behind the clarification of home base's orientation was simple and well explained by Chadwick in the 1874 *DeWitt's* guide:

> The [home] base [is] to be fixed in the ground with one corner pointing towards the pitcher's position, so as to insure the pitcher's having the full width of the home base to pitch over, instead of the one foot of width he would have were the base to be placed with the square side facing him.[24]

The rules for the season of 1875 further clarified the position of home base. An addition to rule 1, section 6, required that home base be positioned such that the corner that faces the pitcher "touch the foul ball lines where they meet at the home base corner."[25] This amendment moved home base from a position centered on its corner of the infield diamond to a location completely in foul territory. While the infield diagram found in the 1875 *Beadle's* guide failed to reflect this move of home base, the diagram in the *DeWitt's* guide of that year did show the change.

To understand the reason behind this rule change, it is necessary to review what was known as the "fair-foul" hit. The fair-foul hit was a particular technique of hitting that took advantage of the fair and foul ball rules of the day. These rules, from "Rule V - The Batting Department," were as follows:

> 11) If the ball from a fair stroke of the bat first touches the ground, the person of a player, or any other object, either in front of, or on, the foul ball lines, it shall be considered fair.

> 12) If the ball from a fair stroke of the bat first touches the ground, the person of a player, or any other object behind the foul ball lines, it shall be declared foul; and the ball so hit shall be called foul by the umpire even before touching the ground, if it be seen falling foul.[26]

In summary, a ball that initially landed in fair territory, regardless of whether it stayed in fair territory or whether it passed first or third base in fair territory, was a fair ball. A fair-foul hit was one in which the batter deftly hit the ball such that it first touched the ground in fair territory and then bounded into foul territory. Often the fielders would have to run a great distance into foul territory to retrieve such a hit ball. To shorten this distance, the first and third basemen would play quite close to the foul lines, which subsequently opened up large gaps in the infield and allowed what would otherwise be easy ground ball outs to safely make it to the outfield as hits.

Henry Chadwick, among others, was eager to lessen the impact of the fair-foul hit. To meet this end, he proposed adding a tenth man (or "right shortstop") to each team so that the large gaps in the infield would be narrowed.[27] Chadwick popularized this idea by writing special sections in both the *Beadle's* and *DeWitt's* guides of 1874 suggesting the use of the 10-man rule. However, though the *Beadle's* guide of 1875 as well as the *DeWitt's* guides from 1875 to 1882 continued to have sections clearly implying that the 10-man rule was the norm for organized baseball, the 10-man game was never adopted into the official rules of the game.

The rule change for 1875 called for home base to move from its former position, centered on its corner of the diamond, back approximately 8-1/2 inches, such that it was located completely in foul territory. This change also moved the batter back a distance into foul territory and thus made it more difficult for him to successfully make a fair-foul hit.[28] This change

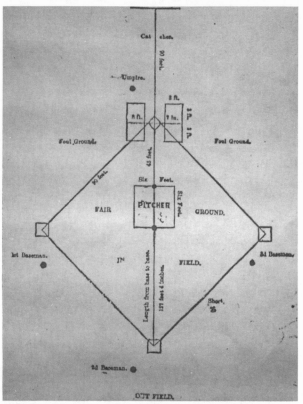

Plate H

in the batter's position did not solve the "problem" of fair-foul hitting; in 1877, the fair-foul hit was eliminated from the game altogether by changing the definition of a fair ball essentially to the modern rule.

The Emergence of the National League—For 1876, the inaugural season of the National League, the rules of the game called for an infield diamond that had the following characteristics: The four bases each covered 12 inches square; home base was located in foul territory, its front corner touching the junction of the first and third base lines; the first, second, and third bases were centered on their respective corners of the infield square, and oriented such that two corners of each base touched the base lines. The orientation of the first, second, and third bases, as well as the exact position of the second base, were still only implied by the diagrams that supplemented the published rules. Furthermore, while the diagram printed in the new 1876 *Spalding's Official Base Ball Guide* correctly showed this layout of the infield, the diagram in the 1876 *Beadle's* guide still failed to show home base in foul territory.

For the year of 1876 alone, the rules in both *Beadle's* and *DeWitt's* guides, but not those in the *Spalding* guide, allowed home base to be composed of wood. By the following year, however, none of the guides mentioned a wooden home base.

Two major changes in the infield diamond rules were introduced for the season of 1877. The first change moved home base for the second time in three years. This time home base was to be positioned "wholly within the diamond. One corner of said base shall face the pitcher's position, and two sides shall form part of the foul lines."[29] With this change, and after two years of printing erroneous diagrams, the 1877 *Beadle's* guide finally contained a diagram that correctly reflected the state of the infield diamond, home base being shown completely in fair territory.

The second infield change for 1877 concerned the size of the bases. "The first, second and third bases must cover a space equal to fifteen inches square...."[30] Home base remained a square foot in size.

Whereas the infield diagram in the 1877 *Beadle's* guide still showed the first, second, and third bases rotated 45 degrees from their current orientation (see plate H), the diagrams in the 1877 *DeWitt's* and *Spalding* guides no longer showed the bases in this skewed orientation. Instead, they showed the base sides parallel to the base paths, as they are today. Nevertheless, the orientation of these bases was not explicitly stated in the official rules at the time.[31]

The 1880s—Prior to the 1880 season, the official rules of the game were completely rewritten, rearranged, and, in general, improved. Though much of the wording regarding the layout of the infield diamond was altered, the state of the infield itself remained unchanged. However, the positioning of the first, second, and third bases was made explicit by new wording of the rules: "...the center of each [base] shall be upon a separate corner of the infield...."[32]

No further changes were made to the rules regarding the baseball diamond until 1885. For that season, it was no longer acceptable to have home base made of marble. Home could now be composed only of "white rubber or white stone."[33] The change was made to help prevent players from slipping on the slick marble plate.[34] The rules of the three-year old American Association departed from those of the National League and called for white rubber home bases only.

The only major differences between the infield diamond of 1885 and that of over a century later are the positions of the first and third bases, and the shape of the home base (see plate J). Whereas photographs of the square home base of the era are numerous, clear pictures of the first and third base bags centered on the base paths are quite difficult to locate. This posi-

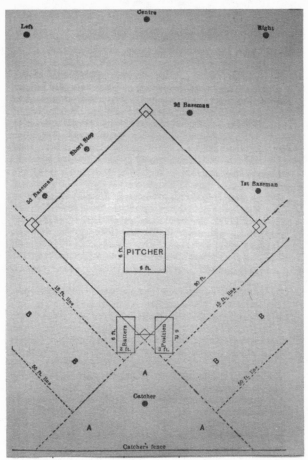

Plate J

to whether the ball was fair or foul. A ball hitting the half of the base that was in fair territory was a fair ball, while a ball hitting the other half of the base was a foul ball. At times, deciding which half of the base had been hit was practically impossible. Moving first and third base completely into fair territory made the decision academic: if the ball hit the base, it had to be a fair ball.

Note that according to the wording of the rule, the first and third bases were to be positioned such that they straddle the base lines to and from second base. However, the diagram that accompanied the rules in the 1887 *Spalding* guide shows the bases positioned as they are today, neatly nestled in their repective corners of the 90-foot infield square (see Plate L). Interestingly, it was the diagram, not the wording of the rule, that prevailed. To this day, second base remains "upon its corner of the infield," while the first and third bases lie wholly within the diamond. This rather strange positioning of second base is often overlooked in modern-day representations of the baseball diamond. Even the cover of *The Macmillan Baseball Encyclopedia* shows an infield diamond with second base erroneously placed wholly within the ninety-foot infield square. Modern day rules avoid any possible conflict between the written rule and the diagram by essentially stating that the diamond should be laid out so that it looks like the diagram

tioning of the bases is best seen in a photograph that was taken prior to the April 29, 1886, opening day game at the Polo Grounds in New York City (see plate K).

The year 1887 brought about a single set of rules embraced by both the National League and the American Association. The two leagues compromised with regard to the layout of the infield diamond: the National League adopted the American Association rule requiring home base to be made only of white rubber. Furthermore, the rules for this season altered the positions of the bases:

> The first, second and third bases must be...so placed that the center of the second base shall be upon its corner of the infield, and the center of the first and third bases shall be on the lines running to and from second base and seven and one-half inches from the foul lines, providing that each base be entirely within the foul lines.[35]

Why change the positions of first and third base? Prior to 1887, if a batted ball hit first or third base, the umpire was faced with a most difficult decision as

Plate K

CORRECT DIAGRAM OF A BALL GROUND

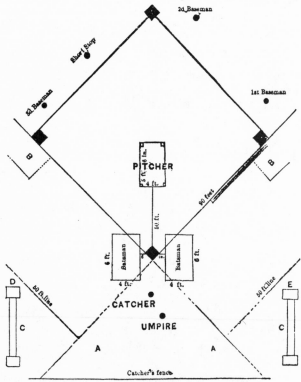

A. A. A.—Ground reserved for Umpire, Batsman and Catcher.
B. B.   —Ground reserved for Captain and Assistant.
C.—Players' Bench.   D.—Visiting Players' Bat Rack.
E.—Home Players' Bat Rack.

Plate L

supplied.

The Modern Baseball Diamond—In 1894, a new, more mathematical and geometrical diagram of the baseball diamond accompanied the *Spalding* guide rules.[36] While the actual layout of the diamond did not change, it was now more precisely defined with labeled points and angles. Henry Chadwick thought the new, complicated description of the infield a bit ridiculous:

> The diagram of the diamond needs a surveyor to lay it out so that it might be made comprehensible to amateurs and novices in the game. What with its "arcs" and its "radiuses" and its algebraic style of description, it is likely to be a greek puzzle to foreign votaries of the game.[37]

As the turn of the century approached, the infield diamond was basically identical to that of today with but one notable exception: the shape of home base. This final significant change to the diamond rules was implemented for the 1900 season. Two triangular areas were added to the front of the square home base such that the front was no longer a point, but a 17-inch wide, flat side of the now familiar five-sided shape. The *Spalding* guide of 1900 explained the reason for the change:

> With the plate placed in accordance with the form of the diamond field, that is, with its corner facing the pitcher instead of one of its sides, a width of 17 inches was presented for the pitcher to throw the ball over instead of 12 inches, the width of each side of the base. But this left the pitcher handicapped by having to "cut the corners" as it is called, besides which the umpire, in judging called balls and strikes, found it difficult to judge the "cut the corner" balls. To obviate this difficulty, the Committee [of Rules], while keeping the square plate in its old place—touching the lines of the diamond on two of its sides—gave it a new form in its fronting the pitcher, by making the front square with its width of 17 inches, the same as from corner to corner, from foul line to foul line. The change made is undoubtedly an advantage alike to the pitcher and umpire, as it enables the pitcher to see the *width* of base he has to throw the ball over better than before, and the umpire can judge called balls and strikes with less difficulty.[38]

The invention of the five-sided home base was claimed by National League pitcher Crazy Schmit. In a letter he sent to *The Sporting News*, Schmit states that he suggested the five-sided home base to James Hart (chairman of the Baseball Rules Committee) two years earlier. After briefly mentioning his invention, Schmit goes on at length to detail his career in a style uncannily reminiscent of Jack Keefe, the "busher" pitcher made famous in Ring Lardner's story *You Know Me, Al.* Recounting the previous season, Schmit writes:

> I pitched some 14 exceptional good games for Cleveland last summer [2-17, 5.86 in 1899]. I am like a gnarled oak and am getting better every year. I may pitch in some smaller league this year. [Charlie] Comiskey says he will give

me a chance when things are settled. I had everything arranged to play for [John] McGraw, but if he goes to St. Louis it is all off.[30]

The majority of Schmit's letter is spent listing excuses for many of his 17 losses with the dismal 1899 Spiders. Unfortunately for Schmit, McGraw did go to St. Louis, and Crazy pitched in only four more major league games, winning none and losing two. Schmit (apparently sensitive of his "Crazy" monicker) ended his letter as follows: "I hope you will not add any nicknames to my name. I remain your humble reader. Frederick Schmit." Whether or not the idea for the five-sided home plate really came from Schmit remains unclear. The fact that he has one of the worst winning percentages (7-36, .163) in baseball history does not.[40]

Former baseball commissioner Ford Frick wrote:

…The establishment of the 90-foot distance between bases must be recognized as the greatest contribution to perfect competition any game has ever known. It is that specification on which our hitting and fielding records are based; that unchanging measurement of success or failure that has set the guidelines for heroes; the great reason why baseball, through the years, has qualified as the most mathematically perfect game ever devised by humankind.[41]

Like Red Smith, Frick describes the baseball diamond as being "perfect." It is the awkward-looking home plate, the strange positioning of the second base, and the first and third bases nestled snugly in their corners of this 90-foot square that we embrace as perfection.

CHRONOLOGY OF BASEBALL DIAMOND RULE CHANGES

1845 First written rules of baseball set down by the Knickerbocker Base Ball Club of New York City.
Distance across infield diamond (home to second and first to third) is set at forty-two paces.
1857 New set of rules adopted at first convention of baseball players.
The sides of the infield square are thirty yards.
First, second, and third bases must each cover a square foot in area and are canvas bags filled with sawdust or sand.
Home base is circular and made of iron.
1860 In Beadle's guide explanatory section, Henry Chadwick suggests that first, second, and third bases be fourteen by seventeen inches and that home base be at least nine inches in diameter.
1861 Rule requires that chalk lines be drawn between home and first and home and third.
1867 Beadle's guide publishes first truly representational diagram of baseball diamond.
1868 Home base changed from a circle to a square.
Size of home base same as that of first, second, and third bases.
Clarification in the rules states that the base bag, not the post to which the bag should be attached, is to be considered the base. This rule dropped in 1876 according to Spalding guide; 1877 according to Beadle's and DeWitt's guides.
1869 In DeWitt's guide explanatory section, Henry Chadwick suggests first, second, and third bases be eighteen inches square.
1872 Beadle's and DeWitt's guides no longer contain explanatory sections. Discrepancy between suggested sizes of first, second, and third bases (fourteen by seventeen inches versus eighteen inches square) is thus removed.
Home base required to be made of white marble or stone.
1874 Foul line rule implies home, first, and third bases are centered on foul lines.
1875 Home base required to have one point facing pitcher and is positioned wholly in foul territory.
1876 Beadle's and DeWitt's guides allow wooden home base; Spalding guide does not.
1877 Home base moved wholly into fair territory.
First, second, and third bases are to cover fifteen inches square. Home base still to cover twelve inches square.
Fair-foul hit removed from the game, as definition of fair and foul balls are changed.
Spalding and DeWitt's guide diagrams show bases with sides parallel to base paths. Beadle's guide will continue to show first, second, and third bases rotated 45 degrees from their modern orientation through 1881, the final year of its publication.
Beadle's and DeWitt's guides no longer allow wooden home base.
1885 National League home base made of white rubber or stone. American Association home base made only of white rubber.
1887 National League and American Association adopt same set of rules.
Home base made only of white rubber.
First and third bases moved into fair territory.
1894 New geometric diagram of baseball diamond adopted.
1900 Home base changed to five-sided shape.

Acknowledgements

Thanks go to Tom Heitz, Liane Hirabayashi, Fred Ivor-Campbell, Larry Webster, and the library staffs of both the National Baseball Library in Cooperstown, New York, and the paul Ziffren Sports Resource Center at the Amateur Athletic Foundation of Los Angeles.
[1] Kevin Nelson, Baseball's Greatest Quotes (New York: Simon and Schuster, 1982), 183.
[2] For example, the distance between first and second base on the modern infield diamond is, at its shortest, 88 feet 1.5 inches.
[3] Harold Seymour, Baseball: The Early Years, vol. 1 of Baseball (New York: Oxford

University Press, 1960-1990), 15-18.

[4] John Thorn, "The True Father of Baseball," chap. 1 in *Total Baseball* (New York: HarperCollins Publishers, HarperPerennial, 1993), 6.

[5] Frederick Ivor-Campbell argued in favor of this scalable pace in his research presentation "Why Forty-Two Paces?" at the 23rd SABR National Convention, June 26, 1993. Ivor-Campbell also noted that deliberate pacing for an adult male can reasonably yield a three-foot pace and, thus, an infield square with sides ninety feet in length.

[6] A similar diagram and set of rules were published in *The Spirit of the Times*, 12 May 1855.

[7] The initial convention was held January 22, 1857, but the rules were officially accepted at a later meeting, held on February 25, 1857. Not until the convention of the following year, held March 10, 1858, did the organization name itself the "National Association of Base Ball Players."

[8] Ibid., 6.

[9] Frederick Ivor-Campbell argued in favor of this scalable pace in his research presentation, "Why Forty-Two Paces?" at the 23rd SABR National Convention , June 26, 1993. Ivor-Campbell also noted that deliberate pacing for an adult male can reasonably yield a three-foot pace and, thus, an infield square with sides ninety feet in length.

[10] Henry Chadwick, ed., *Beadle's Dime Base-Ball Player*, (New York: Irwin P. Beadle & Co., 1860), 18.

[11] Ibid.

[12] According to an article in *The New York Clipper*, 20 May 1865, bases a cubic foot in size were used in Philadelphia in 1860. However, it is unclear that the game in which these bases were used was what one would refer to as baseball. Certainly the use of such bases was not the norm for the era.

[13] One of the earliest patents of a baseball base is U.S. Patent No. 75,076. The device is a base that is attached to a stake by means of a swiveling cap. The diagram accompanying the description of the patent shows the canvas base to be circular, though it is clearly not intended for use as a home base. It is unknown whether the device was ever manufactured.

[14] Henry Chadwick, *Beadle's Dime Base-Ball Player*, (New York: Beadle & Co., 1861), 12.

[15] According to the 1861 *Beadle's* guide, some clubs had adopted this rule during the season of 1860.

[16] Henry Chadwick, ed., *Beadle's Dime Base-Ball Player*, (New York: Beadle & Co., 1868), 17.

[17] Curiously, *The New York Clipper*, 21 December 1867 and 28 December 1867, failed to make note of the change of home from a circle to a square in articles detailing the rule changes for the upcoming 1868 season.

[18] Henry Chadwick, ed., *The Base-Ball Guide for 1869*, (New York: Robert M. DeWitt, 1869), 30.

[19] Henry Chadwick, ed., *Beadle's Dime Base-Ball Player*, (New York: Beadle & Co., 1868), 17. In Appendix 4, "Rules and Scoring" of *Total Baseball*, (New York:HarperCollins Publishers, HarperPerennial, 1993), Dennis Bingham and Tom Heitz state that this rule was dropped in 1876. While the 1876 *Spalding* guide no longer includes this rule, both the *Beadle's* and *DeWitt's* guides of that year do. All three guides omit the rule for 1877.

[20] Henry Chadwick, *The Base-Ball Guide for 1872*, (New York: Robert M. DeWitt, 1872), 111.

[21] Henry Chadwick, ed., *Beadle's Dime Base-Ball Player*, (New York: Beadle & Adams, 1874), 76.

[22] Henry Chadwick, *DeWitt's Base-Ball Guide for 1874*, (New York: Robert M. DeWitt, 1874), 76.

[23] Henry Chadwick, ed., *Beadle's Dime Base-Ball Player*, (New York: Beadle & Co., 1869), 14.

[24] Ibid.

[25] Henry Chadwick, *DeWitt's Base-Ball Guide for 1875*, (New York: Robert M. DeWitt, 1875), 74.

[26] Ibid., 83.

[26] John Thorn, telephone conversation with author, 11 June 1993.

[27] The idea of a ten-man game was not new. Not uncommonly, box scores of baseball games from the 1860s showed ten men per team, the extra man noted as playing "RS" or right shortstop.

[28] While the batter's box moved back 8-1/2 inches with the move of home base, the same season of 1875 called for a change in the lines of the batter's box that resulted in the batter being moved an extra foot away from fair territory.

[29] Henry Chadwick, *DeWitt's Base-Ball Guide for 1877*, (New York: Robert M. DeWitt, 1877), 64.

[30] Ibid.

[31] From 1867 to 1881, the final year of its publication, the *Beadle's* guide diagram of the baseball infield showed the first, second, and third bases to be rotated 45 degrees from their modern orientation.

[32] *Spalding's Base Ball Guide for 1880*, (Chicago: A.G. Spalding & Bros., 1880), 59.

[33] *Spalding's Base Ball Guide for 1885*, (New York: A.G. Spalding & Bros., 1885), 108.

[34] *The Sporting Life*, 26 November 1884, p. 3.

[35] *Spalding's Base Ball Guide for 1887*, (Chicago: A.G. Spalding & Bros., 1887), 107.

[36] By this time both the *Beadle's* and *DeWitt's* guides were no longer published. *Beadle's* last year of publication was 1881, while *DeWitt's* was 1885.

[37] Henry Chadwick, ed., *Spalding's Base Ball Guide for 1894*, (New York: American Sports Publishing Company, 1894), 152.

[38] Henry Chadwick, ed., *Spalding's Official Base Ball Guide*, (New York: American Sports Publishing Company, 1900), 201.

[39] "The New Home Plate," *The Sporting News*, 24 March 1900.

[40] Jack Wadsworth has the worst won-loss percentage for a pitcher with at least five victories: 6-38, .136. However, as of the end of the 1993 season, Anthony Young's record stood at 5-35, .143.

[41] Ford Frick, *Games, Asterisks, and People: Memoirs of a Lucky Fan*, (New York: Crown Publishers, Inc., 1973), 9. Note that, like Red Smith, Frick erroneously states the distance between bases to be ninety feet.

PLATES

A   *Early Baseball Diamond Diagram*. The New York Clipper, *13 December 1856.*

B   *"Diagram of a Base Ball Field." Henry Chadwick, ed.,* Beadle's Dime Base-Ball Player, *(New York: Beadle & Co., 1862).*

C   *Brooklyn Atlantics versus Philadelphia Athletics, 22 October 1866. John Thorn and Mark Rucker,* The National Pastime 3, no. 1 (Spring 1984), 24.

D   Rockingham Nine, Portsmouth, New Hampshire, 1865. John Thorn and Mark Rucker, The National Pastime 3, no. 1 (Spring 1984), 8.

E   Beadle's Diagram for 1867. Henry Chadwick, ed., Beadle's Dime Base-Ball Player, (New York: Beadle & Co., 1867).

F   Brooklyn Atlantics versus Philadelphia Athletics, 7 September 1868. The New York Clipper, 12 September 1868.

G   Beadle's Diagram for 1869. Henry Chadwick, ed., Beadle's Dime Base-Ball Player, (New York: Beadle & Co., 1869).

H   "Diagram of the Diamond Field." Henry Chadwick, ed.,

Beadle's Dime Base-Ball Player, (New York: Beadle & Adams, 1877).

J   "Diagram of a Ball Ground." A.G. Spalding and Lewis Meacham, eds., Spalding's Official Base Ball Guide for 1878, (Chicago: A.G. Spalding & Bro., 1878), 3.

K   Boston Beaneaters versus New York Giants, 29 April 1886. John Thorn and Mark Rucker, The National Pastime 3, no. 1 (Spring 1984), 50.

L   "Correct Diagram of a Ball Ground." Spalding's Base Ball Guide for 1887, (Chicago: A.G. Spalding & Bros., 1887), 4.

Baseball's best bench

While doing a random stroll through The Sports Encyclopedia: Baseball, I came upon the astounding accomplishments of the 1921 Cleveland Indians' bench players. Although the Tribe finished 4-1/2 games behind the Yankees that year, it was not for the lack of a good supporting cast.

Twelve players were listed below the starting eight for Manager Tris Speaker, half of whom had 131 or more at bats. The six who didn't play much included four catchers who had 22 hits in 75 at bats (.293).

The six others represent the finest collection of subs any manager ever had. Tioga George Burns was the first guy off the bench, hitting .361 and slugging .480 (without an homers). He backed up Doc Johnston at first base.

Jack Graney was in his penultimate season, and like Tioga, he hit his career high (.299). Joe Wood was the number one outfield reserve, also in his next-to-last season in the bigs. Wood proved what a remarkable athlete he was by having five fine years as an outfielder after his Hall-of-Fame caliber pitching career was brought to an abrupt end because of arm miseries. Smoky Joe also managed his career high in 1921 (.366 and .562). His four homeruns were one more than Speaker hit in 312 more at bats.

Riggs Stephenson was Billy Wambsganns' backup at second base. Riggs must have been no fun to have in the locker room, because I can't think of any other reason why his .330 batting average as a second and third baseman earned him only a ticket to the minors. Was Wamby's triple play all that important, to cancel out his .250 average? Also, Riggsie was in his rookie year, barely out of the University of Alabama.

Joe Evans was the final member of the J.V. outfield. He hit .333, giving the second-string garden a clean sweep in the batting race ahead of the starting outfield of Elmer Smith, Charlie Jamieson, and Tristram E.

The final member of the big six bench was Les Nunamaker. He hit .359, another career high. And combined with starter Steve O'Neill's .322 this represented one of the top backstop platoons in history. Incidentally, two of the bit-playing bench men were pretty fine catchers: Art Wilson, at the end of his career; and Luke Sewell, at the beginning of his. Pinch Thomas was a decent third receiver, too.

The Tribe's bench average that year was .341 (compared to the Varsity's .299). I doubt there ever was a better bench.

—Cappy Gagnon

The Gowell Claset Saga: 2-0, 9.53

"One of these things just doesn't belong here. . ."

Jamie Selko

Sometimes, when you're cruising through the Big Mac, something just kinda catches your eye. You do a doubletake to see if your eyes have deceived you, and lo! you've stumbled onto a gem. If you're like me, sometimes the gem is Nyls Nyman's first year, or Johnny Tsitouris, 1962—but much more often it's a one-liner, and usually one with a bit of a tarnish. Gowell Claset's line is the one that probably made a greater impression on me than any other. For years, I tried to get a handle on the incongruity inherent in his winning percentage as opposed to his ERA. Finally, unable to reconcile the two disparate figures, I did what should have been done long ago—I looked it up.

Gowell Sylvester "Lefty" Claset, pride of Battle Creek, made the Connie Mack A's at the start of their final tumble from the top, 1933. Many of the stars of the 1929-'30-'31 machine were gone, others were aging fast, especially the pitchers, with only Grove both still there and still in form. Gowell was huge for the time, a strapping 6'3", 210 pound broth of a lad of 25. Apparently, sports writers had trouble with his first name, it being two syllables and all, for he was referred to as Dowell, Cowell and Gowell during his brief sojourn in the bigs. His last name also gave them problems, sometimes being rendered Closet.

He made his first appearance early on in the season, April 12 to be exact, coming in in relief of Tony Frietas, who had been pinch-hit for by Parke

Jamie Selko lives in Eugen, Oregon.

Coleman in the seventh with the A's trailing the Senators 2-1. He pitched the eighth and gave up three hits and a walk. The A's were down 4-1 when he exited. Gowell then didn't get called on to pitch until April 22, when he again came in in a game started by Frietas. Tony had been manhandled by the Yankees, and this time Gowell followed Roy Mahaffey. The Athletics were behind 8-7 when he came in in the eighth, which he got through unscathed. In the ninth, though, he tired, allowing the Yanks to score a run in the 1/3 inning he pitched. His totals for the game included three hits and two walks.

Following this outing, he did not pitch again for a month, until May 22. By this time, the A's had suffered eight rainouts and two "coldouts". The rest seemed to have done him good, however, as he relieved Frietas (again) in a game against the Browns with the score tied 4-4 in the sixth. He pitched an inning without allowing a runner. Grove came in to pitch the seventh, eighth, and ninth, eventually picking up credit for a 6-5 Athletics win. (Historic aside No. 1: this was the period during which Connie Mack had decided to use Lefty as a relief pitcher. This was the second of five games in a row in which he was to pitch, and in which he picked up three wins and two saves. He was then rested during a blowout, picked up a save, sat out another blowout, and finally came in in a double header to record a win and a save. So, he pitched in eight out of 10 games, garnering four wins and four saves before Mr. Mack returned him to the starting rotation.)

Two days later, big Gowell was called on to put out the fire again. Coming in for Cain with two out in the fourth and the Browns ahead 4-1, he got the last out of the fourth. When the A's batted in the fifth, they did it in earnest, scoring five runs, putting them up 6-4 and making it Gowell's game to win. After holding the Browns scoreless in the fifth and sixth, he began the seventh with two walks and was pulled for Lefty.

In this, the longest scoreless outing of his major league career, he gave up no hits, walked three and got his only strikeout, along with win number one. (By the way, Lefty only had to pitch an inning for the save, as in the sixth inning, Shibe Park was hit by lightning, starting a fire which resulted in the game being called.)

On May 28th, Gowell relieved Rube Walberg who had given up 13 hits in 7-1/3 innings, entering the game with the A's on the short end of a 7-5 score. He worked a tough 2/3 inning, allowing but one hit, his third consecutive scoreless outing, covering a total of four innings. On the 30th, Gowell worked his fourth game in nine days, coming in in relief of Lefty who had pitched a scoreless ninth and tenth against the White Sox, and had left with the score tied 6-6. In the top of the eleventh, the A's scored two, but in the bottom of the inning, Gowell gave up two, blowing what would have been a win for Grove (which I'm sure Lefty handled with

Gowell Claset

equanimity). The A's came back to score three more in the top of the twelfth, and the big man held the Sox scoreless in their half of the inning to chalk up win number two.

On June 3, Gowell worked what would prove to be his longest stint in the majors—three innings. Once again, he came in for Walberg who had walked five and given up two hits in 1-1/3 inning. Gowell gave up a run in the third, after the A's had scored 11 runs in the top of the inning. He pitched a scoreless fourth, and went into the fifth with an 11-4 lead, when disaster struck. He was able to get but two outs in the inning, and had to be relieved by Jim Peterson. It was Peterson who cost Gowell a victory, which would have made him 3-0, 9.53, as he gave up the go-ahead runs to the Yanks in what would eventually be a 17-11 A's loss.

Gowell's swan song was the June 7 game against the Senators. Connie picked him to start at home, apparently deciding to throw him into the deep end to see if he could swim. It was not to be a pretty sight. Claset was bombed for five runs in the first, but Connie kept him in when the A's came back to score four in their at bat. He was unable to retire a single batter in the second, the Nats scoring five more times. Miraculously, even here G. Sylvester was able to avoid the loss, as the game went into extra innings! Let's let Shirly Povich of the *Washington Post* describe what went on in the extra frames:

> Connie Mack had his nerve with him in the tenth…he put in young Raymond Coombs, a nephew of the old iron man of the A's, Jack Coombs. Young Coombs had never pitched for anybody except Duke University before, and sure enough Heinie Manush smacked him for a single to right right off the bat. Cronin bunted him to third and Goose Goslin pinch hit for Dave Harris and scored Heinie with a bounce to Bishop over Coombs head that put Washington ahead 14-13.

But, in the home half of the tenth with an A's runner on and Jimmie Foxx at bat, a deluge hit the park and the game was called with the score reverting back to 13-13. (Historical aside #2: Not only did this rain prevent Coombs from getting a loss—or, more probably, picking up what would have proven to be his only big league win, but he was not to pitch again for over a month, not making his "official" debut until July 8.)

Well, that's Gowell's story. I bet he told his grandkids that he was undefeated in the major leagues, and by gum and by golly, he was. You can look it up!

YEAR	TEAM	LG	G	CG	W	L	%	IP	H	ER	SO	BB	ERA
\multicolumn{14}{l}{Gowell Sylvester Claset "Lefty" 6'3-1/2" 210 11/26/07-3/8/81}
1926	K-MU	MI	8	2	2	3	.400	51	74	-	22	34	-
	KAL	CNT	2	2	1	1	.500	13	17	-	6	9	-
	MISS	PCL	2	0	0	0	.000	6	-	-	-	-	-
1927	NOT IN O.B.												
1928	WHLG	MAL	31	-	14	11	.566	211	183	58	128	70	2.48
1929	WMPT	NYP	36	-	9	15	.375	211	214	113	78	92	4.82
1930	MONT	IL	36	15	17	10	.630	217	244	103	94	91	4.27
1931	"	"	43	15	16	14	.533	235	227	92	109	121	3.52
1932	"	"	47	16	23	13	.639	282	280	112	144	115	3.57
1933	PHI	AL	8	0	2	0	1.000	11	23	12	1	11	9.82
	BALT	IL	28	10	7	10	.412	157	195	109	52	82	5.96
1934	ST.P	AA	36	-	7	11	.389	165	236	117	58	65	6.38
1935	"	"	13	-	2	2	.500	57	82	33	26	23	5.21
	ELM	NYP	16	-	3	6	.333	71	81	40	21	38	5.07
1936	"	"	32	16	8	14	.364	199	234	92	37	65	4.16
	Minor League		330	-	111	110	.502	1875	1987	869	755	805	4.33

(Note: ERA figured on 1805 IP)

Stats courtesy of Art Cantu

1926 Michigan State and Central League stats by Ray Nemec

Teammates With the Numbers

Group firepower

"Biff" Brecher and Albey M. Reiner

Discerning students of the game know that, though baseball emphasizes individual skills, the greatest pleasure comes from the meshing of those in-dividual components into a great *team*. When we define a great baseball player, we ask two questions: first: did he perform at a very high level consistently over many years? and, second, did his teams win? There were some real greats who spent whole careers in or near the basement— Ralph Kiner, winning one home run championship after another on the pa-thetic Pirates of the late '40s; the in-comparable Ernie Banks on the dreary Cubs for over two decades. But, in the end, the ob-jective of baseball is not to put up big numbers, but to win. It is

no coincidence that most Hall of Famers were sur-rounded by other excellent players. That's why they won. Ruth and Gehrig, Aaron and Mathews, Mays and McCovey, the names come sliding off the tongue together naturally for every baseball fan.

Most fans have a special affection for gifted team-mates who play together well year after year, maturing and growing old gracefully together. We think of the Dodger in-field of the '70s — Garvey, Lopes, Russell, and Cey; of the Tigers' Whitaker and Trammell; of Yount, Molitor, and Gantner in Milwaukee. Yount, Molitor and Gantner set a career record which will almost certainly never be broken. They amassed more hits as teammates than any other three men in history. From 1978, the first year all three played together, through 1992, they garnered a total

Sam Rice and Joe Judge: the champs.

"Biff" Brecher and **Albey M. Reiner** *are Brooklyn Dodger fans who have not yet recovered from the blow.*

of 6,381 hits—2,455 for Yount, 2,261 for Molitor, and 1,665 for Gantner. In the process, they passed the hit total of the Pirates trio consisting of the Waner brothers and Pie Traynor—5,748. Yount and Molitor are also high on the list of all-time duos, at number 4. Only the Waner brothers, Clemente and Mazeroski and the old Senator duo of Sam Rice and Joe Judge are ahead of them.

One group of teammates stands out from the rest on the historic team hit parade—the Boys of Summer, perhaps the most beloved team in history, was also clearly the best hitting team of all time. The great Brooklyn Dodgers of the late '40s and early '50s had six stars who stayed together for nine years, putting up really big numbers every year. By the time they were through, they had banged out 8,305 hits. No team has ever exhibited such longevity and consistency. They are *way* ahead of their nearest rivals, the Yankees' Murderers' Row.

The following Tables list significant teammate hit combos over the years. Table 1 contains the names of duos from the modern era who have amassed 4,000 or more career hits while playing for the same team. Table 2 shows trios who have collected at least 5,000

hits. Table 3 shows larger groupings with over 6,000 hits. Table 4 presents a few combinations that did not quite make it. We have arbitrarily decreed that a player must participate in at least ten games for a season to count toward the record. While we are reasonably sure we have collected all the relevant duos, we suspect that there are a significant number of larger groups that could be added. We invite the readers to suggest additional names.

While compiling this information, we were struck by several interesting points. First, it rarely helps to add more players to the list. As you do so, you invariably shrink the number of years in which the players played concurrently. Second, despite the feared sluggers who have graced their roster over the years, no Yankees are on the duo list, although the Murderers' Row line-up is on the list for trios and multiple players. Ruth and Gehrig fell 226 hits shy of the 4,000-hit mark. Third, note that another recent superstar, George Brett, made the duo list with three different teammates—Frank White, Willie Wilson, and Hal McRae. That group is also Number 5 on the all-time multiple player list. Fourth, the all-time leading duo, Sam Rice and Joe Judge, was quite a surprise.

Offensive Teammates

Table 1: Duos with More than 4000 Hits

Player	Team	Years	Hits
S. Rice-Judge	Senators	15-17, 19-32	4996
P. & W. Waner	Pirates	27-40	4994*
Clemente-Mazeroski	Pirates	56-72	4895
Yount-Molitor	Brewers	78-92	4716
Brett-F. White	Royals	73-87	4713
J. Rice-D. Evans	Red Sox	74-89	4636
Williams-Santo	Cubs	60-73	4563
Trammell-Whitaker	Tigers	77-94	4556
Cobb-Crawford	Tigers	05-17	4502
Rose-Perez	Reds	64-76	4382
Brett-W. Wilson	Royals	76-87	4346
Mathews-Aaron	Braves	54-66	4332
Yount-Gantner	Brewers	76-91	4276
Clarke-Wagner	Pirates	00-11	4247
Brett-McRae	Royals	73-87	4143
Cobb-Veach	Tigers	12-23	4107
Musial-Schoendienst	Cardinals	46-55, 61-63	4102
Rose-Bench	Reds	67-78	4034

*The Waners also played on the same Braves team for part of 1941 and the same Dodgers team in 1944. Some enterprising researcher could check to see how many hits they collected together at those times. These extra hits might put them in first place.

Table 2: Trios with More than 5000 Hits

Yount-Molitor-Gantner	Brewers	78-91	5996
Banks-Santo-Williams	Cubs	60-71	5455
Gehrig-Ruth-Combs	Yankees	25-34	5326
Traynor-Waner-Waner	Pirates	27-35	5185
Gehrig-Combs-Lazzeri	Yankees	26-35	5166
Perez-Rose-Bench	Reds	64-76	5041

Table 3: Groups with More than 6000 Hits

Reese-Furillo-Robinson-Snider-Hodges-Campanella	Dodgers	48-56	8305!
Brett-McRae-Wilson-White	Royals	77-87	6728
Gehrig-Ruth-Combs-Lazzeri	Yankees	26-34	6281

Table 4: Close, But no Seegar

Powell-B. Robinson	Orioles	61-74	3861
Ruth-Gehrig	Yankees	23, 25-34	3774
Yount-Cecil Cooper	Brewers	77-87	3636
Rice-Burleson-Yastrzemski-Lynn-Fisk-Evans	Red Sox	74-80	5812
Garvey-Russell-Cey-Lopes	Dodgers	72-81	5499

Disenfranchised All-Stars of 1945

Hard luck in career years

Charlie Bevis

Goody Rosen was having a career year at mid-season 1945, batting .363 as the center fielder for the Brooklyn Dodgers, third best in the National League. So was Washington knuckleball pitcher Roger Wolff, having compiled a 9-5 record at the 1945 All-Star break for the second-place Senators.

Both Rosen and Wolff could have expected to be named to their respective league's All-Star squads for 1945. Neither was. They weren't snubbed by the managers charged with the team selections nor were they injured or unable to play. There were no managers or players in the 1945 All-Star Game—it was canceled!

Since its beginning in 1933, the All-Star Game has survived adverse weather conditions (1952, 1961 & 1969) and a player strike (1981), but in 1945 it couldn't overcome federal government travel restrictions imposed by the Office of Defense Transportation.

Instead of a July 10 All-Star Game at Boston's Fenway Park, seven exhibition games were played around the country on July 9 and 10. There were five intra-city games between competing American League and National League teams—highlighted by the Yankees-Giants contest at the Polo Grounds— one intra-state game between the Reds and the Indians, and one inter-sectional game.

The ODT had refused to grant the Tigers permission to detour 62 miles to Pittsburgh to play the Pirates, so these two teams didn't participate in the exhibition series. But the ODT did allow the Dodgers to take a circuitous route from Brooklyn to Cincinnati by way of the nation's capital so that they could play the Senators on July 10.

It was this July 10 game that Rosen and Wolff had to settle for in lieu of a July 10 All-Star appearance, as the Senators defeated the Dodgers 4-3. Rosen went 0 for 3 while Wolff pitched effectively in three innings of relief.

Although there were no official All-Star squads chosen in 1945, *The Sporting News* and the Associated Press each published its own selections for hypothetical National and American League All-Star squads in early July. These selections are listed in the accompanying tables.

The 1945 non-All-Star Game has spawned an unusual category of players who should have been selected to represent their leagues in the annual exhibition classic but never got another opportunity to participate in any All-Star Game.

Of the 63 players selected for the two hypothetical All-Star squads, 27 would have been first-time All-Stars. Just nine of these received another shot at the All-Star Game. Thus 18 1945 players are Disenfranchised All-Stars, having been selected to one or both of the hypothetical teams but never again being selected for the mid-summer classic.

Charlie Bevis is the son of the shortstop on the 1932 semi-pro Bevis family baseball team, subject of his July 1994 piece in Yankee magazine. He has written a number of articles on baseball history and is currently writing a biography of Mickey Cochrane.

Catchers

Among the complete unanimity in the choices for catchers in each league were two players shown in capitalized letters in Table 1 who would have been first-time All-Stars, Mike Tresh and Ken O'Dea.

Tresh of the White Sox probably would have started the All-Star Game for the American League, based on his first half performance in comparison to long-time veterans Rick Ferrell and Frankie Hayes. In his seventh season with Chicago, Tresh was hitting .253 with his usual compliment of 0 home runs. Tresh was best known for hitting only two career home runs, 787 games and 2,568 at bats apart, in 1940 and 1948—and for fathering son Tom, who went on to play with pennant-winning Yankee teams in the 1960s.

O'Dea, a backup on the St. Louis Cardinal pennant winners of 1942-44, finally got his starting shot in 1945, when Walker Cooper went into the Navy on May 1. O'Dea made All-Star status on a three-catcher squad behind Phil Masi of the Boston Braves, who was hitting .335 at midseason, and veteran Ernie Lombardi. By year-end, though, O'Dea would be sharing duties with rookie Del Rice, while another rookie, Joe Garagiola, took over for the pennant-winning 1946 Cardinals as O'Dea was traded to the Braves to back up Masi.

Infielders

The five players for whom this would have been the only All-Star selection are highlighted in Table 2. In the National League, Marty Marion was such a dominant shortstop that one hypothetical team had three third basemen rather than selecting a backup shortstop.

Dodger youngster Eddie Basinski, 22, was an interesting choice for backup shortstop on the other list. Basinski, a violinist in the off-season with the Buffalo Philharmonic Orchestra, was signed by the Dodgers out of the University of Buffalo after a tryout although he hadn't played baseball in either high school or college. Pee Wee Reese returned to play shortstop in 1946 for the Dodgers and "Fiddler" Basinski played just 56 more major league games thereafter.

Nick Etten of the Yankees was having a great season in 1945, taking a shot at the Triple Crown. Etten led the American League with 111 RBIs, was second in homeruns with 18, and finished with a .285 batting average, not far behind Snuffy Stirnweiss' .309 league-leading mark. At 31, Etten would play only one more season with the Yankees, and he would miss the pennant winning years to come.

At least second baseman Eddie Mayo had the satisfaction of playing in a World Series, as the Tigers won the American League pennant in 1945 and went on to defeat the Cubs in seven games. Mayo's play during the season earned him runner-up status for MVP, behind teammate Hal Newhouser.

There was a split decision for backup third baseman behind 38-year-old White Sox sensation Tony Cuccinello, leading the American League in batting at midseason with a .328 average. Mark Christman of the Browns would play four more years after the war. Oscar Grimes of the Yankees, like Etten, had only one more full season.

Christman could be a controversial choice on the TSN squad as he had played less than half of the first half of the season. However, with Browns manager Luke Sewell as the would-be A.L. manager of the 1945 All-Star team on the heels of the Browns' 1944 pennant, Christman very well could have been chosen as back-up third baseman based on his previous year's performance.

Outfielders

Rosen, one of the four outfielders highlighted in Table 3 who were denied their one shot at All-Star selection, was in what was to be the best season of his career. After his great first half, Rosen did not fade in the second half. He finished third in the National League at .325, behind Cavaretta at .355 and Holmes at .352. Rosen was traded to crosstown rival the New York Giants early in the 1946 season, his finale, as Pete Reiser returned to patrol center at Ebbets Field.

Cardinal Buster Adams also had a career year in 1945, finishing third in home runs with 22, fifth in RBs with 109, and second in total bases with 279. When the St. Louis regulars returned the next year, Adams became the Cardinals ace pinch hitter on the 1946 pennant winner.

Thirty-year-old rookie Vance Dinges of the Philadelphia Blue Jays, a.k.a. Phillies, also had a great first half, hitting at a .328 clip for the last-place National League entry. However, Dinges had a not-so-great second half, and finished with a .287 batting average. He'd only play one more major league season after 1945.

In the American League, the Philadelphia A's Bobby Estalella was having a great season as well, which would be his last as a regular. Estalella, one of the first Cuban born major leaguers, batted .299 to finish fourth in the American League batting race.

Pitchers

Wolff was one of the seven pitchers noted in Table 4 who missed their only shot at All-Star status in 1945. The 34-year-old knuckleballer finished the season with a 20-10 record and 2.12 earned run average, third best in the American League. Wolff pitched just two more seasons in the majors.

Cleveland's Steve Gromek had a 19-9 record at year-end, third best winning percentage in the American League. As one of the younger 1945 All-Stars at 25, Gromek went on to play 12 more years in the majors.

Russ Christopher of the A's did not have a good second half. After an outstanding first half record of 11-5, he finished with a disappointing 13-13 mark for Connie Mack's 1945 entry. Christopher became the top reliever for the 1948 World Champion Cleveland Indians.

Red Barrett of the Cardinals experienced the most wins among the four National League pitchers, topping the circuit with 23 victories, easily the best season of his career. Barrett finished third in the 1945 National League MVP voting.

Hank Wyse was right behind Barrett with 22 wins, and finished fifth in Earned Run Average, to lead the Cubs to the National League pennant. Young Hal Gregg of the Dodgers and Blix Donnelly of the Cardinals both had .500 second halves following their promising first half performances. Gregg would finish with 139 strikeouts, second best in the National League.

Many of the Disenfranchised 1945 All-Stars had the best season of their major league career. After getting their chance to excel, most of them took a back seat when veterans returned from the service.

Illustrating this point are the four members of the Disenfranchised 1945 All-Stars who played with the St. Louis Cardinals, the sandwich season between Cardinal pennant-winning years of 1944 and 1946. O'Dea, Donnelly, Barrett and Adams were key members of the 1945 club. But just Barrett and Adams were with the 1946 pennant winners at season's end—Barrett as a reliever and spot starter, and Adams mainly as a pinch hitter. Neither saw action in the seven-game World Series that year.

Quality of play in 1945 has been maligned by some baseball historians, who use one-armed outfielder Pete Gray of the St. Louis Browns as an example. Others have defended the 1945 season, citing the lack of outrageous statistics by veteran players from the previous seasons.

The recent induction into the Hall of Fame of Newhouser, the American League Most Valuable Player in 1945, reminds us that the accomplishments of players like Rosen and Wolff, who happened to peak during World War II, deserve more recognition.

ODT

The 1945 All-Star Game had been confirmed at a February 3 owners meeting, with all proceeds to be donated to war relief. However, on February 21 J. Monroe Johnson, the Director of ODT, announced that a 25 percent cut in travel had been requested of major league baseball.

To keep the regular season intact, the owners agreed to cancel the All-Star Game, since National League President Ford Frick had estimated it would save 500,000 passenger miles, due not just to players, but to all the press and officials who would travel to Boston. The World Series was even in doubt at that point. ODT announced it would be allowed "only if transportation and war conditions at the time permit."

After Germany surrendered in May, some fans had hope that the All-Star Game would be restored.

"They ought to stop yapping about that sort of thing," Johnson was quoted in reply. "Conditions are far worse now. Sports will be lucky to play out the regular schedules this summer and fall unless Japan quickly folds up, relieving the burden on transportation. It already has been demonstrated in redeployment following Germany's defeat that the impact on sports, like everything else, will be terrific."

In June, Mike Todd, a New York theatrical producer then with the USO in France, tried to set up an All-Star Game to be played in Nuremberg Stadium in Germany so that 120,000 GIs could attend it. But nothing came of it.

1945 All-Star "Selections"

Explanations: The Player's batting average (BA) is that at the time of the All-Star break; for pitchers won-loss record (W-L) is similar. TSN signifies the hypothetical team selected by *The Sporting News*; AP signifies the hypothetical team chosen in an Associated Press poll of major league managers. An "X" denotes that player was chosen for that organization's hypothetical team. "Past" and "Future" refer to regular All-Star Game selections before and after 1945; number of times selected with last/next year in parentheses. Names in capital letters are of "disenfranchised All-Stars" of 1945.

Table 1. Catchers

Player	Team	Pos	BA	TSN	AP	Past	Future
American League							
Rick Ferrell	WAS	C	.238	X	X	7 (1944)	0
Frankie Hayes	CLE	C	.240	X	X	4 (1944)	1 (1946)
MIKE TRESH	CHI	C	.253	X	X	0	0
National League							
Ernie Lombardi	NY	C	.296	X	X	7 (1943)	0
Phil Masi	BOS	C	.335	X	X	0	3 (1946)
KEN O'DEA	STL	C	.263	X	X	0	0

Table 2. Infielders

Player	Team	Pos	BA	TSN	AP	Past	Future
American League							
NICK ETTEN	NY	1B	.294	X	X	0	0
George McQuinn	STL	1B	.265	-	X	4 (1944)	2 (1947)
Dick Siebert	PHI	1B	.265	X	-	1 (1943)	0
EDDIE MAYO	DET	2B	.292	X	X	0	0
Snuffy Stirnweiss	NY	2B	.309	X	X	0	1 (1946)
MARK CHRISTMAN	STL	3B	.322	X	-	0	0
Tony Cuccinello	CHI	3B	.328	X	X	2 (1938)	0
OSCAR GRIMES	NY	3B	.276	-	X	0	0
Lou Boudreau	CLE	SS	.274	X	X	5 (1944)	2 (1947)
Vern Stephens	STL	SS	.318	X	X	2 (1944)	5 (1946)
National League							
Phil Cavaretta	CHI	1B	.372	X	X	1 (1944)	2 (1946)
Frank McCormick	CIN	1B	.293	X	X	7 (1944)	1 (1946)
Don Johnson	CHI	2B	.309	X	X	1 (1944)	0
Emil Verban	STL	2B	.281	X	X	0	2 (1946)
Bob Elliott	PIT	3B	.281	X	X	3 (1944)	3 (1947)
Stan Hack	CHI	3B	.327	-	X	4 (1943)	0
Whitey Kurowski	STL	3B	.330	X	X	2 (1944)	2 (1946)
Marty Marion	STL	SS	.253	X	X	2 (1944)	5 (1946)
EDDIE BASINSKI	BRO	SS	.299	X	-	0	0

Table 3. Outfielders

Player	Team	Pos	BA	TSN	AP	Past	Future
American League							
George Case	WAS	OF	.327	X	X	3 (1944)	0
Doc Cramer	DET	OF	.278	X	X	5 (1940)	0
Roy Cullenbine	DET	OF	.265	X	-	2 (1944)	0
BOBBY ESTALELLA	PHI	OF	.292	X	-	0	0
Hank Greenberg	DET	OF	.286	-	X	4 (1940)	0

Name	Team	Pos				Past	Future
Jeff Heath	CLE	OF	.315	-	X	2 (1943)	0
Bob Johnson	BOS	OF	.297	X	X	7 (1944)	0
Wally Moses	CHI	OF	.278	-	X	1 (1937)	0
					National League		
BUSTER ADAMS	STL	OF	.300	X	-	0	0
VANCE DINGES	PHI	OF	.328	X	-	0	0
Tommy Holmes	BOS	OF	.401	X	X	0	1 (1948)
Bill Nicholson	CHI	OF	.259	X	X	4 (1944)	0
Mel Ott	NY	OF	.325	X	X	11 (1944)	0
Andy Pafko	CHI	OF	.301	-	X	0	4 (1947)
GOODY ROSEN	BRO	OF	.363	X	X	0	0
Dixie Walker	BRO	OF	.299	-	X	2 (1944)	2 (1946)

Table 4. Pitchers

					American League		
Name	Team	Pos	W-L	TSN	AP	Past	Future
Al Benton	DET	P	7-1	X	-	2 (1942)	0
Hank Borowy	NY	P	10-5	X	X	1 (1944)	0
RUSS CHRISTOPHER	PHI	P	11-5	X	X	0	0
Dave Ferriss	BOS	P	14-2	X	X	0	1 (1946)
STEVE GROMEK	CLE	P	9-5	X	X	0	0
Jack Kramer	STL	P	8-7	X	-	0	2 (1946)
Thornton Lee	CHI	P	9-6	-	X	1 (1941)	0
Dutch Leonard	WAS	P	9-3	X	X	3 (1944)	1 (1951)
Hal Newhouser	DET	P	13-5	X	X	3 (1944)	3 (1946)
Allie Reynolds	CLE	P	8-7	-	X	0	5 (1949)
ROGER WOLFF	WAS	P	9-5	X	-	0	0
					National League		
RED BARRETT	STL	P	10-6	X	X	0	0
Mort Cooper	BOS	P	8-1	X	X	2 (1943)	1 (1946)
Paul Derringer	CHI	P	9-6	X	-	6 (1942)	0
BLIX DONNELLY	STL	P	4-6	X	-	0	0
HAL GREGG	BRO	P	10-5	X	X	0	0
Van Lingo Mungo	NY	P	9-4	-	X	3 (1937)	0
Claude Passeau	CHI	P	10-2	X	X	3 (1943)	1 (1946)
Preacher Roe	PIT	P	6-6	X	X	0	4 (1949)
Rip Sewall	PIT	P	9-7	-	X	2 (1944)	1 (1946)
Bill Voiselle	NY	P	10-7	X	-	1 (1944)	0
HANK WYSE	CHI	P	10-5	-	X	0	0

Games Ahead and Games Behind

A stat for evaluating pitchers

James C. Kaufman and Alan S. Kaufman

Teams are compared with a single statistic to decide pennants: Games Ahead/Games Behind. While it has its limitations, the stat is compellingly simple and truly reflects baseball's bottom line. We decided to evaluate pitchers based on the Games Ahead/ Games Behind stat, computing it conventionally, the way it is used to determine each team's standing in its division.

The main benefit of this stat is to permit quick comparisons between teams (or pitchers) with different numbers of decisions. For example, when teams have played the same number of games, then all you have to do is compare their number of wins to determine how many games one team is behind another. When they have played different numbers of games (e.g., if one team is 31-21 and another is 30-15), comparing wins doesn't help much. The Games Ahead stat tells us that the second team (with one fewer win) is actually 2.5 Games Ahead.

A benefit of Games Ahead compared to simple winning percentage is that it is a *practical* stat that translates directly to the number of games a team or pitcher must win to catch up with its or his opponent. For pitchers, Games Ahead is really a bottom-line stat. The number of games won is important and so is

ERA; but the name of the game is to maximize the number of wins and minimize the number of losses. A pitcher who accomplishes that feat consistently will lead his team to the pennant.

The attached chart shows the major league leaders in "Games Ahead" from Al Spalding in 1876 to Tommy Glavine in 1993 and Jummy Key in 1994, along with the number of games they finished ahead of the next pitcher. In '93, Greg Maddux (20-10) won his second straight NL Cy Young trophy, but in view of the airtight Division race in the NL West, a case can be made for Glavine (22-6) as being more instrumental in the Braves' narrow triumph over the Giants. The Atlanta lefty edged the Giants' John Burkett (22-7) and the Astros' Mark Portugal (18-4) for the ML Games Ahead crown. In 1992, Glavine also paced the NL in Games Ahead (despite losing that Cy Young to Maddux as well), though he trailed ML leader Jack Morris.

The Games Ahead method isn't intended to replace the existing ways of evaluating pitchers; it's just another angle. Some notable findings:

Walter Johnson led all ML pitchers by 7 games in 1913, the modern record. Lefty Grove holds down the second and third spots. Old Hoss Radbourn is the all-time leader with an 8-game bulge in 1884. Denny McLain's 4-game edge in 1968 is the largest margin of the past half-century.

Though the chart only lists ML leaders, Jack Chesbro led all AL pitchers by 9.5 games in 1904, the all-time record for one league. The modern NL record

James C. Kaufman and Alan S. Kaufman are the authors of The Worst Baseball Pitchers of All Time (McFarland, 1993), to be published and in revised form by Citadel Press in April, 1995. Alan is Research Professor at the University of Alabama, and is the author of psychological texts and test that are used throughout the world. James is a freelance writer and former journalist who has published may works of fiction, non-fiction, and poetry.

is 5 games, set by Dizzy Dean in 1934 and tied by Don Newcombe in 1956.

Grove and Tom Seaver are the only modern pitchers to lead the majors four times; Seaver led during three different decades. Pete Alexander and Sandy Koufax led the majors three times, each doing it in consecutive years. Counting pre-1900 seasons, Cy Young also led four times; Kid Nichols was a three-time champ and finished second twice.

It's not in the chart, but we also computed who finished the most games *behind* the leader each season. Jose DeLeon finished 16.5 games behind Bob Welch in 1990 and 18.5 games behind Doc Gooden in '85 (when DeLeon was 2-19) to join Hall-of-Famer Red Ruffing and ex-Mets Roger Craig and Jerry Koosman—among others—as two-time tail-enders. DeLeon's 18.5 Games Behind equalled Craig's futility with the '63 Mets; you've got to go back to 1934, when Si Johnson trailed Dizzy Dean by 19 games, to find a pitcher who finished a more distant last. The worst mark of this century is Happy Jack Townsend's 25-game deficit in 1904; the worst ever is the 35.5 games that an 18-year-old rookie named Larry McKeon (18-41) finished behind Radbourn (60-12) in 1884.

Besides Ruffing, the list of tail-enders includes Hall of Famers Candy Cummings, Tim Keefe, Burleigh Grimes, Jesse Haines and Robin Roberts. It also numbers Lee Richmond in 1882, who had pitched the

majors' first perfect game two years earlier; Don Larsen, who pitched the only World Series perfect game; and Virgil Trucks, who pitched two no-hitters the same year he finished 17.5 Games Behind. Among Anthony Young's notable feats in 1993, when his 27 straight losses and 1-16 mark made headlines, was the fact that he finished 15.5 games behind Glavine's Games Ahead pace.

Ruffing went from Games Behind chump in 1928-29 to Games Ahead champ in 1938. Also going from bottom to top were Will White, Paul Derringer, and Preacher Roe. The opposite path was taken by Roberts, McLain, Jim Bunning and Rick Sutcliffe.

The All-time Games Ahead champ, regardless of year, is no contest: Radbourn, in 1884, was +48 (wins minus losses) in his 60-12 season to finish 5.5 games ahead of John Clarkson's 53-16 mark one year later. Since 1900, there's a three-way tie at the top—the +29 records turned in by Jack Chesbro (41-12), Smoky Joe Wood (34-5) and Walter Johnson (36-7). The leaders since 1930 are Grove's +27 and McLain's +25 the seasons each won 31 games; Ron Guidry's +22 in 1978 is the best since expansion. The worst record ever by a Games Ahead champ was Roger Clemens' +11 in '87 (20-9).

Kirk McCaskill (10-19) and Rod Nichols (2-11) set a record in 1991. They finished only 10.5 games behind the leaders, the best "worst" ever.

Games Ahead (GA) "Champs" (1876-1994)

Year	ML Leader	(W-L)	GA	Year	ML Leader	(W-L)	GA
1876	Spalding	(47-13)	4	1895	C. Young	(35-10)	
1877	Bond	(40-17)	6.5		Hoffer	(31-6)	6.5
1878	Bond	(40-19)	6	1896	Hoffer	(25-7)	1
1879	Ward	(47-17)	3	1897	Nichols	(31-11)	0.5
1880	Corcoran	(43-14)	5.5	1898	Nichols	(31-12)	0.5
1881	Corcoran	(31-14)	1.5	1899	Hughes	(28-6)	1.5
1882	W. White	(40-12)	7	1900	McGinnity	(29-9)	3
1883	Radbourn	(49-25)	1.5	1901	C. Young	(33-10)	3
1884	Radbourn	(60-12)	8	1902	Chesbro	(28-6)	0.5
1885	Clarkson	(53-16)	2	1903	C. Young	(28-9)	0.5
1886	Baldwin	(42-13)	2	1904	Chesbro	(41-12)	1
1887	Kilroy	(46-19)	2	1905	Mathewson	(31-8)	4
1888	S. King	(45-21)	0.5	1906	M. Brown	(26-6)	2.5
1889	Clarkson	(49-19)	0.5	1907	Donovan	(25-4)	2.5
1890	Gleason	(38-17)	0.5	1908	Mathewson	(37-11)	0.5
1891	Hutchinson	(44-19)	1	1909	Mullin	(29-8)	1
1892	C. Young	(36-12)	2.5	1910	Coombs	(31-9)	1
1893	Nichols/Killen	(34-14)	1	1911	Marquard	(24-7)	0.5
1894	Meekin	(33-9)	0.5	1912	J. Wood	(34-5)	4.5

Year	ML Leader	(W-L)	GA	Year	ML Leader	(W-L)	GA
1913	W. Johnson	(36-7)	7	1952	Roberts	(28-7)	2
1914	B. James	(26-7)	0.5	1953	Spahn	(23-7)	1
1915	Alexander	(31-10)	3	1954	Lemon	(23-7)	1
1916	Alexander	(33-12)	3.5	1955	Newcombe	(20-5)	2
1917	Alexander	(30-13)	0.5	1956	Newcombe	(27-7)	3.5
1918	Vaughn	(22-10)		1957	Bunning	(20-8)	0.5
	Hendrix	(19-7)	0.5	1958	Turley	(21-7)	1.5
1919	Cicotte	(29-7)	3	1959	Face	(18-1)	2.5
1920	Bagby	(31-12)	2	1960	Broglio	(21-9)	0.5
1921	Mays	(27-9)	1.5	1961	Ford	(25-4)	3.5
1922	Bush	(26-7)	2.5	1962	Purkey	(23-5)	0.5
1923	Luque	(27-8)	3	1963	Koufax	(25-5)	1.5
1924	Vance	(28-6)	3	1964	Koufax/Bunker	(19-5)	0.5
1925	S. Coveleski	(20-5)	1	1965	Koufax	(26-8)	2
1926	Uhle	(27-11)	1	1966	Marichal	(25-6)	0.5
1927	Hoyt	(22-7)	0.5	1967	Lonborg	(22-9)	0.5
1928	Benton	(25-9)		1968	McLain	(31-6)	4
	Grove	(24-8)		1969	Seaver	(25-7)	1.5
	Hoyt	(23-7)		1970	Cuellar	(24-8)	
	Crowder	(21-5)	2		Gibson	(23-7)	0.5
1929	Earnshaw	(24-8)	1	1971	Blue	(24-8)	
1930	Grove	(28-5)	5.5		McNally	(21-5)	2
1931	Grove	(31-4)	6.5	1972	Carlton	(27-10)	1.5
1932	Gomez	(24-7)	0.5	1973	Hunter	(21-5)	1.5
1933	Grove	(24-8)	1	1974	Messersmith	(20-6)	0.5
1934	Dean	(30-7)	1	1975	Seaver	(22-9)	0.5
1935	Dean	(28-12)	1	1976	Carlton/Garland	(20-7)	0.5
1936	Hubbell	(26-6)	4	1977	Seaver	(21-6)	
1937	Hubbell	(22-8)			Candelaria	(20-5)	1
	J. Allen	(15-1)	0.5	1978	Guidry	(25-3)	3.5
1938	Ruffing	(21-7)	0.5	1979	Flanagan	(23-9)	1
1939	Derringer	(25-7)	1	1980	Stone	(25-7)	1.5
1940	Feller	(27-11)		1981	Seaver	(14-2)	1
	B. Newsom	(21-5)	1.5	1982	P. Niekro	(17-4)	0.5
1941	Riddle	(19-4)	1	1983	Dotson	(22-7)	0.5
1942	Hughson	(22-6)		1984	Sutcliffe	(20-6)	1
	Bonham	(21-5)	0.5	1985	Gooden	(24-4)	2
1943	Chandler	(20-4)	1.5	1986	Clemens	(24-4)	3.5
1944	Newhouser	(29-9)	2.5	1987	Clemens	(20-9)	0.5
1945	Newhouser	(25-9)	1	1988	Viola	(24-7)	
1946	Ferriss	(25-6)	1		Cone	(20-3)	1
1947	Jansen	(21-5)	1	1989	Saberhagen	(23-6)	2.5
1948	Bearden/Brecheen	(20-7)		1990	Welch	(27-6)	2.5
	Kramer	(18-5)	1	1991	Smiley/Erickson	(20-8)	0.5
1949	Parnell	(25-7)	0.5	1992	Morris	(21-6)	1
1950	Maglie	(18-4)	Z0.5	1993	Glavine	(22-6)	0.5
1951	Roe	(22-3)	1	1994	Key	(17-4)	1

Grace Under Pressure

Don Newcombe's performance in clutch situations

Guy Waterman

Big Don Newcombe was one of baseball's dominant pitchers of the 1950s. Mainstay righthander of the last great Brooklyn Dodger teams, Newk won 17 games as a late-called rookie in 1949, 19 games in 1950 and 20 in 1951. Then, following a stint in the service, he came back to win 20 games again in 1955 and a magnificent 27 in 1956.

Newcombe also pioneered as the first black pitcher to appear in the regular rotation of a twentieth century major league team. This role placed him under unprecedented social and psychological pressures.

Jackie Robinson had been the first black to cross the color line in 1947, but when Jackie went to the plate, he was one lone black man facing a team of nine entrenched white men, one of whom (the pitcher) controlled the ball. That was mighty tough on Robinson, but a comfort perhaps to his white opponents.

When Newcombe began to pitch regularly for the 1949 Dodgers, the racial roles were reversed. Now Southern white batters, who had never played with blacks or been required to treat them as equals in any walk of life, suddenly found themselves going up to the plate to face a big black man standing tall on a mound just sixty feet away, backed by eight united black and white teammates. Furthermore, this big

black man had that hard white ball in *his* hand, and he obviously *was* big (6' 4", 220 pounds) and could throw that ball *very* fast and, on occasion, dangerously close to a batter's head.

This reversal of roles placed Newcombe in a social and psychological setting unprecedented in baseball history, a tremendous pressure to bear for a 23-year-old rookie.[1]

The "Choke" Charge—The charge was levelled against Newcombe for many years, based on a half dozen post-season games, that he could not stand up to pressure, that he "choked" in the clutch, that he lost the big games. Newcombe himself was keenly aware of this charge. In a 1962 interview, he recalled the whispers he heard even at the height of his career in 1956:

"People were talking about my 'choking up.'…not being able to win a big game…being 'gutless.'…and all that stuff."[2]

In 1956 a writeup in *The Sporting News*, discussing the Most Valuable Player Award, expressed surprise that Newcombe won, calling attention to "two dismal failures in the [World Series] with the Yankees" and alleging that Sal Maglie (13-5, versus Newcombe's 27-7 in 1956) might have won instead:

Newcombe's failure to come through in the last weeks of the Brooklyn pennant drive while Maglie made himself the leader of the effort,…developed the impression

Guy Waterman is co-author (with his wife, Laura) of several books on recreational history. In other incarnations, he may have been a nightclub piano player, a Washington speechwriter, and a Vermont backwoods homesteader-mountain climber.

that...Salvatore, with his 13-5, would get the prize.[3]

This, despite Newcombe's post-All-Star break record of 18-2. But after a loss in the 1956 World Series, a parking lot attendant accosted Newcombe with the worst kind of accusation:

"Can't you take competition? What's the matter, Newk, are you gutless?"[4]

In 1957 the *Saturday Evening Post* called Newcombe "one of the most maligned pitchers in baseball."[5] As late as 1975 the stigma endured. In *The Dodgers*, published that year, Tommy Holmes closed his passage on Newcombe with this comment:

"The misfortunes he encountered in games with the pennant at stake and in World Series competition detracted greatly from his reputation."[6]

These charges are serious—but are they merited? How well did Don Newcombe perform under pressure? In fairness to the man and to the historical record, this question deserves a careful, objective answer. Let's look at the record.

1949: A rookie comes through—Newcombe came up to the Dodgers in May, 1949, a year of a very close pennant race between Brooklyn and St. Louis. Though a raw rookie, just turning 23 in June, Newk was thrown into the starting rotation. As the race tightened during the last six weeks of the season, Newcombe was repeatedly handed pressure-packed assignments. On August 8, 1949, with the Dodgers and Cards deadlocked at 63 wins and 39 losses each, Newcombe faced Brooklyn's cross-town rivals, the New York Giants, and won a 2-1 squeaker; had he lost, the Brooks would have fallen from first place, as the Redbirds won that day. Later that month Brooklyn and St. Louis went head to head, the Dodgers now trailing by two games. Newcombe drew a start against Cardinal lefthander Al Brazle, whose record was 13-5 going into the game. Newk responded with a six-hit shutout, cutting the Cards' lead to a single game. A contemporary report of the game indicates the amount of pressure involved in that game:

Less than twenty-four hours earlier the Dodgers were on the brink of the obscurity that goes with a runner-up finish, but late yesterday afternoon they were breathing defiance into the faces of the Cardinals, convinced that theirs was a team destined to win the National League pennant.

The convincer was a 6-0, six-hit victory that Don Newcombe hurled...

...The gallant Brooks fashioned back-to-back conquests Tuesday night and yesterday, captured the two "must" games, and now feel certain that the top prize will go to them.

Newcombe's work in this crucial contest was a pitching masterpiece . . .[7]

Nevertheless, by late September St. Louis had assumed the lead again. With four games remaining, one full game back, Newcombe and Preacher Roe pitched a double-header against the Boston Braves, on September 29, 1949. When Roe won the first game and the radio reported the Cards losing to Pittsburgh, the teams were deadlocked: surely a pressure situation for a 23-year-old rookie, going against the Braves' 32-year-old ace, Johnny Sain, a 24-game winner the previous year. Newcombe responded by winning the big game with a four-hit shutout.

On the last day of the season, October 2, 1949, the pennant still not clinched, Shotton started Newcombe again, with only two days' rest. Obviously the Brooklyn manager felt his best hope lay with the young star, despite his inexperience. The Dodgers won that key game, though Newcombe did not pitch well and was relieved in the fourth inning.

For the World Series opener on October 5, 1949, Shotton again picked Newcombe for the starting role, again with just two day's rest. Through eight strong innings, Newcombe overpowered the awesome Yankee lineup, holding them to four hits, with no walks, striking out 11. It was an amazing feat for an inexperienced and overworked 23-year-old, pioneering as the first black starter in a Series. The only trouble was that New York's Allie Reynolds was even better that day, holding the powerful Brooklyn batters to *two* hits. In the ninth, Tommy Henrich caught Newcombe's one mistake of the day, sending it over the fence for a tough 1-0 verdict. But who succumbed to pressure that day? Newcombe, who pitched masterfully save for that one mistake? Or the vaunted Dodger hitters who couldn't get anything going against Reynolds?

In a second Series start that year, on October 8, Newcombe lost again, knocked out in the fourth inning en route to a 6-4 loss. Clearly that was not one of his better performances. Be it noted: he was pitching with just two days' rest for the third time in a row.

1950: Winning the big ones in September—In 1950 the Dodgers again trailed in September, this time 7-1/2 games behind the Philadelphia Phillies (the "Whiz Kids" of that year) whom they faced for a crucial double-header on September 6. This was an absolutely critical twin bill for the desperate Brooks. Newcombe stepped into that pressure-laden scenario and won a close opener, 2-0, yielding but three hits. Having come through brilliantly there, he proceeded to start the second game as well. Bear in mind, this was no meaningless season-end contest in which to stage a gimmick like having one pitcher start both games, in the style of Iron Man McGinnity of the Dark Ages. This was a key double-header, a do-or-die situation for the Dodgers. Having pitched so brilliantly in the opener, Newcombe would have continued his shutout streak through the second game had it not been for fielding misplays by the normally excellent rightfielder, Carl Furillo, which led to two tainted Phillie runs. Newk left in the seventh, trailing 2-1, but Brooklyn rallied for three runs to sweep the crucial two games and stay alive in the pennant race.

Still, by September 23, the Dodgers were seven games out when Newcombe faced Philadelphia's ace, the future Hall of Famer, Robin Roberts. In many face-to-face duels, Roberts had beaten Newcombe before. But in this pressure situation, Newcombe edged Roberts, 3-2.

On October 1, the last day of the season, Brooklyn faced Philadelphia again, with the race still undecided. A Dodger win would tie it up and force a playoff. Newcombe again faced Roberts. Once again Newk pitched magnificently, holding the Phils to one poorly-earned run for nine innings. (Snider and Robinson failed to agree on who would catch a weak pop fly by Del Ennis which either of them might have caught; this put a runner into scoring position who should not have been there.) But Brooklyn's batters could not get more than one run off the great Roberts either, so the game went into the tenth inning. In that frame, Dick Sisler's story-book three-run homer broke the tie and the hearts of Dodger fans. Yes, Newcombe lost this big one—but he might so easily have won in nine innings had others done their jobs as well as he did his.

1951: Trying to Stop the Giants' Rush—In 1951 Newcombe played a hero's role in the Dodgers' des-

Don Newcombe at the height of his powers.

perate struggle to hold their eroding lead over the fast-charging Giants.

On September 8, when the big Dodger lead of August was beginning to blow away, Newk faced the Giants and stopped them on two hits ("an overpowering exhibition," said the *New York Times*).[8]

On September 29, with just two days' rest, Newk faced his old nemesis, Robin Roberts and, in a "must" game, beat him with a seven-hit shutout, the *Times* commenting:

"Facing near-elimination from the National League pennant race, the Dodgers and big Don Newcombe rose magnificently to the challenge."[9]

The very next day, Newk stepped into an urgent relief role, hurling 5-2/3 innings of shutout relief which held the door open for an eventual Dodger win, 9-8 in 14 innings. This amazing sequence of 14-2/3 shutout innings in two successive days occurred just two days before he was asked yet again to take the ball—and start the famous playoff game against the Giants on October 2.

On that fateful day the overworked Newcombe held the powerful Giants to just one run through eight innings. Even then, had Branca (or Labine or Erskine) done his job and got Bobby Thomson out, Newcombe would forever after have been cited as the man who came through in the clutch to win that decisive playoff game. Instead there came the "shot heard 'round the world" and Brooklyn was once more in second place.

The Dodger ace missed all of 1952 and 1953 on account of military service, and part of 1954 as well, the year of the Giants and Dusty Rhodes' pinch homeruns and Willie Mays' dash to deepest centerfield—not part of this story.

The mid-1950s mainstay for pennant winners—In 1955 the Dodgers won an easy race by a 13-1/2 game margin, so pressure was not present. In 1956 it was again close, with Dodger pitchers facing a lot of "must" games. Newcombe came through with his finest year, going 27-7 to win both the Cy Young Award (its first year) and the National League Most Valuable Player. Repeatedly, Newcombe won key victories when the race was tightest. On August 2 he beat the challenging Braves with a four-hit shutout; the *Times'* report next day started: "Don Newcombe won the 'big one' yesterday…"[10] He ran up a scoreless string of 39-2/3 innings right in the heat of the pennant race, then won critical close games in September—3-1 in eleven innings against the Giants on September 7, a three-hit shutout over the Cubs on September 15,

followed by two easy victories, then a heartbreaker loss to Roberts on September 26, and finally a last-day pennant-clincher on September 30. (The last was admittedly a sloppy 8-6 contest in which the offense played a more vital role than the winning pitcher.)

Toward a Just Evaluation—Newcombe lost World

Series games in 1955 and 1956, and these, combined with his 1949 Series losses and those weak final innings in the 1950 and 1951 finales, fueled countless whispers that he couldn't win the big ones. I hope that a more just evaluation may be derived from the foregoing review of his performance in pressure-packed pennant races, plus a realistic look at how well he came through in that first game of 1949, the 1950 season finale, and the 1951 playoff. Given any degree of reasonable support from his teammates, three of those key games would have ended in Newcombe victories, just as so many key pennant games had.

Often overlooked is that other ace pitchers lost crucial games too. (Every game has a loser.) Reynolds, winner of that 1-0 1949 Series opener, had drawn a much more important assignment in the second-to-last game of the regular season that year, a game the Yankees literally had to win to stay alive. Reynolds "choked," if that phrase must be used, allowing the Red Sox to take a 4-0 lead; subsequent Yankee pitching and hitting overcame the deficit. Whitey Ford, winningest pitcher in Series history and renowned as a clutch performer, lost two games in the 1963 Classic, one a 2-1 squeaker. It is not recorded that anyone charged he folded under pressure. That great competitor Bob Gibson failed to win the crucial seventh game in 1968. Let no fool try to accuse Gibson of "choking."

When his first major league manager, Burt Shotton, was asked to comment on one of Newcombe's close losses in 1949, he put it in proper perspective:

What do I think of him? I think he's human, that's all. He just had a bad game in him, the same as every damn one of us in this business, and it came out. Certainly there's nothing else I could think of the boy. He's a great pitcher and he'll be back in there delivering when we need him.[11]

After his 1956 Series losses, President Dwight D. Eisenhower wrote a letter to Newcombe, advising him to forget the Series and remember his performance in the close pennant race. Wrote Ike: "Every athlete in every sport in the world knows that some days things just don't break right."[12] Sportswriter Dick Young summed it up years later with the reminder: "The thing to remember is that Don Newcombe was asked to pitch the big ones."[13]

Don Newcombe in his prime was an impressive, complex, and powerful figure. He faced pressures and hostilities unprecedented for young black pitchers of his time. In later years his career came to an early end amid the disgrace of alcoholism. Yet the big man overcame that enemy too and returned to become a counsellor to big league athletes on coping with the fatal temptations of alcohol and drug abuse. In 1979 he received the Ernie Meld Award as the "figure who has contributed greatly to the overall image of professional baseball both on and off the field." Prior winners had included such other admirable role-models as Ernie Banks, Roberto Clemente, and Phil Niekro.

Young players had good reason to heed his message. No one knew better than Don Newcombe the meaning of pressure. Taking his life as a whole in perspective, no one responded with greater courage.

Notes
1. The unprecedented pressures on Newcombe as the first black pitcher in regular rotation has been examined in detail in Guy Waterman, "Racial Pioneering on the Mound: Don Newcombe's Social and Psychological Ordeal," *NINE: A Journal of Baseball History and Social Policy Perspective*, Volume 1, Number 2 (Spring 1993), pp. 185-195.
2. *The Sporting News*, June 9, 1962.
3. *The Sporting News*, November 28, 1956, p. 10.
4. Michael Brown, quoted in Don Newcombe, "I'm No Quitter," *Saturday Evening Post*, March 9, 1957, p. 27.
5. *Ibid.* (headline).
6. Tommy Holmes *The Dodgers*, (New York: Macmillan, 1975), p. 113.
7. "Dodgers Blank Cards, Trail by Game," *New York Times*, August 25, 1949, p. 27.
8. "Dodgers Crush Giants, 9-0," *New York times*, September 9, 1951, p. S-1.
9. "Newcombe Halts Phils, 5-0, Aided by Pafko 2-Run Homer," *New York Times*, September 30, 1951, p. S-1.
10. "Dodgers Beat Braves Third in Row," *New York Times*, August 3, 1956, p. 13.
11. Burt Shotten, quoted in "Big Don Looms as Dodgers' Hurler for 2nd Series Game," *Afro-American*, October 8, 1949, p. 19.
12. Dwight D. Eisenhower, quoted in Newcombe, "I'm No Quitter," p. 27.
13. Dick Young, *The Sporting News*, October 16, 1973.

The Johnny Cooney Caper

Johnny Cooney was with the Braves for 10 years, 1921-30, with a pitching record of 34-44. He played some outfield and first base, batted .300 or better four different times in limited plate appearances, and never hit a homerun. In 1935, he was born again as an outfielder with the Dodgers. He became the Bums' regular center fielder in 1936-37, hit well, but was still looking for his first four-bagger. Then it was back to the Braves as an outfielder in 1938. In 1939, his 15th National League season, at age 38, he cracked two homeruns in two days. Then he reverted to form, never again hitting a circuit clout, although he played through 1944. In 3,372 at bats over 20 years, he hit two homeruns.

—Don Nelson

If God Owned the Angels...

A look back at the major leagues' first twentieth-century expansion

Tom Ruane

On October 17, 1960, the National League voted to expand to ten teams in 1962 with the addition of entries in New York and Houston. Beaten to the punch, the American League issued a surprise announcement nine days later. The surprise wasn't so much their decision to expand to ten teams, but to jump the gun on the N.L. by adding the new teams (in Los Angeles and Washington) in the spring of 1961.

So began the first wave of expansion in modern baseball history. For the A.L. entries, it looked like a recipe for disaster. An ownership group for the Washington franchise had been selected on November 17, but the league went into the annual winter meetings with the Los Angeles franchise still up in the air. The Dodgers wanted to delay the move of another team into their area, while the A.L. countered with a proposal for both leagues to expand to nine teams in 1961 with inter-league play. The N.L. refused, saying that four months simply wasn't enough time to get a club ready to play.

The A.L. disagreed and on December 6, rejecting a proposal by Charlie Finley, selected a group of owners for Los Angeles headed by Gene Autry. They'd already missed the major-minor league draft and had only a week to prepare for the expansion draft.

Tom Ruane lives and researches in Poughkeepsie, New York.

Pushed back a day by a severe snowstorm, the expansion draft took place in Boston on December 14, 1960. Each of the eight existing clubs provided a list of 15 players, selected from their 40-man reserve list, who would be made available to the new teams. At least seven had to have been on their 25-man rosters as of September 1st. The Angels and Senators were required to pick 28 players from these lists, four from each club. In addition, each expansion team had to take at least 10 pitchers, two catchers, six infielders and four outfielders.

This was similar to the draft on October 10, 1961, to stock the National League teams. Most of the differences seemed to favor the N.L. entries. They'd had a year to scout and prepare for the draft instead of a week. There was no requirement that a team pick a certain number of players by position. In addition to the 15-man lists, each existing club also had to make available two additional players from their 25-man roster. Half of these so-called "premium" players would be doled out in a supplemental draft.

The disadvantages? One was that the talent pool had already been diluted by the previous expansion draft. But the largest potential disadvantage—and the one generating the most argument at the time—was that the N.L. teams had been able to formulate their expansion lists prior to the deadline for setting their 40-man winter rosters. Since a team will typically release marginal players at that time in order to protect minor league prospects, these fringe players could not be included on the A.L. lists of available players. Promising younger players, or more valuable veterans, had to be added instead.

At the time, the feeling was that the National League teams were getting a raw deal. The owners of the Houston Colts threatened to give their franchise back to the league if the player pool wasn't improved. George Weiss of the Mets and Paul Richards of the Colts made a special appeal to the league's other general managers at a meeting held during the World Series. Even A.L. officials joined in the criticism.

Bing Devine, Cardinal general manager and one of the plan's architects, offered a weak defense, saying that the league had never promised the new clubs "pennant contending teams or even first-division outfits," and that he was "sure the Colts and Mets didn't enter the league with the expectation that we'd furnish them—at any price—with a sure-fire pennant winner."

He wasn't kidding. No one was going to confuse either the Mets or the Colts with a first-division outfit for a long, long time. The Angels, on the other hand, would find themselves in first place on July 4, 1962, in the middle of only their second season, and would finish that year a solid third-place team.

Table 1 shows the comparative records of the two league's expansion teams for their first five years.

Table 1					
American League			**National League**		
1961	131- 191	.407	1962	104- 216	.325
1962	146- 177	.452	1963	117- 207	.361
1963	126- 197	.390	1964	117- 205	.363
1964	144- 180	.445	1965	115- 209	.355
1965	145- 179	.448	1966	125- 198	.387
Total	692- 924	.428		578-1035	.358

Not only were the A.L. teams better each year, but the *worst* year for the Angels and Senators (1963) was still better than the *best* year for the Mets and the Colts/Astros (1966). The average A.L. expansion team over this period had a record of 69-92, while the N.L. teams averaged 58-104. Things got so bad for the Mets and Colts that a special draft was held for them following the 1963 season.

Why were the A.L. teams so much better? Were the players the Mets and Colts had to choose from that much worse than the ones made available to the Angels and Senators? With 20-20 hindsight, how good a team could the Mets have been if they'd concentrated on picking the best players available instead of washed-up ex-Dodgers? If an omniscient general manager had been running the Angels instead of Fred Haney, could they have won the pennant in 1962? In 1961?

In order to (at least partially) answer these questions, I need to be able to analyze the sources of talent these teams relied upon: the expansion draft, player purchases, free agent signees and trades. Fortunately, much of this information is available. We know (for the most part) who was on those expansion lists, what players were sold during 1961 and 1962 and who were signed as free agents. And while we don't know what trades could've been made (just as we don't know what players could've been purchased), we do know who was traded and for whom.

Since one of the things I'll want to do is compare players, both individually and in groups, I'll need some way of measuring talent. For this study I'll be using the Marginal Player Rating (MPR)[1], a variation of the Total Player Rating used by Thorn and Palmer in Total Baseball. MPR, described in more detail in the Notes, represents a player's contribution, expressed in wins, over what a marginal or replacement-value player would've done. An average regular or starting pitcher will have a MPR somewhere between 1 and 2, while a negative MPR (converted to zero for this study) means that the player probably shouldn't be in the major leagues.

Let's start with the 1960 A.L. draft. Table 2 shows the list of players the existing clubs made available to the Angels and Senators. Pitchers are listed first and a W or L after the name indicates that the player was drafted by either Washington or Los Angeles.

In addition to these players, Los Angeles selected two players from a minor league pool and Washington three. The Angels picked up Steve Bilko and Albie Pearson, while the Senators added Leo Burke, Joe McClain and Haywood Sullivan. Following the draft, the two teams swapped Davis and Mahoney, Aspromonte and Veal, Hamlin and Zipfel, Chance and Hicks.

Table 3 shows the lists (as far as I can tell) of the National League players made available to the Mets and Astros during the 1961 draft. Here an H or N after the name indicates that player was drafted by either Houston or New York.

Some of this is conjecture. Since the Reds were heading into the World Series at the time this information was released, much of their list was kept secret. The press printed a "best guess" of the rest as well as the names of the "premium" players to be made available after the initial phase. In addition, the Giants' list contained only 14 names, an oversight that went unmentioned (and uncorrected) in the pa-

Table 2

BALTIMORE	BOSTON	CHICAGO	CLEVELAND	DETROIT	KANSAS CITY	MINNESOTA	NEW YORK
Dean Chance-W	Bob Carlson	Alan Brice	Ted Bowsfield-L	P. Burnside-W	Ray Blemker	Pete Cimino	Luis Arroyo
Steve Dalkowski	Jerry Casale-L	Dick Donovan-W	J. Klippstein-W	Wyman Carey	Bob Davis-W	Tex Clevenger-L	Eli Grba-L
Billy Hoeft	Arnie Earley	Ed Hobaugh-W	Mike Lee	Pat Dobson	Ned Garver-L	R. Hernandez-W	Gerald Heintz
Gordon Jones	Dave Hillman	Turk Lown	Carl Mathias-W	Dick Egan	Don Larsen	Hector Maestri-W	Duke Maas-L
Ron Moeller-L	Darrell Massey	Ken McBride-L	Don Newcombe	A. Gatewood-L	Joe Petrokovic	Tom McAvoy	Bob Meyer
	Fred Newman-L	Gerry Staley	Dave Tyriver	Joe Grzenda	Howie Reed	Tom Morgan	Bobby Shantz-W
Bob Boyd	T. Sturdivant-W			Alan Koch	Ken Sanders	H. Woodeshick-W	Roland Sheldon
Clint Courtney	Ted Wills	Earl Averill-L	K. Aspromonte-W	Dave Sisler-W			Ted Wieand
Walt Dropo	Wilbur Wood	Joe Ginsberg	Steve Demeter	Bob Sprout-L	Hank Bauer	Julio Becquer-L	
Gene Green-W		Billy Goodman	Don Dillard		Chester Boak-W	Steve Korcheck	Fritz Brickell
Chuck Hinton-W	Jim Fregosi-L	Joe Hicks-L	Marty Keough-W	Harry Chiti	Frank Cipriani	Hal Naragon	Bob Cerv-L
Billy Klaus-W	Don Gile	T. Kluszewski-L	Jim King-W	Neil Chrisley	Pete Daley-W	John Schaive-W	Alan Hall
James Liggett	Jim Mahoney-L	Dean Look	Gene Leek-L	Dick Gernert	Dutch Dotterer-W	F.Throneberry-L	Ken Hunt-L
Don Ross-L	Rip Repulski	Jim McAnany-L	Gordon Lund	Bob Rodgers-L	Ken Hamlin-W	J. Valdivielso	Dale Long-W
G. Woodling-W	Ed Sadowski-L	Jim Rivera	Joe Morgan	Coot Veal-L	Jay Hankins	Elmer Valo	Gil McDougal
Frank Zupo	Willie Tasby-W	Earl Torgeson	Red Wilson				

Table 3

CHICAGO	CINCINNATI	LOS ANGELES	MILWAUKEE	PHILADELPHIA	PITTSBURG	ST. LOUIS	SAN FRANCISCO
Dick Burwell	Harvey Alex	Nelson Chittum	Johnny Antonelli	Ray Culp	Al Jackson-N	Craig Anderson-N	Don Choate
Dick Drott-H	Marv Fodor	Roger Craig-N	Bob Botz	Ruben Gomez	Clem Labine	Al Cicotte	Ray Daviault-N
Mel Wright	Ken Johnson-H	Jim Golden-H	Ken MacKenzie	Bruce Gruber	W. Mizell	Kerry McDaniel	Dick Denton
	Sherman Jones-N	Rene Valdes	Seth Morehead	Jess Hickman-H	Curt Raydon	Clint Stark	Ed Feldman
Richie Ashburn	Howie Nunn	Rick Warren	Dennis Overby	Ken Lehman	Bobby Shantz-H	Bill Wakefield	Eddie Fisher
Walter Bales	Orlando Pena		Paul Roof-H	Robin Roberts	Jim Umbricht-H		Sam Jones-H
Lou Bishop	Ray Ripplemeyer	Bob Aspromonte-H				C. Cannizzaro-N	Billy Loes
Ed Bouchee-N		Sheldon Brodsky	Bob Boyd	Dick Allen	J. Christopher-N	Roberto Herrara	Dom Zanni
Sam Drake-N	Rogelio Alvarez	Mel Corbo	Neil Chrisley	C. Coleman-N	Norm Housely	Jim Hickman-N	
George Freese	Gus Bell-N	Gil Hodges-W	Gino Cimoli	Pancho Herrera	Johnny Logan	Gary Kolb	Ernie Bowman
Al Heist-H	Elio Chacon-N	Norm Larker-H	John DeMerit-N	Al Kenders	Roman Mejias-H	Don Landrum	Eddie Bressoud-H
Jim McAnany	Vic Davalillo	Al Norris	Felix Mantilla-N	Bob Sadowski	Henry Mitchell	Bob Lillis-H	Dick Dietz
Jim McKnight	Dick Gernert-H	Ralph Plummer	Wayne McDonald	B. G. Smith-N	Walt Moryn	Gerry Marx	Hobie Landrith-N
Paul Popovich	Fred Hopke	Norm Sherry	Merritt Ranew-H	Elmer Valo	Rocky Nelson	Ed Olivares-H	Jim Marshall
Mel Roach	Darrell Johnson	Gene Wallace	Phil Roof	Ken Walters	Elmo Plaskett	R. Schoendienst	John Weekly
Moe Thacker		Gordon Windhorn	Sammy White				

pers of the day.

Table 4 shows the probable players made available during the "premium" phase

Table 4

CHICAGO	CINCINNATI	LOS ANGELES	MILWAUKEE
Don Zimmer-N	Jay Hook-N	Dick Farrell-H	Al Spangler-H
Jim Brewer	Don Blasingame	Daryl Spencer	Don McMahon
Barney Schultz	Wally Post		Bob Taylor

PHILADELPHIA	PITTSBURG	ST. LOUIS	SAN FRANCISCO
Lee Walls-N	Hal Smith-H	Bob Miller-N	Joe Amalfitano-H
Dallas Green	Don Leppert	Alex Grammas	Billy O'Dell
			Dick Lemay

The selected player (the one we're sure about) is listed first. In the case of the Cubs, Reds, Braves and Giants, there was some confusion as to the premium players and both guesses are listed.

Which draft had more talent? Table 5 shows the total MPR wins for all players available in each draft, the total selected by the expansion teams, as well as the percentage of talent selected. The three columns are intended to cover short, medium and long-range value and contain the sum of MPR wins for the years indicated.[2]

In terms of MPR wins, there was actually slightly

more talent available to the National League teams, both in the short and the long term, than to the American League teams. Surprisingly, the Mets and Colts as a group didn't seem to do much worse at finding short-range talent than the Angels and Senators.

Table 5

1960 American League Draft

	61	61-65	61+
Available:	51.4	172.5	291.8
Selected:	29.8	130.5	172.7
PCT:	58.0	75.7	59.2

1961 National League Draft

	62	62-66	62+
Available:	53.0	177.7	299.9
Selected:	28.6	87.3	116.7
PCT:	54.0	49.1	38.9

But the breakdown by team on Table 6 tells another story.

It now becomes clear why the Mets had such a disastrous start. Pretty much *all* the talent drafted by the National League teams was picked up by the Colts. 11 players were drafted that year that would have an MPR of 1.0 or higher in 1962; all 11 were

Table 6

Years following draft

	1	1-5	1+
Angels	15.2	66.9	102.6
Senators	14.6	63.6	70.1
Colts	24.4	52.3	61.6
Mets	4.2	35.0	55.1

drafted by the Colts. It seems incredible that out of the 53.0 MPR wins available in the draft, the Mets could've found 22 players that between them totaled only 4.2 wins—Ed Bressoud by himself had more than that. What might not be obvious is why Houston didn't have a better record than 64-96, as they clearly out-drafted even the Angels.

More on that later. First, Table 7 shows the top ten players available in each draft.

Table 7

1960 American League Draft

	61		61-65		61+
*Donovan	4.5	*Fregosi	14.9	Wood	37.9
Hoeft	4.3	*Chance	14.7	*Fregosi	37.8
*McBride	3.7	*Shantz	9.4	*Chance	26.3
Arroyo	3.7	*Woodeshick	8.7	Dobson	16.5
Morgan	3.5	*McBride	8.4	Sanders	14.7
*Grba	2.5	*Hinton	8.2	*Woodeshick	11.7
Lown	2.5	*Donovan	7.4	*Shantz	9.4
*Bowsfield	2.4	*Klippstein	7.4	*Hinton	8.6
*Shantz	2.2	Hoeft	7.3	*McBride	8.4
*Woodling	1.9	*Newman	7.2	*Klippstein	8.0

1961 National League Draft:

	62		62-66		62+
*Bressoud	5.2	Allen	18.1	Allen	49.7
*Farrell	3.7	*Bressoud	12.3	Fisher	19.7
Roberts	3.5	Fisher	12.1	*Miller	18.2
Fisher	3.4	Roberts	11.2	*Bressoud	12.3
*Shantz	3.0	*Miller	8.3	Culp	12.0
Ashburn	2.3	*Johnson	8.0	Dietz	12.0
*Umbricht	2.1	*Farrell	7.3	Pena	11.9
Zanni	1.7	*Shantz	7.3	*Johnson	11.3
Pena	1.6	*Jackson	6.9	Roberts	11.2
*Larker	1.5	*Mantilla	6.2	*Farrell	11.0

Here, an asterisk means that player was selected in the draft. A few things to note:

1) nearly all of the short-range talent that was overlooked in the A.L. draft was veteran relief pitching. Since the Angels eventually picked up Morgan, one of the best, this hardly hurt them.

2) almost none of the medium-range talent was missed by the A.L. teams. By 1964, *none* of the bypassed position players had any hits in major league baseball. The story in the National League was quite different. From the Phillies alone, they failed to draft the 1963 Rookie Pitcher of the Year (Ray Culp) as well as the 1964

Rookie of the Year (Dick Allen). Not only did they miss 3 out of 4 of the top players in this range, but most of the players they did select had their best sea-

sons elsewhere. Among the top players, only Ken Johnson and Dick Farrell would collect the majority of their MPR wins for the team that drafted them.

3) the only long-range oversights made by the Angels and Senators were late-blooming pitchers. In 1971, Wilbur Wood and Pat Dobson would win 22 and 20 games, respectively, and Ken Sanders would be the best relief pitcher in baseball. A lot of other teams missed seeing their potential as well; prior to their big seasons, Sanders had been released, Wood sold and Dobson traded twice.

One difference between the A.L. and N.L. drafts was in the number of players selected. The A.L. teams had to pick 28 each, or 56 out of the 120 available players. The N.L. teams could take between 16 and 24 players from these lists. Houston selected 19 and New York only 18 during this phase. They each had to pick four more players apiece during the "premium" phase of the draft. So while each team could've selected as many as 28 players, they didn't have to take more than 20. In retrospect this might have been a disadvantage for the Mets and Colts. Between them, they only picked 16 pitchers. By contrast, the Angels and Senators selected 25, the last two being Dean Chance and Dick Donovan, who would both win 20 games and lead their leagues in ERA.

Still, how important was the draft as a source of immediate talent to the expansion teams? Table 8 shows the percentage of the total at-bats and innings pitched that were produced by the players selected in the draft.[3]

Table 8

	At-Bats	%	Innings	%	Avg.
Angels:	2149/5040	42.6	834/1438	58.0	50.3
Senators:	3798/4953	76.7	689/1425	48.4	62.5
Colts:	3553/5168	68.8	693/1454	47.7	58.2
Mets:	2284/5110	44.7	1057/1430	73.9	59.3

But these numbers underestimate the draft's importance because they don't include players obtained in trades. After both drafts, the expansion teams dealt some of those they'd selected.

Table 9 shows the players they got in return.

Table 9

	At-Bats	%	Innings	%	Avg.
Angels:	3274/5040	65.0	1104/1438	76.8	70.9
Senators	4380/4953	88.4	931/1425	65.3	76.9
Colts:	4110/5168	79.5	886/1454	60.9	70.2
Mets:	3419/5110	66.9	1077/1430	75.3	71.1

A look at these trades goes a long way to explaining why the Colts didn't do better during their inaugural season. They sent their most valuable short-term talent, Ed Bressoud, to Boston for a disappointing Don Buddin. They swapped Bobby Shantz, another of their best picks, to the Cards for two players who between them had 0.1 MPR wins left in their careers. While at the other extreme, the Angels swapped a group of players like Jim McAnany, Tex Clevenger and Ken Hamlin for three future all-stars: Leon Wagner, Billy Moran and Lee Thomas.

The new teams traded 16 of the drafted players before the end of their first season. Table 10 shows how they did in those trades.

Table 10									
	MPR obtained			lost			difference		
	1	1-5	1+	1	1-5	1+	1	1-5	1+
Angels:	3.4	28.3	29.7	0.9	1.8	2.4	+2.5	+26.5	+27.3
Senators:	5.6	18.3	18.3	3.8	22.3	25.3	+1.8	-4.0	-7.0
Colts:	1.5	5.6	5.6	8.4	19.7	19.9	-6.9	-14.1	-14.3
Mets:	0.8	0.8	0.8	0.5	1.8	1.8	+0.3	-1.0	-1.0

It's a little surprising how little trading the Mets did. Immediately following the draft, George Weiss, the president of the Mets, looked over the roster of his 22 selections and told the press:

> Please don't think that this is the line-up which will open the season. Trades and money will change it. I'd say two-thirds of this group will be with us in spring training in St. Petersburg.

As it turned out, 21 of the 22 players would play next season for the Mets. Only Lee Walls, sent to the Dodgers along with a bucket of cash for Charlie Neal, would be dealt away prior to spring training. Eventually, the Mets would start dealing, trading away most of the medium-range talent they drafted. Felix Mantilla, Al Jackson and Bob Miller would all have their best seasons elsewhere. Of their combined 21.4 MPR wins, all but 1.9 of them would come for other teams.

If you adjust the earlier chart of the talent drafted by each team to account for the trades made during the first year, you get the figures in Table 11.

Table 11			
Years following draft			
	1	1-5	1+
Angels:	17.7	93.4	129.9
Senators:	16.4	59.6	63.1
Colts:	17.5	38.2	47.3
Mets:	4.5	34.0	54.1

Table 12 shows how that compares with each team's winning percentage.

Table 12				
Years following draft				
	1		1-5	
Angels:	17.7	.435	93.4	.474
Senators:	16.4	.379	59.6	.382
Colts:	17.5	.400	38.2	.412
Mets:	4.5	.250	34.0	.322

The Colts did better than expected given their medium-range draft results, much of this due to their emerging farm system. Normally, it took about five seasons for a young player to work his way through the minors and make an impact on the parent team, but by the end of their second season the Colts featured the first all-rookie line-up. And it wasn't just a gimmick—included in that line-up were future all-stars Joe Morgan, Jimmy Wynn, Rusty Staub and Jerry Grote.

But in the first few years at least, an expansion team can count on little help from home-grown talent. The only other significant source of players available during that period are free agents (which back then meant players who had been released) and players for sale. It's impossible to know what players, given enough money, *could* have been purchased, but we do know what players were sold and what free agents were signed. This gives us a good idea of what talent, apart from the expansion draft, was available to the new teams. From the A.L. draft to the end of the 1961 season, 36 players were purchased or signed as free agents at the major league level. Table 13 shows the MPR breakdown.

Table 13				
	Players	1	1-5	1-
Total	36	11.1	32.9	39.1
Angels:	7	6.5	16.6	22.8
Senators:	2	0.1	0.4	0.4

The next year, 41 players were purchased or signed as free agents at the major league level. Table 14 shows their MPR breakdown.

Table	14			
	Players	1	1-5	1-
Total	41	16.9	45.7	68.2
Mets:	11	4.8	7.3	7.9
Colts:	6	3.1	10.1	21.6

Table 15 shows the players who were the top five players sold or signed as free agents.

Table 15			
1960-1961:			
	61		61-
*Tom Morgan	3.5	*Ron Kline	15.4
*Ron Kline	1.5	*Tom Morgan	4.9
Dick Brown	1.1	Dick Brown	3.8
*Rocky Bridges	0.9	Ed Rakow	3.3
Chuck Essegian	0.8	Wes Covington	2.9
1961-1962:			
	62		62-
Robin Roberts	3.5	*Don McMahon	21.5
*Don McMahon	3.0	Moe Drabowski	15.2
*Richie Ashburn	2.3	Robin Roberts	11.2
Joe Nuxhall	2.0	Joe Nuxhall	6.8
*Frank Thomas	1.6	*Richie Ashburn	2.3

An asterisk means that the player was picked up by an expansion team.

Relief pitchers comprised the bulk of the long-range talent. With the exception of the Angels' Tom Morgan, all of the valuable relief pitchers (Kline, McMahon and Drabowski) had their best season with other teams.

More talent was moved in this fashion during the Mets and Colts first year than during the Angels and Senators. So once again, the N.L. teams' poor showing doesn't seem to have been due to a lack of available talent. But it also should be noted that purchases and free agents were a much thinner source of talent in both years than the expansion draft.

And while the Angels' domination in purchasing players and signing free-agents is a little deceptive (they did let Ron Kline get away before his best seasons), this was yet another category in which they excelled. How well could've they done with an all-knowing general manager?—probably not that much better than they did. To be sure, some of it was dumb luck. At the conclusion of the draft, the Senators wanted to add a fifth outfielder. They offered Fred Haney a list of 3 or 4 unfamiliar players to pick from in exchange for Joe Hicks. "Well, I don't know who to take," he said. "Hell, I'll take a chance on Chance."

Of course the team could've been improved. An omniscient general manager probably would've picked up Dick Donovan and Chuck Hinton (both late picks by Washington), who, considering their outstanding 1962 seasons (Donovan winning 20 games and Hinton hitting .310), would've made the Yankees even more uncomfortable that summer. As it was, the Angels found themselves in a pennant race

during their second season, something no other expansion team has been able to accomplish in any of their first four seasons.

Just as it's hard to examine all the blunders made by the Mets during their first season and imagine an first-year team doing a worse job, it's not easy to look at what the Angels accomplished without regarding it as an upper-bound on the amount of short-term success an expansion team can enjoy. What's amazing is that, picking from similar groups of players, and with only days to prepare instead of a year, the Angels were able to win 65 more games over the first two years than the Mets.

In 1968, both leagues would expand again. The rules would be different, with the established teams providing lists of protected (rather than available) players, but once more the A.L. teams would be far better than their N.L. counterparts. The Kansas City Royals, while not matching the immediate success of the Angels, would end up with the best five-year record of any expansion team. It wouldn't be until 1976 that the American League would have truly awful expansion teams, when the Blue Jays and Mariners would enter the league and approach, but not reach, the five-year record of futility set by the Mets and Colts.

Unfortunately, a similar analysis of how these later expansion teams did is not possible at present. The protected lists were never entirely leaked to the press as the first (and the most recent) ones were. And the passage of time (25 years in the case of the 1968 expansion) hasn't made the league offices any more willing to declassify this information. So for the time being, we don't know just how good the Royals (or the Expos or the Mariners) could've been—whether players like Dick Allen or Ray Culp were overlooked or whether they did as good a job as possible with the meager talent made available to them.

Notes:

1. Total Player Rating (TPR), used by Thorn and Palmer in Total Baseball, measures a player's value (expressed in wins) over an average performance at his position. A team consisting entirely of players with TPRs of zero would be expected to win about half their games. By itself, then, this is not a particularly good indicator of talent since it treats an average player as having no value.

What's missing from the formula is the difference between an average player (again expressed in wins) over a replacement-value player. This should take into account service—an average player who played regularly should be more valuable than one sitting on the bench. For simplicity, I have measured service in terms of plate appearances for position players and a combination of innings pitched and relief appearances for pitchers. In order to determine the formula, I assumed that a team consisting entirely of replacement-value players would have a winning percentage of .350. I used the performance of first-year expansion teams as a rough approximation of this.

Over the course of a season, then, a team consisting entirely of players with TPRs of zero would win about 25 more games than a team of replacement-value players. Figuring about 13 of those wins would come from the position players, who'd have about 5600-6000 plate appearances a year (depending upon the use of the DH), I gave all position players credit for one win for each 450 plate appearances. The pitching wins were also divided up rather arbitrarily; assuming 1450 innings and about 200 relief appearance a year, I gave all pitchers a win for every 160 innings pitched and another for every 80 relief appearances.

These wins were added to the player's TPR to yield his Marginal Player Rating (MPR). For this study, I converted all negative MPRs to zero. A negative MPR simply means that the player was worse than a replacement-value player at his position (not uncommon for an expansion team) and I didn't want to treat a terrible player who played regularly as worse than an inferior player cut during spring training.

2. Where more than one player was suggested as the other "premium" player (for example, Don McMahon and Bob Taylor from the Braves), I have averaged their MPRs.

3. The players swapped by the Angels and Senators immediately following the draft are included in the A.L. figures.

No Kidding

As the 1994 baseball season recedes into the record books, it may be of interest to say a few words about one of the game's great unsung heroes. I am referring to Juan Ponce de Leon, who was born in Madrid in 1460, broke into professional baseball in 1874 at an age when most players are well past their primes, played intermittently with the National, American, Federal, and other leagues over a 69-year period, and died in St. Augustine, Florida in 1963 at the ripe old age of 503.

Juan (a.k.a. Kid de Leon, the Castilian Kid and Kid Madrid) was a pretty fair ballplayer, with a batting average of .306, 992 RBIs, and 235 stolen bases in 19 seasons played. However, his amazing vital statistics alone would be enough to enshrine him among baseball's (near-) immortals, not to mention the fact that he was probably the first player of Hispanic descent to make it in the big time. Why did the Kid wait so long before launching his career? First of all, as every schoolchild knows, he spent his early years searching for the legendary Fountain of Youth. (Indeed, there is some evidence that he actually found it.) It should also be remembered that the game of baseball was not invented until de Leon was well into middle age. (A persistent report that he was seen in his mid-200's with a Spanish Triple A team was discredited a long time ago.)

I came upon this astounding information recently while leafing through the huge Total Baseball encyclopedia, which gives Kid de Leon's complete stats for illustrative purposes on page 631 in the section explaining the use of the all-time player register. Some skeptics will probably come forward to claim that the whole thing is just a put-on, and it is curious that the Kid doesn't appear in the actual register. However, the two men who put Total Baseball together, John Thorn and Pete Palmer, are well known as serious-minded, dedicated baseball scholars, and it hardly seems likely that they would attempt to perpetrate a hoax of such magnitude on their readers.

—Louis Jay Herman

Alonso Perry in the Dominican Republic

A dominant force

José de Jesus Jiménez, M.D.

Baseball in the Dominican Republic began in1891, when a group of Cuban sportsmen headed by the brothers Ignacio and Ubaldo Alomá introduced the game in the country.

In the first 29 years of this century, short series were played among local teams. At times, we were visited by professional teams from Cuba and Puerto Rico. There was no professional baseball from 1929 to 1935 starting again in 1936. In 1937, great baseball came to the D.R., when a group of stars from the Negro Leagues in the U.S., including men like Leroy Matlock, Satchel Paige, Joshua Gibson, Lazaro Salazar, Martin Dihigo, and Sam Bankhead visited the country. The Dominican capital was represented by the team "Ciudad Trujillo". This team won the 36-game season championship. Other teams were "Aguilas Cibaenas" (The Eagles) from Santiago and the Estrellas Orientales (Oriental Stars) from San Pedro de Macoris. The "Ciudad Trujillo" team was a fusion of the two traditional teams in our capital: Licey and Escogido. This fusion did not last long. In fact, after 1937, there was no professional baseball in the D.R. until 1951.

That year, the summer season lasted from May 5 up to September 24, with teams in Santo Domingo, in the capital (then named Ciudad Trujillo)—with both Licey and Escogido, in Santiago, with the Eagles, and in San Pedro de Macoris with the Oriental Stars.

From 1951 through 1954, the season was divided into two rounds of 27 games each. The winners of the first and second rounds had to face off in the final series in order to decide the national championship. Games were played Saturday afternoon and Sundays: one in the morning and the other in the afternoon.

Alonso Perry, a 6'3", 200-lb. veteran of the Negro Leagues played his first Dominican profession game as first baseman and cleanup hitter for Licey. In his first game he got no hits, but from then on he connected for one or more in 27 straight games, a record for Dominican baseball. He ended the regular season at .400 (36-for 90), with nine homeruns. In the final series against Escogido, he was named Most Valuable Player after connecting in five straight games, deciding the last contest with a grand slam.

In 1952, Perry played the full season, batted.327, and lead the league with 11 homeruns. Licey lost the final series against the Eagles four games to three.

In 1953, Perry set a still-standing record of 53 runs batted in. He was also leader in homers (11) and stolen bases (16)—only time in anyone has ever accomplished that double in the D.R. In the final series between the Eagles and the Licey Tigers, Perry was the leader in batting: 8 hits in 21 at bats for an average of .381. The series was finally won by the Tigers four games to one.

Perry again led the league in 1954, with an average of .336, and he carried his team to the final series against the Estrellas Orientales. The series was won by the Stars.

Jose de Jesus Jimenez, M.D. is a SABR member who lives in the Dominican Republic.

In 1955, Dominican baseball became affiliated with Organized Baseball, and became winter baseball, sometimes played, for the first time, under lights. The Dominican League of Professional Baseball was created. The teams were the traditional ones: Aguilas, Licey (Tigers), Escogido and Estrellas Orientales. The affiliation with organized baseball in the United States, and the switch to winter ball allowed the Dominican teams to bring many more excellent players from the U.S.

In1955, the modern stadium "Quisqueya" was inaugurated in our capital. The 1955-56 season started on October 23 and finished February 5, 1956. There was a single regular season, then with a semi-final series and finally, the winner of the semifinal series had to face the winner of the regular season. In that inaugural season, Perry batted .325 and was leader in doubles with 12.

Perry had an off-year in1956-57, and many Licey fans started to think that the old idol was reaching an end. But Perry came back to win the batting title the next year, with an average of .332. His last season in Dominican baseball was 1958-59. This time playing with the Estrellas Orientales, his total of 49 homers set a record that stood until Ricardo Carty hit 50 in 1973-74. Perry is considered the non-Dominican player with the best career in the history of Dominican baseball. His final batting average was .310.

Perry was born in Alabama in 1923. He played in the Negro Leagues in the U.S. from 1940 to 1950. He was originally a pitcher, but was later switched to first base so that his potent bat would be in the lineup every day. He never played in the major leagues, as he certainly would have if he'd been white. He also played in Mexico from 1955 until 1963. With Diabolos Rojos in 1956, he won the Mexican League triple crown: 392-28-118.

Alonso Perry in the Dominican Republic

Year	Team	G	AB	R	RBI	H	BA	1B	2B	3B	HR	TB	SA	BB	SO	SB
1951	Licey	25	90	27	32	36	.400	22	4	1	9	69	767	21	2	10
1952	Licey	45	162	29	38	53	.327	32	9	1	11	97	599	17	14	5
1953	Licey	56	229	40	53	67	.293	41	11	4	11	119	519	23	10	16
1954	Licey	42	146	29	29	49	.336	29	11	1	8	86	589	32	5	6
1955-56	Licey	53	209	29	31	68	.325	46	13	6	3	102	478	14	16	2
1956-57	Licey	46	159	19	19	40	.252	32	7	1	0	49	308	24	19	2
1957-58	Licey	51	202	18	23	67	.332	54	8	2	3	88	436	14	24	1
1958-59	Estrellas Orientales	60	233	27	27	63	.270	48	9	2	4	88	378	12	16	0
Totals		378	1430	218	252	443	.310	304	72	18	49	698	488	157	106	42

The DiMaggio Streak: How Big a Deal *was* It?

Other players actually had a better chance

Charles Blahous

Charles Blahous lives in Alexandria, Virginia.

Joe DiMaggio's 56-game hitting streak is rightly praised in song and story as a herculean feat of consistency. And yet I would be willing to wager that few recognize just how improbable, how flukish this achievement was, even for the great DiMaggio. In this article I want to pose and to answer the question, "Even given the high level of performance established by Joe DiMaggio in 1941, how unlikely was it for Joe to put his hits together in a way that produced a 56-game streak?" And, once we answer that, to ask, "Is there anyone who actually would have had a better chance, statistically speaking, to produce this astounding result?"

Many statisticians have attempted to estimate the improbability of DiMaggio's hitting streak using the frequencies of occurrence of hits throughout baseball as a basis. Of course, the likelihood of such a streak varies dramatically as a function of hit probability per at bat (batting average), such that the chances of a .250 hitter putting such a streak together are negligible when compared to a .375 hitter. DiMaggio's chances of putting together such a streak were greatly enhanced because he was one of the leading hitters for average in the game. Given the quality of DiMaggio's hitting in 1941, and the large numbers of at bats afforded him by being in the middle of the Yankee lineup, how likely was the streak in purely statistical terms?

For the purposes of this study we will ignore walks and hit batsmen, and other plate appearances in which an at bat is not assigned, instead of trying to estimate the chances that DiMaggio had to turn a walk into a hit. Since hits can only occur in plate appearances in which an at bat is charged, we can define his opportunities for hits as being his at bats, even though in some unquantifiable sense, this is not true. However, given that we are only trying to measure the unlikelihood of his hits being arranged in such a way as to produce a streak, and are not interested in changing the total number of hits, taking DiMaggio's .357 average as an assigned frequency of hit production, this is an assumption consistent with our aims.

A player's chances of getting a hit in a game are a function of two things: his success rate per at bat, and his number of at bats. Joe's chance of getting a hit in 1941 was .357 per at bat, which is to say that his chance of making an out was .643. In a given number of at bats, his chance of getting at least one hit is, conveniently, one minus his chance of getting no hits. Thus, we simply take his chance of not getting a hit, .643, and raise it to the power equal to the number of his at bats. In 1941, Joe averaged 3.89 at bats per game, meaning that his chance of going without during each game was 0.179. Ergo, in each game, Joe's chances of getting at least one hit were 82.1 percent.

If your chances of getting at least one hit in each game are .821, your chances of getting at least one hit in each of a span of 56 games is .821 to power 56, or .0000160. That represents Joe's chance, given a 56-game span, of getting at least one hit in every game.

Now, Joe played 139 games in 1941, meaning that he had 84 56-game spans. His chances of putting together a 56-game streak in any one of them is, again, one minus his chances of never getting a 56-game streak. This amounts to .00134, which is to say that Joe had a 0.134 percent chance in 1941, given his .357 average and total number of at bats, of hitting in 56 straight games.

One way to put this in perspective is to note how many identical 1941 seasons Joe would have had to play before he would have had an even-money chance of putting together a 56-game streak. Taking the chances of his failing to put together such a streak, and raising them exponentially to the number of seasons played, you get into the 517th season before Joe's chances of doing it somewhere along the way are better than 50-50.

Now, bear in mind that Joe has to play each of these seasons at the level that he established in 1941. Even the career-average-level Joe DiMaggio would have to play for much longer to have a 50-50 chance of turning the trick.

It should be obvious from the above derivation that Joe DiMaggio, great player that he was, was not the most likely man to produce a 56-game streak, at least on the basis of probability. Perhaps he alone had the consistency and temperament to pull it off. Yet, there are a number of other twentieth-century players who had seasons with a better chance to do it than Joe, thanks to their high batting averages and at bats per game. A list of some strong candidates follows:

Player	Yr.	Avg.	Chance of Streak	Yrs to 50-50
Nap Lajoie	1901	.426	18.9 percent	4
Ty Cobb	1911	.420	12.4 percent	6
Ty Cobb	1912	.409	4.6 percent	15
George Sisler	1920	.407	8.7 percent	8
George Sisler	1922	.420	15.6 percent	5
Rogers Hornsby	1922	.401	5.3 percent	13
Rogers Hornsby	1924	.424	4.5 percent	16
Al Simmons	1925	.387	5.8 percent	12
Lefty O'Doul	1929	.398	6.4 percent	11
Bill Terry	1930	.401	6.7 percent	11
Joe DiMaggio	1941	.357	0.13 percent	517

You can easily see how minor fluctuations in batting average can cause large differences in a player's chances of putting together a long streak. Batting average is clearly the most important factor, closely followed by at bats per game, and finally by number of games played (streak opportunities).

You may find it incredible that Nap Lajoie's chances of putting together a 56-game hitting streak in 1901 were almost one in five. Your instincts are right. There is a fallacy underlying these figures that we have yet to analyze.

The above data assume that the batter plays his games in perfectly consistent conditions. But of course, Joe DiMaggio did not receive 3.89 at bats in every game of 1941. Sometimes he had five, and sometimes only two. This has a large effect on a player's chances to put together a long streak, for the simple reason that a two at-bat game takes away from his chances more than a six at-bat game adds to them (already, at five at bats, chances of getting one hit are very good, and are not significantly added to in the sixth at bat, whereas failure to get a third chance is statistically likely to be crucial). The further we stray from perfect at-bat consistency, the more a player's chances diminish. Indeed, even moving from 3.89 to the real-world discrete figures of three or four at bats has a detrimental effect.

Nap Lajoie is listed as having 4.15 at bats for every game in 1901. Suppose, in a given 56-game streak, he had one game with two at bats, 11 with three, 28 with four, 12 with five, three with six, and one with seven at bats. Normally, with perfect at-bat consistency, his chances of a streak over those 56 games would be 0.276 percent. The variation in at-bat numbers by itself reduces the result to 0.107 percent, reduces his chances during the season of having such a streak from 18.9 percent to 7.7 percent, and increases the number of years from four to nine that he would have to hit .426 in this manner to have a 50-50 shot.

Nine years may not seem like a long time to have to play before the 56-game streak becomes an even-money proposition, but, of course, no one has ever hit .426 over nine years, and it's highly unlikely that anyone ever will. It is further testimony to DiMaggio's achievement that, even when Lajoie was hitting at what seems like an now unattainable pace, the chances were more than 90 percent against him.

Still, Lajoie's streak potential does seem very high, perhaps unrealistically high, given the curious fact that *Total Baseball* does not list him as having achieved even a 30-game hitting streak in 1901, which he would have been overwhelmingly likely to do at at least some point, even with random fluctuations in his at bats per game. In every game, on average, that Lajoie played that year, he had a full 90 percent chance of coming away with at least one hit, making a 30-game streak quite likely at some point. His failure to be listed as having one may seem a bit odd. It is worth noting that the next best "streak candidates, " George Sisler in 1922 and Ty Cobb in 1911, had hitting streaks of 41 and 40 games, respectively.

Lajoie's record is particularly problematic in view of the fact that Murphy's biography of Lajoie lists him as having a .422 average for 1901 instead of the .426 credited him by *Total Baseball*. Moreover, even Murphy's figure is higher than that supposed for some time, until an error in Lajoie's record was rectified and nine hits were restored to him. In short, the lack of a long streak is not the only way in which Lajoie's records for 1901 are a bit unusual. This and the fact that in the American League of 1901, a foul did not count as a strike, means that the reader may be justified in viewing Ty Cobb, George Sisler, and Rogers Hornsby as the twentieth-century players most qualified to hold this particular record. That DiMaggio, or for that matter Pete Rose, possesses a streak longer than Sisler's or Cobb's, is an astounding feat of consistency and concentration.

The discerning reader may wonder how these calculations take proper account of the influences of pitching and opposing defense, the latter factor perhaps particularly coming to mind in view of the way that DiMaggio's streak came to an end. In a sense, our computations took these factors into account when we accepted DiMaggio's .357 batting average as a given commodity. That batting average resulted from a complex interaction of DiMaggio's hitting ability with the skill of the pitchers he faced, as well as the defenses arrayed against him. Since we know the cumulative result of those interactions, and are merely trying to figure the likelihood of the hits being arranged in a certain way, we do not need to know how they worked together to produce the .357 result— that is, so long as we assume that DiMaggio had the same chance of getting a hit in each of the 56 games.

In the real world, as we have seen, DiMaggio did not have the same chance in every game, due for example, to the differing number of at bats from game to game. When we face this reality, we also lose the luxury of ignoring the specific influences of pitching and other factors. Just as it matters, for example, whether DiMaggio had two four at-bat games or one each of two at-bat and six at-bat games, it also matters whether he faced the better pitcher in the two at-bat versus the six at-bat game, as his hit chances would be affected accordingly. If we were to estimate

Nap Lajoie

DiMaggio's streak chances with perfect rigor, we would have to know not only the opposing pitchers' statistical profiles, but also the precise way in which pitchers' and fielders' skills worked together with DiMaggio's abilities, to affect his chances in every at bat. Although game designers have over the years assumed that offensive and pitching/defensive statistics each contribute exactly 50 percent to the statistical profile associated with every at bat, this is an assumption, not a known fact. Instead of risking the introduction of a new error based on that assumption, I have chosen to accept the errors of approximation resulting from ignoring specific influences of pitchers during the streak.

During his 56-game hitting streak, DiMaggio had three games with two at bats, 11 with three, 26 with four, and 16 with five. A .357 hitter, with that distribution of games, would have had a 0.00000796 chance of getting at least one hit in every one of them. Over the course of the season, DiMaggio, with 84 such chances to have streaks, would have had a 0.0668 percent chance of coming up with one by season's end.

What this all means is that Joe DiMaggio, given his .357 batting average and the at-bat chances that he received, did something that he shouldn't have been expected to do unless he hit that way for 1,038 years. Given the infrequency today with which any batters hit even .357, it looks like DiMaggio's mark may be with us for a long, long time.

Baseball Axiom No. 22

All generalizations about nineteenth-century pitching are false...
including this one

Robert E. Shipley

Timothy John Keefe, a most versatile nineteenth-century hurler, won 342 major league games between 1880 and 1893. Of these 342 wins, six were achieved while lobbing underhand from a 4-ft. by 6-ft. box with its front line located 45 from home plate, 35 while tossing underhand from a 4-ft. by 6-ft. box with the front line 50 feet from home plate, 110 while throwing sidearm and overhand from this same 4-ft. by 6-ft. box, 42 while firing overhand from a 4-ft. by 7-ft. box with its front line located 50 feet from home, 122 while hurling overhand from the back line of a 4-ft. by 5-1/2-ft. box with a front line located 50 feet from home, 17 while pitching overhand from the back line of a 4-ft. by 6-ft. box with the front line located 51 feet from home, and 10 while flinging overhand from a pitching slab located 60 feet, six inches from home plate.

Confusing? Try this.

Timothy John Keefe, a nineteenth-century Hall-of-Famer, won 342 games between 1880 and 1893. Of these 342 wins, 193 were achieved during years when the batter could call for pitch locations either above the waist and below the shoulders (High) or below the waist and above the knees (Low); 149 were achieved during years when the batter enjoyed no such privilege.

Or this.

Timothy John Keefe, a nineteenth-century star who pitched in three major leagues between 1880-1893, won 342 games. Of these 342 victories, six occurred when three strikes were needed for a strikeout and eight balls for a walk, 155 happened when three strikes were needed for a strikeout and seven balls for a walk, 32 took place when three strikes were needed for a strikeout and six balls for a walk, 35 were achieved when four strikes were needed for a strikeout and five balls for a walk, 35 also were achieved during conditions where three strikes were needed for a strikeout and five balls for a walk, and 79 were gained when three strikes equalled a strikeout and four balls a walk.

The point of this unusual litany is simply to illustrate what a strange and alien terrain nineteenth-century baseball is for the modern fan. A period of constant experimentation and change, it does not lend itself to superficial description or analysis. Fitting none of our operative frames of reference regarding the sport, it must be analyzed and investigated on its own terms and in sufficient detail to ensure that we are accurately describing and understanding what actually occurred at the particular time under study.

No facile generalizations can be made about baseball during the nineteenth century. The period was just too dynamic and fluid to allow for this. One could even argue that there was no one phenomenon that could be justly labeled as nineteenth-century base-

Robert E. Shipley *lives in Aston, Pennsylvania*

ball.

Unfortunately, many researchers and statisticians have instead approached the topic of nineteenth-century baseball as if it were a static universe, a monolith with little variation or nuance. How else to explain the plethora of topics and lists such as "Nineteenth-Century Stars," "Nineteenth-Century Pitching Leaders," and "Nineteenth-Century Baseball" that reverberate through the literature. The main variation that is sometimes allowed is the infrequent division of the nineteenth century into pre-1893 vs. 1893-1899 (or 1893-1900) periods in recognition of the modern pitching distance of 60 feet, six inches beginning in 1893. While a good start, this framework is also doomed to miss much of the richness and nuance of the age—especially with regard to the 1880s, the most dynamic period of experimentation and change in baseball history.

Nowhere is this variation and dynamism more apparent than in regard to pitching rules and conditions. As Henry Chadwick frequently stated in the annual *Spalding* guides and elsewhere, major league rules committees were constantly attempting to legislate a balance between pitching and hitting. They quickly learned that the easiest way to do this was to affect pitching conditions by changing basic governing rules. While most pitchers did not survive as long nor through as many rule changes as "Sir" Timothy Keefe, any nineteenth-century hurler who pitched for more than one season faced some version of "future shock" when he stepped into the pitching box or on the slab for the first time each spring.

It must have been difficult for hurlers of the day to keep all of the changes straight. It is even more difficult for the modern student of the game to keep everything in chronological (and just plain logical) order. Secondary source material, some of it written by exceptional baseball scholars who have forgotten more about the game than most of us will ever know, often contradict one another, and sometimes even themselves, concerning nineteenth-century rule changes and the years in which they occurred. Moreover, sources that do appear to be fairly complete as well as factually accurate are usually not very easy to follow, at least not for those like me who have trouble pouring mud out of a hiking boot unless directions have been printed on the heel.

My own personal solution to this situation appears in the accompanying matrix chart entitled "Pitching Conditions." I used *Spalding* and *Reach* guides to determine the exact year, wording and result of all rule changes that affected pitching significantly during the nineteenth century. Using the chart, you can find the basic pitching conditions for any given year.

While most of the logic of the chart is self-evident, two further explanations are required. One, distance from home plate is expressed as what I call the "pivot" distance, or the approximate distance from the pitcher's pivot (back) foot to home plate. This avoids the problem of comparing apples and oranges and it establishes a common baseline throughout the years. It shows the *actual* pitching distance for the years between 1887-1892 when rules stipulated that the pitcher must plant his foot on the back line of the pitching box and then move forward only one step. The only point of confusion occurs for the years 1876-1886 when pitchers could move within a box. For these instances I have assumed that the pitchers delivered with their front feet as close to the front line of the box as possible, so I assumed a pivot distance 3-1/2 feet behind this. Hence a pitcher throwing from a box with a front line 45 feet from home plate would have a pivot distance of 45 feet plus 3-1/2 feet, or 48-1/2 feet. This column also points out several misconceptions about pitching distance that have sometimes been perpetuated in the literature. Most obvious of these is the fact that the 1893 change to 60 feet, six inches was an effective increase of five feet, not 10 feet, six inches as is sometimes incorrectly stated. (And, as has been pointed out by others before, the figure of "60'6"" was not a surveyor's error, but a logical increase of five feet from the existing standard.)

The second point is that some things that may have also affected pitching conditions have not been included due to impact and space considerations. For example, the fact that most players did not wear gloves until the late 1880s or early 1890s is not included here. Neither is the change in the rule allowing an out for a foul ball caught on one bounce (1883-NL; 1884-UA; 1885-AA). Nor is the fact that substitutions were not allowed except for injuries and, in some instances the consent of the opposing team, until 1889 when one "free" substitution was allowed. Nonetheless, all major rule changes and conditions that had a significant impact have been included here.

On one level this matrix serves as another illustration of the complexities and variation inherent in the pitching profession during that era. On another level, however, it can be seen as a heuristic device, a starting point if you will, for learning more about nineteenth century baseball through the use of comparing and contrasting individual and league performances for specific periods with common rules and conditions.

The possibilities are abundant. A few examples: Who were the premier underhand pitchers throwing from a pivot distance of 48-1/2 feet? From 53-1/2 feet? Which pitchers fared better or worse as the number of balls for a walk decreased? Which pitchers and hitters did best in surviving significant rule changes? How did Hall-of-Famers do in individual eras and how did they survive major rule transitions? How did non-HOFers perform? Are there some who deserve more recognition for excelling during certain specific eras? Beyond these descriptive comparisons, the more important question of why some responded comparatively better to change than others could be addressed. And finally, how were aggregate batting and pitching statistics affected by particular rule changes?

I cannot hope to answer all of these questions here, nor will I try. However, I have prepared a short exercise to illustrate the promise of such an approach. Beginning with what I consider to be the two most critical conditions on the chart—"Pivot Foot Distance" and "Allowable Pitching Motion"—I established five logical eras within which to compare pitching performances:

I. Underhand Delivery With Pivot Distance of 48-1/2 feet (1876-1880)

II. Underhand Delivery With Pivot Distance of 53-1/2 feet (1881-1882)

III. Shoulder Height Restriction/No Restriction Delivery With Pivot Distance of 53-1/2 feet (1883-1886)

IV. No Restriction Delivery With Pivot Distance of 55-1/2 feet & 57-1/2 feet. (1887-1892)

V. No Restriction Delivery With Pivot Distance of 60-1/2 feet (1893-1900)

One could well argue for a different breakdown based on the same criteria. For example, the first underhand category could be broken into two subcategories based on the period of 1876-1877 when pitchers threw more like softball pitchers today (below the hip with no bent elbow) vs. 1878-1880 when pitchers were allowed to throw more like Dick Hall or Kent Tekulve (below the waist with bent elbow). One could also opt for a separate category called "Shoulder Height Restriction with Pivot Distance of 53-1/2 feet" which would cover 1883 for the National League, 1884 for the Union Association and 1883-June, 1885 for the American Association.

I chose to do neither because the primary sources of the time frequently noted how difficult it was for um-

pires to enforce such motion restrictions. In his book *American's National Game*, Spalding noted that the "below the hip with no bent elbow" rule had to be changed since very few pitchers could throw that way and umpires therefore "permitted the unlawful delivery of the ball rather than stop the game and disappoint the crowd." Spalding also noted the change in 1878 to allow pitching below the waist caused many pitchers to circumvent the rule by wearing their belts abnormally high. In regard to the 1883 rule on allowing shoulder height deliveries, Spalding noted that this was subject to pitcher deception and that it was "differently construed by different umpires." In the 1884 *Spalding* guide, Henry Chadwick stated that by the latter half of 1883 umpires were liberally allowing overhand pitching rather than the shoulder height restriction because it was difficult to judge and enforce. (The penalty for disregarding the rule in 1883 was only for the umpire to call a "foul balk." Two "foul balks" in one inning gave the batter first base and advanced the runners one base.) Very clearly, pitching motion restrictions were difficult to detect and enforce as long as they were not outrageously obvious. It could even be postulated that during any period under consideration there were certainly some pitchers who were "cheating" to the next level—throwing sidearm in an underhand era, tossing overhand in the era of shoulder height restriction, etc. Hence, I have chosen to lump similar motions together.

A case could also be made for including conditions experienced under Player's League rules in 1890 as a separate category since the pivot distance was effectively set at 57 feet as opposed to 55-1/2 feet for the National League and American Association during the same year. In this case I chose to set up just one category for the time period from 1887-1892 since the experience of the Player's League was so short-lived and affected so few pitchers.

Using these categories I then derived the top ten pitchers based on three different pitching statistics—Wins, ERA, and Hits Per Game—for each. The results of this exercise appear in the chart entitled "Nineteenth-Century Pitching Leaders." Several preliminary points of interest are suggested by the chart. A few of them:

1. 16 pitchers achieved successful enough transitions so that they made a list of top pitchers in at least two different eras. Four made lists in three different eras: Jim McCormick (non-HOF), Pud Galvin (HOF), Mickey Welch (HOF), and Tony Mullane (non-HOF).

Pud Galvin

NBL

hand era. In addition to the aforementioned McCormick, Galvin, and Welch, only Hoss Radbourn (HOF) and Tony Mullane (non-HOF) made the transition and kept their top ranking. Radbourn is something of a special case, since by most accounts he continued to throw in the same submarine style throughout his career.

4. Of the 18 top sidearm/overhand pitchers throwing from 53-1/2 feet in Group III (1883-1886), only six made it to top ranking in a later era: Mickey Welch, Tony Mullane, Tim Keefe (HOF), Charlie Buffinton (non-HOF), John Clarkson (HOF), and Bob Caruthers (non-HOF).

5. The top ranked overhand pitchers from 55-1/2 feet to 57 feet in Group IV (1887-1892) fared the least successfully of any group in making the transition to a later era. Of 19 pitchers in Group IV, only three—all HOFers—made the transition successfully enough to 60 feet, six inches to make a top ten list in the applicable categories: Kid Nichols, Cy Young, and

1/2-ft. pivot distance fared best of any group making transitions. Of the twelve pitchers appearing in Group I (1876-1880), seven reached top ten ranking in some category in at least one other era. Three of them reached top ranking in at least two additional eras, thus making the transition successfully from underhand at the shortest pivot distance to overhand or no restriction pitching: Jim McCormick, Pud Galvin, and Mickey Welch.

3. Of all the top pitchers tossing underhand either from 48-1/2 feet or 53-1/2 feet (Group I and II), only five made it to the top level of success in the over-

6. Some HOFers only achieved top ranking in one era (e.g., Al Spalding) and some didn't make it in any era (e.g., Candy Cummings).

7. Some non-HOFers deserve additional recognition, arguably for HOF status, but at the very least for a greater place in baseball history. Most obvious are the two non-HOFers who achieved top ranking in three different eras; Jim McCormick (career: 265-214 .553) and Tony Mullane (career: 284-220 .563). Additional credit should also be focused on at least three top pitchers who made their mark predominately during the two underhand eras: Tommy Bond (career:

193-115 .627), Will White (career: 229-166 .580), and Larry Corcoran (career: 177-89 .665). Vic Willis (career 249-205 .548), a Group V pitcher who lost a close vote a few years ago for the HOF, also deserve special mention for achieving the top ERA and lowest Hits Per Game of any pitcher during those years.

Of course, you can argue that more logical and meaningful categories and groupings can be developed from the earlier rule/condition matrix than the five groups I chose for this preliminary analysis. And that is just fine. The matrix lends itself to interpretation and re-interpretation. Its chief strength is flexibility, not finality; it should serve to open de-

Mickey Welch

bate, not close it.

Reality is almost always more complex than the Zen paintings we create in our minds to reduce the world to logical and more manageable proportions. So it is with the world of nineteenth-century baseball, and in particular, nineteenth-century pitching. I hope the proposals noted here will fall upon fertile ground and open up new opportunities for research and interpretation. At the very least, the subject should not

again be broached without keeping in mind the absolute truth of Baseball Axiom No. 22—generally speaking, of course.

PITCHING CONDITIONS
1876-1900

YEAR	PIVOT FOOT DISTANCE	ALLOWABLE PITCHING MOTION	PITCHING AREA	NO. OF STRIKES	NO. OF BALLS	OTHER/RELATED RULES (BY YEAR)
1876	48'6"	UNDERHAND BELOW HIP WITH NO BENT ELBOW.	6'x 6' BOX	4 (BATTER GIVEN A WARNING	9	BATTER CALLS FOR HIGH OR LOW PITCH (1876-86)
1877	(45' TO FRONT OF			STRIKE		
1878	BOX; APPROX. 3'6" MORE		(45' FROM HOME)	BEFORE FINAL		PITCHER CAN USE TWO-STEP DELIVERY IN BOX (187686)
1879	TO PIVOT FOOT)	UNDERHAND BELOW WAIST;	4'x 6' BOX	STRIKE)		UMPIRE CAN CALL

Year	Distance	Delivery Motion	Box			Rules
1880		BENT ELBOW ALLOWED.	(45')		8	FOR NEW BALL AT END OF INNING (1882); ANYTIME (1883PRESENT)
1881						
1882						
1883	53'6" (50' TO FRONT OF BOX; APPROX. 3'6" MORE TO PIVOT FOOT)	ANY MOTION W/ SIDEARM SHOULDER HEIGHT RESTRICTION	4'x 6' BOX (50' FROM HOME)	3	7	HIT BY PITCH TO FIRST (1884-1891 AA; 1887-PRESENT NL)
1884 AA						
1884 UA						
1884 NL					6	NO RAISED LEG IN WINDUP NL (1-01/2 MONTHS 1885)
1885 AA					7	FLAT BAT ALLOWED (1885-92)
1885 NL					6	
1886 AA		ANY MOTION W/O RESTRICTION	4'x 7' BOX (50' FROM HOME)			BATTER CAN NO LONGER CALL FOR HIGH OR LOW; (1887PRESENT)
1886 NL					7	
1887	55'6" (BACK LINE OF BOX)	(END OF 1883 TO PRESENT NL AND PL; 7 JUNE 1885 TO 1891-AA)	4'x 5'6" BOX (50' FROM HOME)	4	5	PITCHER MUST KEEP FOOT ON BACK LINE OF BOX AND MOVE FORWARD ONLY ONE STEP (NL 1887-92; PL1890)
1888						
1889						
1890 PL	57' (BACK LINE)		4'x 6' BOX (51')			DEFACING OF BALL PROHIBITED (1890 PRESENT)
1890 NL				3		
1891	55'6" (BACK LINE OF BOX)		4'x 5'6" BOX (50' FROM HOME)		4	PITCHER MUST KEEP FOOT ON SLAB AND MOVE FORWARD ONLY ONE STEP (1893 PRESENT)
1892						
1893-1900	60'6"		PITCHING SLAB (60/6")			

NL = NATIONAL LEAGUE   UA = UNION ASSOCIATION
AA = AMERICAN ASSOCIATION   PL = PLAYERS LEAGUE

19TH CENTURY PITCHING LEADERS
(MINIMUM 100 INNINGS PER YEAR AVERAGE)

WINS			ERA			HITS PER GAME		

I. UNDERHAND DELIVERY WITH 48'6" PIVOT DISTANCE (1876 - 1880)

TOMMY BOND	NL	180	AL SPALDING	NL	1.78	LARRY CORCORAN	NL	6.78
MONTE WARD	NL	108	MONTE WARD	NL	1.85	LEE RICHMOND	NL	8.18

WILL WHITE	NL	93	JIM DEVLIN	NL	1.90	MONTE WARD	NL	8.19
GEORGE BRADLEY	NL	89	LARRY CORCORAN	NL	1.95	JIM MCCORMICK	NL	8.82
TERRY LARKIN	NL	89	WILL WHITE	NL	1.99	JIM DEVLIN	NL	9.02
JIM MCCORMICK	NL	70	JIM MCCORMICK	NL	2.07	MICKEY WELCH	NL	9.02
JIM DEVLIN	NL	65	TOMMY BOND	NL	2.11	GEORGE BRADLEY	NL	9.11
PUD GALVIN	NL	57	LEE RICHMOND	NL	2.15	TOMMY BOND	NL	9.17
AL SPALDING	NL	48	GEORGE BRADLEY	NL	2.22	WILL WHITE	NL	9.20
LARRY CORCORAN	NL	43	TERRY LARKIN	NL	2.44	AL SPALDING	NL	9.32

II.   UNDERHAND DELIVERY WITH 53'6" PIVOT DISTANCE (1881-1882)

JIM MCCORMICK	NL	62	DENNY DRISCOLL	AA	1.21	DENNY DRISCOLL	AA	7.25
LARRY CORCORAN	NL	58	WILL WHITE	NL	1.66	WILL WHITE	NL	7.86
HOSS RADBOURN	NL	58	H. MCCORMICK	NL, AA	2.05	LARRY CORCORAN	NL	7.91
PUD GALVIN	NL	56	LARRY CORCORAN	NL	2.1420	H. MCCORMICK	NL, AA	8.04
JIM WHITNEY	NL	55	TONY MULLANE	NL, AA	2.1424	JIM MCCORMICK	NL	8.30
FRED GOLDSMITH	NL	52	HOSS RADBOURN	NL	2.23	HOSS RADBOURN	NL	8.32
GEORGE DERBY	NL	46	JUMBO MCGINNIS	AA	2.33	TONY MULLANE	NL, AA	8.44
WILL WHITE	NL	40	MONTE WARD	NL	2.34	HARRY SALISBURY	AA	8.46
LEE RICHMOND	NL	39	JIM MCCORMICK	NL	2.41	STUMP WEIDMAN	NL	8.54
MONTE WARD	NL	37	STUMP WEIDMAN	NL	2.45	FRED GOLDSMITH	NL	8.63

III.   SHOULDER HEIGHT RESTRICTION/NO RESTRICTION DELIVERY WITH 53'6" PIVOT DISTANCE (1883-1886)

HOSS RADBOURN	NL	162	HOSS RADBOURN	NL	2.09	TOAD RAMSEY	AA	6.62
TIM KEEFE	AA, NL	152	JOHN CLARKSON	NL	2.10	LADY BALDWIN	UA, NL	6.79
MICKEY WELCH	NL	141	LADY BALDWIN	UA, NL	2.15	TIM KEEFE	AA, NL	7.26
PUD GALVIN	NL, AA	137	BOB CARUTHERS	AA	2.22	MATT KILROY	AA	7.34
GUY HECKER	AA	134	TIM KEEFE	AA, NL	2.25	JOHN CLARKSON	NL	7.50
JIM MCCORMICK	NL, UA	120	HENRY BOYLE	UA, NL	2.26	DAVE FOUTZ	AA	7.53
TONY MULLANE	AA	104	DAVE FOUTZ	AA	2.31	BOB CARUTHERS	AA	7.70
BOBBY MATHEWS	AA	103	JIM MCCORMICK	NL, UA	2.37	TONY MULLANE	AA	7.83
C. BUFFINTON	NL	102	TOAD RAMSEY	AA	2.39	JOHN HEALY	NL	7.92
JOHN CLARKSON	NL	99	GUY HECKER	AA	2.45	CHARLIE SWEENEY	NL, UA	7.93

IV.   NO RESTRICTION DELIVERY WITH 55'6" & 57' PIVOT DISTANCE (1887-1892)

JOHN CLARKSON	NL	204	KID NICHOLS	NL	2.50	AMOS RUSIE	NL	7.36
SILVER KING	AA, P, N	179	CY YOUNG	NL	2.53	JACK STIVETTS	AA, NL	7.70
GUS WEYHING	AA, P, N	177	BILLY RHINES	NL	2.66	ED STEIN	NL	7.83
BOB CARUTHERS	AA, NL	141	SILVER KING	AA, P, N	2.845	TIM KEEFE	NL, PL	.89
MARK BALDWIN	N, AA, P	140	JOHN CLARKSON	NL	2.846	PHIL KNELL	N, P, AA	8.02
TIM KEEFE	NL, PL	139	TIM KEEFE	NL. PL	2.847	BILL HUTCHINSON	NL	8.07
BILL HUTCHINSON	NL	139	BILL HUTCHINSON	NL	2.87	TONY MULLANE	AA, NL	8.14
E. CHAMBERLAIN	AA	131	TONY MULLANE	AA, NL	2.93	MICKEY WELCH	NL	8.21
C. BUFFINTON	N, P, AA	129	MICKEY WELCH	NL	2.96	KID NICHOLS	NL	8.24
TONY MULLANE	AA, NL	124	JESSE DURYEA	AA, NL	2.97	CY YOUNG	NL	8.26

V.   NO RESTRICTION DELIVERY WITH 60'6" PIVOT DISTANCE (1893-1900)

KID NICHOLS	NL	218	VIC WILLIS	NL	3.07	VIC WILLIS	NL	8.08
CY YOUNG	NL	214	AMOS RUSIE	NL	3.08	CY SEYMOUR	NL	8.30
BRICKYD. KENNEDY	NL	161	JESSE TANNEHILL	NL	3.16	AMOS RUSIE	NL	8.64
PINK HAWLEY	NL	154	KID NICHOLS	NL	3.20	TED LEWIS	NL	8.93
CLARK GRIFFITH	NL	152	CY YOUNG	NL	3.22	KID NICHOLS	NL	9.07
TED BREITENSTEIN	NL	149	DOC MCJAMES	NL	3.34	DOC MCJAMES	NL	9.28
AMOS RUSIE	NL	140	CLARK GRIFFITH	NL	3.40	TED BREITENSTEIN	NL	9.46
OVETT MEEKIN	NL	133	NIXEY CALLAHAN	NL	3.49	BILL HOFFER	NL	9.50
GEORGE CUPPY	NL	130	JACK POWELL	NL	3.526	ED DOHENY	NL	9.60
FRANK KILLEN	NL	128	TED LEWIS	NL	3.530	BILL HILL	NL	9.67

Uncovering Satchel Paige's 1935 Season

A summer in North Dakota

Scott Roper

Many of the exploits of Leroy "Satchel" Paige are well known. His two autobiographies, *Pitchin' Man* and *Maybe I'll Pitch Forever*, John Holway's dual biography of Paige and Josh Gibson (*Josh and Satch*), and other works are excellent sources for those who wish to learn more about Paige's career and to get a flavor of Paige's flamboyant personality. However, at least one year in his career lacks substantial documentation, and the extent to which Paige dominated the baseball scene during that season is nearly forgotten. This paper, therefore, is an attempt to shed some light on Satchel Paige's 1935 season, which he spent playing semi-professional baseball in Bismarck, North Dakota.

Most of the information in this paper comes from the 1935 pages of the *Bismarck Tribune*, with supplementary material originating in Paige's autobiographies. Unfortunately, not every game in which Paige pitched was reported upon in the newspapers (at least three games are known to be missing). Still, I was able to compile a partial record of Paige's season, and the record demonstrates the pitcher's importance to Bismarck's drive to national prominence.

The Challenge—In 1933, a local semi-professional

team in Jamestown, North Dakota hired three well-known African American players, Barney Brown and Art and Charley Hancock, to play on its otherwise all-white club. Although the move did not greatly revolutionize the state's semi-pro sports scene—most North Dakota baseball clubs had been integrated for decades—the addition of Negro League stars did threaten Neil Churchill, auto magnate, mayor of the city of Bismarck and manager of his city's semi-pro baseball team.

To Churchill, the state baseball bragging rights were at stake. He knew that he had to counter Jamestown's roster moves, so he contacted Abe Saperstein, a promoter for the Negro Leagues, and asked for the name of "the best Negro pitcher in baseball." After negotiating with the Pittsburgh Crawfords, Churchill obtained the services of Satchel Paige, and Bismarck won the 1933 state baseball championship.

However, 1935 is the year most people remember when they think of Satchel Paige in a Bismarck uniform. On March 24, 1935, fresh from 17 wins in a California winter league, Paige returned to Bismarck's baseball team for the first time since the 1933 state championship. Off the field, he and his new wife Janet had their problems—for instance, the city's white landlords refused to rent them a place to live, so Churchill found them a place to live in an abandoned railroad bunk car. On the field, however, Paige was the most important part of Bismarck's drive to the 1935 national semiprofessional baseball champion-

Scott Roper lives in Tucson, Arizona, is a lifelong baseball fan, and coaches Little League. He has been interested in the question of batting order since 1966 and developed this model in 1990 using an IBM-compatible 80486 computer and programming in BASIC. He encourages comments via CompuServe (ID# 73237,100).

ship.

The Big Season—The sportswriters for the *Bismarck Tribune* expected Paige to lead the club to the "biggest baseball season in [the team's] history." Aside from Paige, the club's lineup initially included Andy Anderson at catcher, infielders Joe Desiderato, Al Leary, Red Haley, and Bob McCarney, and outfielders Bill Borlan, Gus Becker, and Mike Goetz. This was at best a temporary lineup, for Churchill replaced many of those players over the course of the season.

Bismarck opened the season on May 4 in Jamestown. The Jamestown club had released all of its African-American players during the off-season, choosing instead to field an all-white team. (Some of the released players ended up on the Valley City, North Dakota team.) In the opening game, Paige pitched a brilliant five-hitter, striking out 10, walking one, and yielding only two runs. Unfortunately, a passed ball in the eighth and a superior pitching performance by opposing pitcher Ed Bradley won the game for Jamestown, two to one. Paige avenged his loss in the next game, a May 12 shutout over Jamestown. He yielded only three hits, striking out fifteen.

During the month of May, Bismarck is known to have played a total of twelve games, winning nine and losing three. Paige pitched in ten of those games, four as a relief pitcher, winning seven and losing one. He pitched 67.2 innings in that period, gave up 10 runs (all earned), pitched three shutouts, walked eight, struck out 93 batters, and gave up 29 hits. Paige held opposing batters to a .127 batting average, yielded three home runs, and boasted an earned run average of 1.33.

Of course, there were a number of highlights in May that did not always reflect in the statistics. For instance, on May 20, the *Bismarck Tribune* reported that in one of Paige's relief appearances, "The Dusky Ace in his usual colorful style toyed with the Williston stickers, shooting an underhand ball and taking things easy."

Paige hit home the winning runs in games against Valley City and Beulah, and pitched three innings of no-hit relief in one of those games (striking out seven of the nine batters he faced). He also pitched a one-hitter at Devils Lake, a team composed of Cleveland Indians minor leaguers, and won both ends of a double-header against the barnstorming House of David team, a club which featured Grover Cleveland Alexander and Elmer Dean (brother of Dizzy and Paul).

Neil Churchill, knowing that Paige could not carry the team alone, signed a number of other players to supplement his pitcher. Notable among the newcomers were Vern "Moose" Johnson, a power hitting outfielder from Sioux City of the Western League; Negro League veteran "Behoven" ("Lefty") Vincent; and Kansas City Monarchs catcher Quincy Trouppe.

Unfortunately, the *Tribune* did not cover some of the team's June games, so Paige's records for that period are incomplete. What is known is that Bismarck played at least 26 games, many of them in Canadian tournaments. Of those games, the club won 14, lost 11, and tied one game. Paige pitched in 11 of those games, three in relief, winning six, losing one, and pitching to a tie in another. Two of Paige's games were shutouts, including an eight-inning scoreless tie against Chet Brewer and the Kansas City Monarchs in Winnipeg, a game in which Paige struck out 18 Monarchs batters. Paige was shelled once in that span, giving up six earned runs in a June 23 game versus Valley City.

Paige was up to his challenges in June. According to the *Tribune*, "(Chet) Brewer has boasted that he will defeat Paige every time the Capital City colored ace opposes him on the mound but Paige says, 'it just can't be done.'" To back up those words, Paige defeated Brewer and the Monarchs on June 16, 2-1, allowing only two Monarchs runners as far as second base. Much of that credit belonged to Quincy Trouppe, who threw out three runners attempting to steal second base.

Bismarck's July record was much improved over its June record. The club is known to have played at least 34 games, winning 26, losing six, and tying one. Some of this improvement can be credited to Neil Churchill's player additions. Churchill signed pitchers Barney Morris and Harold Bates in June, allowing Paige added rest and Churchill to release "Lefty" Vincent, who was suffering from a tired arm. In July, Churchill signed Negro League veteran Hilton Smith, first baseman Ed Hendee of the New York-Pennsylvania League, second baseman Dan Oberholzer of Minneapolis and Des Moines, and on July 25, Brooklyn Eagles pitcher-catcher Ted "Double Duty" Radcliffe. Paige pitched in only about a third of Bismarck's July games, and won at least five of those contests. He had a record of 16 wins, two losses, and two ties on July 6, and was hitting .211 at that point in the season (14 for 45).

Bismarck finished the season by winning 23 of their last 26 known games, including all seven of their games in the National Semi-Professional Baseball

Satchel Paige's Pitching Performance for Bismarck in 1935 —an incomplete record

DATE	OPPONENT	(D)	IP	R	H	1b	2b	3b	HR	K	BB	Comments
5/4	Jamestown ND	L	8	2	5	4	0	0	1	10	1	CG
5/12	Jamestown ND	W	9	0	3	3	0	0	0	15	1	CG/ShO
5/15	Devils Lake ND	W	9	2	4	3	0	1	0	15	1	CG
5/19	Williston ND	-	4	2	4	2	2	0	0	3	1	Relief
5/23	Valley City ND	W	9	1	3	2	0	0	1	10	0	CG
5/24	Valley City ND	-	6.2	3	6	4	1	0	1	8	1	Relief
5/26	Beulah ND	W	3	0	0	0	0	0	0	7	0	Relief
5/28	Devils Lake ND	W	9	0	1	1	0	0	0	15	1	CG/ShO
5/30	Hs. of David	W	1	0	0	0	0	0	0	2	0	Relief
5/30	Hs. of David	W	9	0	3	3	0	0	0	8	2	CG/ShO
6/2	Jamestown ND	-	3	0	2	2	0	0	0			Relief
6/4	Hs. of David	-										Relief
6/6	K.C. Monarchs	T	8	0	6					18		CG/ShO
6/8	K.C. Monarchs	W		4	7							
6/12	Hs. of David	W	10	2	5							CG
6/16	K.C. Monarchs	W	9	0	5	4	1	0	0	12	1	CG/ShO
6/19	Devils Lake ND	-	3		3				4	0	Relief	
6/20	Devils Lake ND	L										
6/23	Valley City ND	W	9	6	9	8	1	0	0	9	2	CG
6/26	Valley City ND	W	9	1	2					17		CG
6/30	Hs. of David	W	9	4	6	6	0	0	0	15	1	CG
7/4	Mex. Charraros	T	5	0	2	2	0	0	0	9	0	(Rain)CG/ShO
7/7	Jamestown ND	W	9	2	6	6	0	0	0	13	1	CG
7/9	Verden (CAN)	-	3	0								
7/10	(unknown)	W										in Russell CAN
7/12	Mex. Charraros	W	9	1	3	3	0	0	0	13	0	CG
7/13	Mex. Charraros	?										
7/17	Shreveport LA	W		1								
7/19	Jamestown ND	-	4	2								
7/20	Winnipeg MB	?										
7/23	Jamestown ND	?										
7/25	Jamestown ND	W	9	0	3	3	0	0	0	15	0	CG/ShO
7/26	Pierre SD	-	1									Started game
7/28	Can-Am Stars	W	9	1	3							CG
8/1	Devils Lake ND	W		1	5						CG	
8/5	Devils Lake ND	W	9	0	2	2	0	0	0			CG/ShO
8/8	Devils Lake ND	W		2	5					14		CG
8/11	Minn/St. Paul	W	9	6	12	6	4	0	2	11	2	CG
8/16	Monroe LA	W	9	4	7					15		CG
8/18	Wichita KS	S	2.2	1						7		Relief
8/20	Denver	W	9	1	5	5	0	0	0	12	0	CG
8/23	Duncan	W	9	1	5	4	1	0	0	16	1	CG
8/26	Duncan	W	9	2	9	8	0	1	0	14	1	CG
8/30	Dickey	-	1	0	1	1	0	0	0	3	0	Relief
9/2	Hs. of David	W	5									Relief

KEY: (D)= Decision; W= win; L= loss; T= tie; S= save; -= no decision; ?= decision unknown; IP= innings pitched; R= total runs yielded; H= hits yielded; 1b= singles yielded; 2b= doubles yielded; 3b= triples yielded; HR= home runs yielded; BB= walks; K=strikeouts; CG= complete game; ShO= shutout; (Rain)= rain-shortened game.

NOTE: As of 7/7, Paige was reported as having 17 wins, 2 losses, and 2 ties, meaning at least three victories are missing from this list.

Tournament in Wichita, Kansas. Paige pitched in at least 11 games in the final stretch, winning eight, saving one, and losing no games. He is known to have won at least 27 games over the course of Bismarck's season (against two losses and two ties), and may have won more—no pitching decisions were reported in three of Bismarck's victories, and accounts for a handful of other games did not appear in the newspapers.

In the seven-game National Semi-Professional Tournament, Paige shared the pitching duties with Chet Brewer, whom Neil Churchill borrowed from the Kansas City Monarchs. Still, Paige pitched 38-2/3 innings over five of those games, four of which were complete-game victories. (He also recorded one save.) He gave up nine runs (an average of 2.09 per nine innings), and he struck out a tournament record 64 batters. Over his last three games in the tournament, opposing players hit only .190 against him (19 for 100; only two of those hits were extra-base hits). For his performance, Churchill gave Paige a new car.

In spite of his spectacular season, Satchel Paige would have to wait nearly 13 years before joining a major league club. Scouts from the St. Louis Cardinals, Pittsburgh Pirates, Cincinnati Reds, Detroit Tigers, and New York Yankees attended the tournament, but, as the *Bismarck Tribune* noted, they were "Ivory-hunters" looking for white talent, and they were not about to break the unwritten rule barring African Americans from playing in the major leagues. George Barton, a columnist for the *Minneapolis Tribune* in 1935, ventured that Paige "would bring around $100,000 in the open market" if were white.

A journalist for the *Bismarck Tribune* speculated that Paige, "had he been of a lighter hue, would have been grabbed up by the major league scouts long before the national tournament. As it was the dusky hurler received the unanimous choice of the tournament committee for the outstanding pitcher award."

The Season Ends—After the tournament, Bismarck's season quickly wound down. The club played a handful of games in Colorado and Kansas before disbanding after Labor Day. Neil Churchill returned to Bismarck and retired from coaching to concentrate on local politics and on his automobile dealership. His team had won at least 79 games over the course of the season. Except for Al Leary, Barney Morris, and Red Haley, all of whom returned to Bismarck, nearly every player on the team either left for home or joined other teams.

Satchel Paige joined the Kansas City Monarchs after the Bismarck club disbanded. Before he did so, he added one more page to his legend:

> In a recent baseball game between the Bismarck Negro team and the Dickey nine, 'Satchel' Paige, star hurler of the Bismarcks, went to the mound in the final inning at the urgent demand of the fans.

Paige sent all of his fielders to the bench, and proceeded to strike out the first two men to face him. The third batter reached safely on a pop-up to third base, but Paige struck out the next batter to end the game.

Deuces are Wild
On October 2, Cardinal Pepper Martin, the Wild Horse of the Osage, had two hits and two stolen bases and scored the only two runs of the game in a 2-0 win over the Athletics in Game Two of the 1931 World Series. Wild Bill Hallahan pitched the shutout for the Cards, and had a 2-0 record in the Series.

Three's a Charm
On October 3, Dickie Kerr, the White Sox's third-best pitcher (and not in on the fix), pitched a three-hitter, winning 3-0 in Game Three of the 1919 World Series against the Reds.

—Don Nelson

A Case for the DH

The National League's return to dead ball days—

Russell O. Wright

During the periods from 1903-19 (the "dead ball" era) and 1963-68 (when the strike zone was changed), most fans agreed offense and defense were out of balance. The National League has returned to the imbalance of these periods and I recommend the designated hitter as a *proven* way to restore balance. The following graphs from my book *The Evolution of Baseball* demonstrate that (1) the NL is out of balance and (2) the AL avoided a similar imbalance with the DH.

Runs Comparisons—Figure 2-1 shows runs per game by periods for the AL and NL. In three of the five periods the leagues were close together. The AL lead from 1920-41 is primarily due to the Yankees, who outscored the rest of the AL by nearly the same margins by which they outscored the NL, although the Tigers also helped add to the AL margin. The AL lead from 1973-89 is due to the DH. The AL increase over the 1961-72 dip was 10.8 percent while the NL increased only 1.5 percent. In 1973-89, the NL was only 6.5 percent above 1903-19 while the AL was 15.5 percent above.

Looking at the leagues separately, Figure 2-3 shows AL runs per game by five year interval. The 1965-69 dip back to dead ball days was eliminated by the DH, and 1985-89 is just above the 1950-54 peak. We'll see in other graphs that the main effect of the DH is to return the AL to 1942-1960, where a rough balance

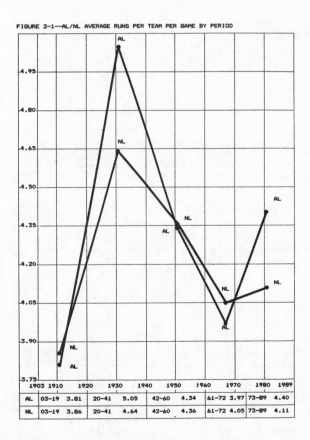

FIGURE 2-1—AL/NL AVERAGE RUNS PER TEAM PER GAME BY PERIOD

	03-19		20-41		42-60		61-72		73-89	
AL	03-19	3.81	20-41	5.05	42-60	4.34	61-72	3.97	73-89	4.40
NL	03-19	3.86	20-41	4.64	42-60	4.36	61-72	4.05	73-89	4.11

was struck between 1903-19 dead ball days and the dominance of the hitters from 1920-41.

For the NL, Figure 2-5 shows runs per game by five year interval. The "deadest" ball interval for the NL was 1915-19 due to the effects of the Federal League in 1915 and WWI in 1917-18. The NL scored more

Russell O. Wright lives in Torrance, California. Graphs are from his book, Evolution of Baseball, (McFarland), and are numbered accordingly.

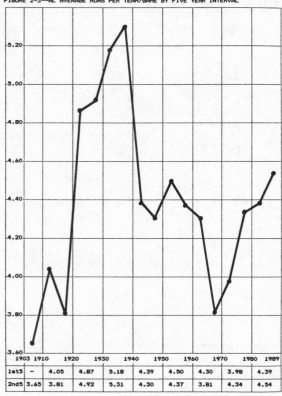

FIGURE 2-3--AL AVERAGE RUNS PER TEAM/GAME BY FIVE YEAR INTERVAL

	1903	1910	1920	1930	1940	1950	1960	1970	1980	1989
1st5	-	4.05	4.87	5.18	4.39	4.50	4.30	3.98	4.39	
2nd5	3.65	3.81	4.92	5.31	4.30	4.37	3.81	4.34	4.54	

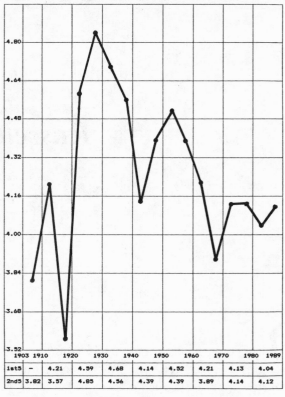

FIGURE 2-5--NL AVERAGE RUNS PER TEAM/GAME BY FIVE YEAR INTERVAL

	1903	1910	1920	1930	1940	1950	1960	1970	1980	1989
1st5	-	4.21	4.59	4.68	4.14	4.52	4.21	4.13	4.04	
2nd5	3.82	3.57	4.85	4.56	4.39	4.39	3.89	4.14	4.12	

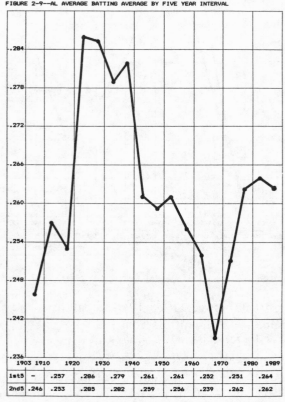

FIGURE 2-9--AL AVERAGE BATTING AVERAGE BY FIVE YEAR INTERVAL

	1903	1910	1920	1930	1940	1950	1960	1970	1980	1989
1st5	-	.257	.286	.279	.261	.261	.252	.251	.264	
2nd5	.246	.253	.285	.282	.259	.256	.239	.262	.262	

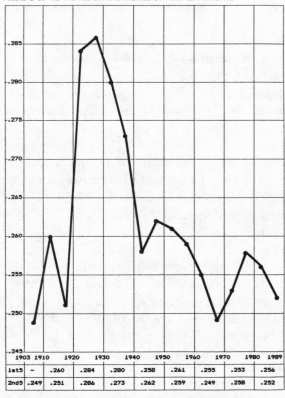

FIGURE 2-11--NL AVERAGE BATTING AVERAGE BY FIVE YEAR INTERVAL

	1903	1910	1920	1930	1940	1950	1960	1970	1980	1989
1st5	-	.260	.284	.280	.258	.261	.255	.253	.256	
2nd5	.249	.251	.286	.273	.262	.259	.249	.258	.252	

FIGURE 3-1--AL/NL AVERAGE HOME RUNS PER TEAM PER GAME BY PERIOD

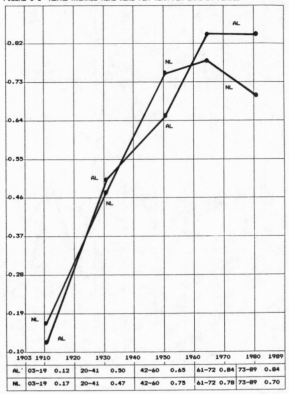

| AL' | 03-19 | 0.12 | 20-41 | 0.50 | 42-60 | 0.65 | 61-72 | 0.84 | 73-89 | 0.84 |
| NL | 03-19 | 0.17 | 20-41 | 0.47 | 42-60 | 0.75 | 61-72 | 0.78 | 73-89 | 0.70 |

FIGURE 3-4--NL AVERAGE HOME RUNS PER TEAM PER GAME BY DECADE

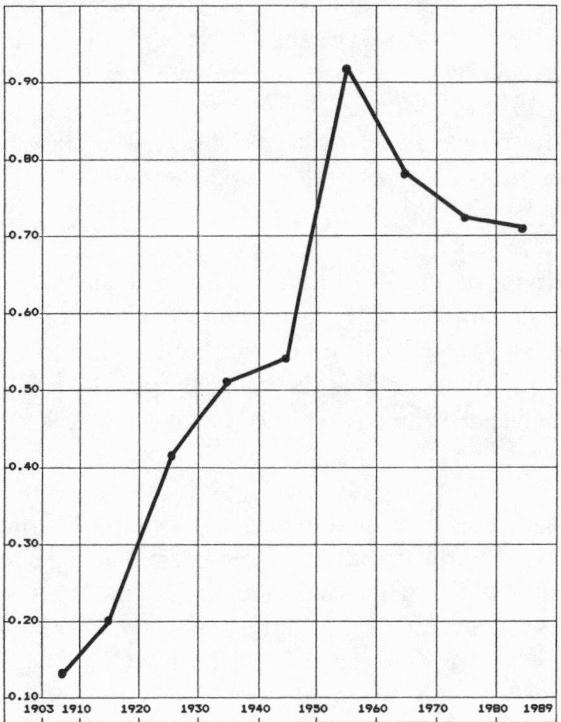

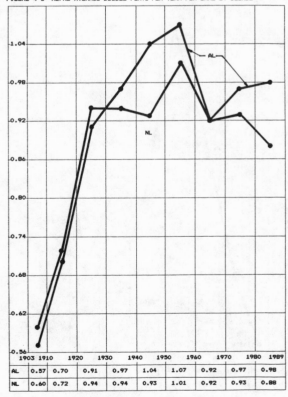

| NL | 0.13 | 0.20 | 0.42 | 0.51 | 0.54 | 0.92 | 0.78 | 0.72 | 0.71 |
| Rank | 9 | 8 | 7 | 6 | 5 | 1 | 2 | 3 | 4 |

FIGURE 4-4--AL/NL AVERAGE STRIKEOUTS PER TEAM PER GAME BY DECADE

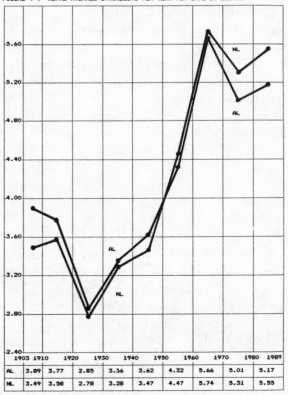

| AL | 3.89 | 3.77 | 2.85 | 3.36 | 3.62 | 4.32 | 5.66 | 5.01 | 5.17 |
| NL | 3.49 | 3.58 | 2.78 | 3.28 | 3.47 | 4.47 | 5.74 | 5.31 | 5.55 |

FIGURE 4-6--AL/NL AVERAGE DOUBLE PLAYS PER TEAM PER GAME BY DECADE

| AL | 0.57 | 0.70 | 0.91 | 0.97 | 1.04 | 1.07 | 0.92 | 0.97 | 0.98 |
| NL | 0.60 | 0.72 | 0.94 | 0.94 | 0.93 | 1.01 | 0.92 | 0.93 | 0.88 |

runs from 1910 through 1914, the middle of the dead ball period, than it did in any interval during the 25 years from 1965-89. And the NL was still declining in 1992. Its level of 3.88 runs per game was its lowest since 1918 outside the 1963-68 period. Runs per game for the five years from 1988-92 were exactly 4.00, lower than all but three prior intervals (1903-09, 1915-19, and 1965-69).

Batting Averages—Turning to batting averages, Figure 2-9 shows AL batting averages by five year interval. The shape is similar to that for runs, except the 1965-69 interval is the worst ever in the history of the league. The DH returned batting averages back to 1950s levels.

But the shape of the graph for NL batting averages in Figure 2-11 is quite different than that for NL runs. There was only a small improvement in batting average after WWII while runs in Figure 2-5 had a second peak in the 1950s (due to the home run barrage of that decade as we'll see in a moment). NL batting averages in 1965-69 equaled the dead ball low of 1903-09, and they've been steadily declining since 1975-79. The five years from 1988-92 at .251 are just barely above the .249 all-time lows for the first nine decades of the century.

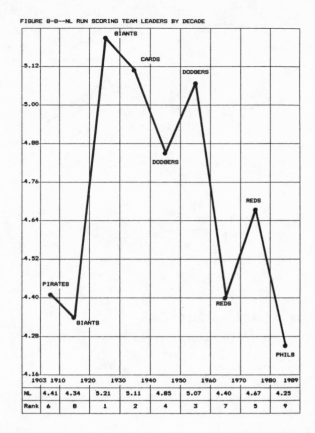

FIGURE 2-8—NL RUN SCORING TEAM LEADERS BY DECADE

	1903	1910	1920	1930	1940	1950	1960	1970	1980	1989
NL	4.41	4.34	5.21	5.11	4.85	5.07	4.40	4.67	4.25	
Rank	6	8	1	2	4	3	7	5	9	

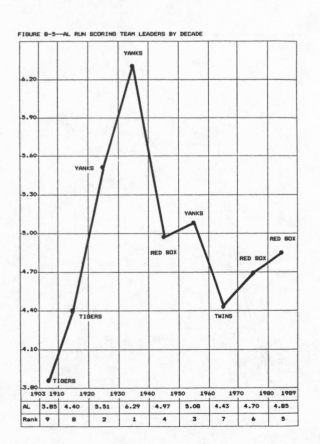

FIGURE 2-5—AL RUN SCORING TEAM LEADERS BY DECADE

	1903	1910	1920	1930	1940	1950	1960	1970	1980	1989
AL	3.85	4.40	5.51	6.29	4.97	5.08	4.43	4.70	4.85	
Rank	9	8	2	1	4	3	7	6	5	

Home Runs—Figure 3-1 shows home runs per game for the NL and AL by period. In spite of such famous home run hitters as Babe Ruth, Lou Gehrig, and Jimmie Foxx, the AL was only slightly ahead of the NL in home runs from 1920-41, and the AL trailed the NL substantially in 1942-60 giving the NL the overall lead through 1972. The biggest margin between the leagues prior to 1972 was the NL's 15 percent lead from 1942-60. But with the DH from 1973-89 the AL stayed even with its 1961-72 level while the NL declined. The biggest margin between the leagues came in 1973-89 when the DH drove the AL to a 20 percent edge over the NL (the margin for the decade of the 1980s was 25 percent in favor of the AL).

The NL decline is seen more clearly in Figure 3-4 which shows NL home runs by decade. The NL increased in home runs in every decade (in spite of the effects of WWII in the 1940s) until the 1963-68 strike zone change caused a sharp decrease from the 1950s to the 1960s. The NL did not recover, and it declined through the 1980s—its lowest decade since the 1940s.

Strikeouts—Another measure confirming the trend

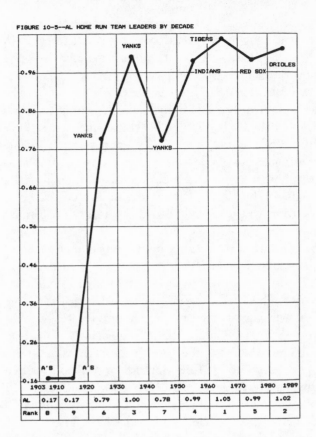

FIGURE 10-5--AL HOME RUN TEAM LEADERS BY DECADE

	1903	1910	1920	1930	1940	1950	1960	1970	1980	1989
AL	0.17	0.17	0.79	1.00	0.78	0.99	1.05	0.99	1.02	
Rank	8	9	6	3	7	4	1	5	2	

decade for each league. The AL and NL were very close until the 1930s, when the AL outscored the NL by a wide margin as we saw in Figure 2-1. The result was that the AL moved ahead of the NL in double plays for the first time. This is because increasing baserunners (especially the number of runners on first) means increasing double plays. This explains the AL peak over the NL through the 1950s, when runs in both leagues were nearly identical—the AL had a huge surge in walks in the years just before and after 1950. All of the original eight AL teams except the Twins set their double play records between 1948 and 1956. The NL surged in walks too, but at a lower level than the AL.

The number of opportunities is so important in double plays that three NL teams (the Phillies, Braves, and Reds) set their curent records in the late 1920s, even though fielding has greatly improved since then. These three teams had plenty of opposing baserunners in the late 1920s as that was the peak period for NL offense and these were the worst three teams in the league during that time.

Both leagues were equally low in double plays in the 1960s due to the death of offense (increasing strikeouts also tend to decrease double plays as the ball is simply put in play less often), and both leagues

is strikeouts as shown in Figure 4-4. The AL led the NL until the 1950s, but the difference between the leagues was small from the 1920s through the 1960s. Strikeouts increased in every decade from the 1920s to the 1960s as pitchers recovered from the rule changes favoring hitters around 1920 and the batters continued the "big swing" approach. The peak decade was the 1960s due to the 1963-68 strike zone change. Reversing the strike zone change and reducing the pitcher's mound caused a dip in the 1970s, but both leagues are increasing again and the 1980s were the second highest decade ever for both.

As we have seen, however, the AL is matching its highs in strikeouts with highs in home runs while the NL hits fewer and fewer home runs even as strikeouts increase. The NL now leads the AL in strikeouts by its largest margin ever, and strikeouts in the NL for the ten years from 1983-92 are 5.77 per game, breaking the record set in the decade of the 1960s. The five years from 1988-92 are higher yet at 5.80. The NL set its all time high for a single year at 6.01 in 1986 (1987 was 6.00). It's clear pitchers dominate hitters in the NL.

Double Plays—Moving to another revealing but less noticed measure, Figure 4-6 shows double plays by

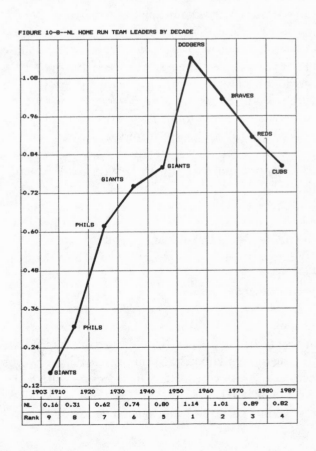

FIGURE 10-8--NL HOME RUN TEAM LEADERS BY DECADE

	1903	1910	1920	1930	1940	1950	1960	1970	1980	1989
NL	0.16	0.31	0.62	0.74	0.80	1.14	1.01	0.89	0.82	
Rank	9	8	7	6	5	1	2	3	4	

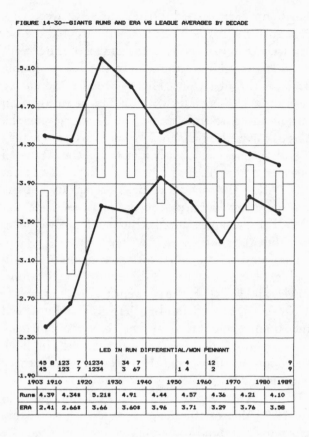

FIGURE 14-30—GIANTS RUNS AND ERA VS LEAGUE AVERAGES BY DECADE

LED IN RUN DIFFERENTIAL/WON PENNANT

45	8 123	7 01234	34 7		4	12			9
45	123	7 1234	3 67		1 4	2			9
1903	1910	1920	1930	1940	1950	1960	1970	1980	1989
Runs	4.39	4.34±	5.21±	4.91	4.44	4.57	4.36	4.21	4.10
ERA	2.41	2.66±	3.66	3.60±	3.96	3.71	3.29	3.76	3.58

had their lowest double play marks since the beginning of the 1920s. Double plays increased in the AL in the 1970s and 1980s with the DH bringing offense back to life, but with lower walk levels total double plays are still below the peaks of the 1940s and 1950s. NL double plays, however, have fallen sharply in the 1980s as NL offense has gone into cardiac arrest (and strikeouts have continued to grow).

Double plays in the 1980s for the NL were back at the same level they were in the late teens even though errors have declined by over 40 percent since then. The NL mark of 0.80 in 1989 was the league's lowest since 1919. Even in 1917, in the middle of the NL's worst offensive period from 1915-19 (as we saw in Figure 2-5), the NL was able to average 0.78 double plays per game. The NL is back into the dead ball era in more ways than just declining runs and batting averages.

League leaders for runs—So far we've been looking at results for the leagues. Now let's look at data for the leading runs and homeruns teams in each league. This data also confirm the NL is in a decline, which the AL avoided with the use of the DH. First we'll look at the leading teams for runs in each decade.

The best AL run-scoring teams in each decade are shown in Figure 8-5. It's easy to see that the Twins in the 1960s led the AL with almost exactly the same runs per game that the Tigers posted in leading the AL from 1910-19. This was due to the 1963-68 strike zone change. The DH brought the AL out of its 1960s dip, but the Red Sox, who led the league in the 1970s and 1980s, couldn't get back even to their league leading levels of the 1940s—let alone the five-plus runs per game the Yankees recorded in leading the league in the 1950s. The leagues have recovered better than the leaders because the leagues are more balanced now. Many measures in *The Evolution of Baseball* show that equity between the teams is at an all time high today.

Figure 8-8 shows the same data for the NL. The Reds in the 1960s led the league with about the same runs per game posted by the leading Pirates and Giants in 1903-09 and 1910-19 respectively. The dead ball era returned to the 1960s in the NL just as it did in the AL. The Big Red Machine of the 1970s pulled the NL above dead ball levels, but it was still well below the levels of the 1940s and 1950s—not to mention the peaks of the 1920s and 1930s. The Phillies then led the NL in the 1980s with the lowest leading average of the century. This was not simply a return to dead ball days. By this measure, the 1980s were the deadest ball decade of them all in the NL.

League leaders for homeruns—If we look at homeruns in the same way, we see a similar pattern in the difference between the two leagues, although home run levels have never returned to anything near the levels of the dead ball period.

Figure 10-5 shows home run leaders for the AL by decade. The huge surge in homeruns in the 1920s and 1930s led by the Yankees stalled a little during the 1940s due to the effects of WWII. The Yankees never led a decade again after the 1940s, but only the Tigers in the 1960s and the Orioles in the 1980s were able to top the record of the 1930s Yankees. This is another of many measures that show how far ahead of all other major league teams the Yankees were in the 1930s.

Not only was there no dead ball "dip" in the AL in the 1960s, no AL team has been able to match the 1960s Tigers for average homeruns in a decade. Runs and batting averages plummeted in the 1960s, but the Tigers kept hitting them out at a record rate (the fact that Tiger Stadium is the greatest homedome of them all didn't hurt). The use of the DH in the AL simply kept leader homeruns near their 1960 peaks (*league* homeruns were at record highs in the 1980s in the AL). But keeping leader homeruns near their peaks was a great achievement compared to results in the NL.

Figure 10-8 shows homerun leaders for the NL. The Dodgers set the major league record for a decade in the 1950s (with the short fence in the LA Coliseum helping to boost the records set earlier in Ebbets Field). This was a culmination of a constant increase in leader homeruns from 1903 onward, the same pattern shown for the league overall in Figure 3-4. But, matching the league pattern again, NL homerun leaders have declined in every decade since the record 1950s.

A different team has led every decade since the 1950s, but each leader has declined from the previous decade. By the 1980s, the Cubs led the league at a level just barely above the league-leading Giants in the 1940s (in spite of the effects of WWII). Overall, NL leaders declined by 28 percent from the 1950s peak to the 1980s (for the league as a whole in Figure 3-4 the decline was 23 percent). AL leaders in the 1980s were 3 percent *above* 1950s levels (for the league as a whole the increase was 16 percent). Once again the AL has avoided a major decline in offense with the use of the DH.

Serious decline for the NL—To give final emphasis to the decline of NL offense, let's look at the decade record of the Giants, the NL leader in runs and home runs (and winning percentage) from 1903-89. Figure 14-30 shows runs per game and ERA by decade for the Giants as compared to the league averages. The league averages are represented by the top of the rectangular box for runs and by the bottom of the box for ERA. The asterisks in the data box at the bottom of the page show when the Giants were first or last in the league in a decade for either measure. A value with an asterisk that was above the league average means a first place finish, a value below the league average means a last place finish (the Giants were first four times but never last).

The graph shows that the dead ball era for the Giants was the 1980s, when they averaged 4.10 runs per game, their lowest in the century—and they were still above the league average (they are the only team in the majors never to fall below the league average in runs for a decade). The lowest year ever for the Giants was 1985, when they averaged only 3.43 runs per game. Even in 1943, during the depths of WWII when the Giants won only 55 games and had their lowest winning percentage of the century at .359, they were able to score 3.58 runs per game (they've fallen below that 1943 level only four times since—in 1956, and again in 1980, 1985, and 1992).

One team does not make a trend. But when the best scoring NL team for the century, the only one that has never fallen below the league average for a decade, has three of its worst four years in 1980, 1985, and 1992, it certainly can be said to be confirming a trend.

And so we end as we began. Defense and offense are out of balance in the NL, and a *proven* remedy is at hand—the DH.

The Cahill Brothers' Night Baseball Experiments

"Inverted calciums" and "flaming arcs"

David Pietrusza

Baseball had experimented with night play ever since Edison had perfected the incandescent bulb. Most of the episodes were crude or even carnival-like, often in backwater venues. Just before World War I, however, a more sophisticated and sustained effort would be made. It would involve not fly-by-night baseball promoters but a trio of highly reputable industrialist-inventors.

The troika was a brother act, the Cahills—George, Thaddeus, and Arthur—who owned a Holyoke, Massachusetts floodlight manufacturing firm. Beginning in 1904 with George in the lead, they developed plans for a logical sideline, night baseball.

Both George and Thaddeus had attended law school, but back in the 1890's had become far more interested in finding new uses for electricity. Thaddeus, for example, invented an electric typewriter, "wireless telephony," "composing machines," and a rather contradictory discovery, "wired wireless devices." In March 1908 it was reported that George had perfected a pitching machine employing compressed air. "I was always fond of baseball," Cahill recalled, "and an enthusiastic player in my schoolboy and college days."

"Night is the natural time for play, for amusement, for relaxation," George once observed in explaining his ardor for night ball. "I believe that man's greatest games, his outdoor manly sports, can be and should be played at night."

In 1908 Cahill put out feelers to organized baseball and a result was this July 18 letter from *Sporting Life* Editor Francis Richter to Cincinnati Reds President August "Garry" Herrmann:

Friend Herrmann:

Mr. George F. Cahill…has invented an electrical apparatus for playing base ball at night on which he has secured completely protecting patents. The invention is practical, the cost being not at all heavy or excessive and appears to be quite feasible—so feasible in fact that Messrs Shibe and Mack of the Athletics had almost completed arrangements for a demonstration at Columbia Park in August when temporarily insuperable obstacles with the authorities arose. In conversing with Mr. Cahill I suggested that you of all men would, for various and obvious reasons, be the one to consult about the trial or introduction of the invention, and he is willing to go to Cincinnati at a moment's notice if you will receive him and give him a fair and full hearing. If the scheme is practical, as I fully believe it is, it is highly important that "organized ball" should control an invention that will have the greatest and most far-reaching effect upon the sport. If it should fall into the hands of speculative outsiders it would surely mean ri-

David Pietrusza is the author of Lights On!: The Story of Night Baseball (A&M). *He was Associate Editor of* Total Baseball *(Third Edition).*

val night-playing leagues. There are great commercial possibilities and probabilities in the invention, which should be kept within the present "charmed circle." I have no financial or other interest in the matter and write simply as a favor to Mr. Cahill (who has given me complete details of his system) and a duty to "organized ball."

Sincerely Yours,
Francis Richter

On August 24, 1908, Herrmann, George Cahill and a team of Cincinnati businessmen announced the formation of the "Night Baseball Development Co.," incorporated at the state capital in Columbus with a capital of $50,000. Herrmann would invest $4,000 personally.

"President Herrmann has great faith in the practicality of the system," observed *Sporting Life*, "If it works successfully every fan who has ever been docked a half day's pay for sneaking out to the ball park will worship Mr. Herrmann. Think of it! Baseball every afternoon and evening. Great double bill. Two frolics daily. Take the children in the afternoon and come back yourself for the night show. Pitchers for today: Ewing and Mathewson at 3:30; Spade and Wiltse at 8 P.M. No tie games. Play never stopped on account of darkness. Stay and see the finish."

By late September three towers ("Not unlike giant oil derricks") had already been erected and completion was promised in "two weeks." Yet a pessimistic edge seemed to be creeping into the venture, with talk of using the illuminating mechanism for "political meetings" if the baseball bubble burst. It was a harbinger of ill fortune; nothing at all happened that season—and friction even grew between the partners over such mundane items as their electrical bills.

Yet, in the New Year hope—and baseball—always returns. An intriguing detail was announced in February 1909. Herrmann's Reds would take on Charles Comiskey's Chicago White Stockings on April 11, following a day game between the two clubs. Only three towers still were in place, but it was promised that the remaining two would soon be raised. "Comiskey," noted the Chicago *Tribune*, "already has manifested much interest in the development of the novel plan. It is believed he will put a team on the field in the evening to oppose the Reds."

Still, that encounter never took place. A March 18, 1909 letter from Cahill to Herrmann reveals that he was unable to resolve "our motor generator question." A trial actually occurred on June 18, 1909, following a regular season match versus the Phils. Five one-hundred foot towers holding 14 arc lights were now erected at the Reds' home, the ornate but hopelessly decrepit Palace of the Fans. One account states that two were over the grandstand and one each at the scoreboard, the bleachers and in left and right field. (I know that doesn't add up to five, but will leave the matter up to next researcher to clarify.)

Arc lights consisted of carbon filaments. The carbon used in Cahill's projectors was as large as baseball bats and a Cahill employee had to stand at the ready by each lamp to reload filaments as the old carbon burned off. Powering this was a huge 250-horsepower, 60-cycle dynamo which Cahill placed under the Grandstand. It had a speed of 345 revolutions per minute and a voltage of 235.

Forty-five hundred customers, including members of both the Reds and Phils, congregated in the stands. A. L. Tearney, President of the Amateur Baseball Managers' League of Chicago, also attended with an eye toward implementing the innovation if he indeed liked what he saw.

Originally, Herrmann had still planned on using Reds players for the exhibition, but fear of injuring his chattels caused him to pull back. Instead Herrmann (obviously losing nerve step by step), secured the services of the local Cincinnati and Covington lodges of the Benevolent Protective Order of Elks—seemingly a more adventurous bunch than the average major leaguer of the day. Herrmann, by the way, was in the running for the post of Grand Exalted Ruler of all of American Elkdom and most of the crowd consisted of lodge brothers, their families and friends. The proceeds would go into a fund to transport the local Elks delegations to the BPOE Convention in Los Angeles—where they would be counted on to support the magnate's candidacy.

Herrmann professed himself as pleased with the results of the night's game: "Night baseball has come to stay. It needs some further development, but with proper lighting conditions—better than this experiment provided—will make the sport immensely popular."

Reds manager (and future Senators major-domo) Clark Griffith was less enthusiastic: "I don't believe night ball is destined to rival the daylight article, but I will say I was much surprised at the ease with which the game was played under to-night. Under improved lighting it will grow more popular."

He had cause for reticence. Infielders reported

no problems, but outfielders did. One fly ball was totally lost and resulted in a home run (There is some disagreement on this last point; one source states: "Errors were marked up against the players more because of their lack of training than the lack of light.")

This was Herrmann's last involvement with Cahill's apparatus. Perhaps, the real story of the evening was found in the box score—15 strikeouts by one hurler, nine by his rival. Visibility must have poor at home plate for that was clearly a huge number of K's for that era. In the outfield the situation may have been even worse. "The 'inverted calciums' out in center field," noted sportswriter Ren Mulford, "were a disappointment.... The game was a novelty and at times took on the elements of a diamond comedy." And while he thought the experiment had proved that such events as football or track could be illuminated, he summed up rather correctly, "It will be a long time before National and American Leaguers are fighting for championships under the glare of the electric lights."

For two weeks after the experiment Cahill's lights illuminated a less prestigious pastime—a carnival. Admission ten cents. Good crowds attended, up to 10,000 per night, but the sideshows did little to add to the dignity of the idea.

Undaunted, the inventor travelled north to Grand Rapids, Michigan. There he had the support of the local Advertisers Club which was billed as the "premier advertising organization of the United States."

What they planned for the evening was pretty hokey, even by bush league standards. A large number of fund-raising souvenirs would be peddled including commemorative pennants on walking canes (donated by Grand Rapids' Herpolsheimer Co.) and red boxes or "bricks" of carmelcorn. "This Brick Builds Grand Rapids" read each container, which held a variety of prizes, mostly cheap noisemakers ("crickets"), but also certificates for such more valuable items as "chairs, neckties, magazine subscriptions—everything on earth."

George Cahill installed his system at Ramona Athletic Park, home of the city's Central League franchise, for a July 7 exhibition. Cooperating with him and the Advertisers were the Grand Rapids—Muskegon Power Company and the Grand Rapids Railway Company. Thirty "flaming arcs" were installed, 12 over the grandstand and 18 along the sides of the playing field. Augmenting them were 10 "mammoth" searchlights, placed so fly balls could be discerned. All told 55,000 watts of power were in place.

The Grand Rapids team had started slowly that season, losing 14 consecutive games in June, but had recently shot up to third place. Their competition would be the tough first-place Potters from Zanesville, Ohio.

Financially the game was a roaring success, everything the Advertising Club could have desired. 4,300 witnessed Grand Rapids triumph 11-10 in a seven inning contest. Over one thousand dollars was raised for next year's pageant.

Earlier in the day Grand Rapids and Zanesville had played a regular season contest, with the home club prevailing 2-1 in ten innings. The evening's affair could not, however, be an official contest, as Central League rules specified that games could not start later than two hours before sunset. The night game was hardly as scientific as the afternoon's; in fact, it was a farce.

It must have been suspected that the system was not strong enough. Before the exhibition, ground rules were laid out that any misjudged fly ball or muffed grounder would be scored as a hit. Only dropped throws would be scored as miscues.

Managers Raidy of Grand Rapids and Montgomery of Zanesville ordered their batters to go easy, and for awhile they did so, although even half-heartedly hit balls could be tough to snag in semi-darkness. "After a run or so was scored," revealed the Grand Rapids *Evening Press* "they were content to hit the pill as directly at the pitcher or another infielder as possible and then loaf down the first base line while being thrown out."

In the sixth frame, however, all wraps were off and the runs came in bunches. All told there were five homers, four triples, and six doubles.

The Grand Rapids *Herald* reported "outfielders had their troubles in judging the balls lofted in their direction but the light was perfect for the batters, and how they did land on the ball."

Cahill's system would have one last test—at Chicago. On January 18, 1910, Herrmann wrote to fellow magnate, Chicago White Sox owner Charles Comiskey, to join in the nightball venture. Two days later, Comiskey was on board—"I will invest in your proposition."

On August 20, 1910 Comiskey, about to embark on an Illinois River houseboat trip, took time out to announce that a three-night multi-sport trial of Cahill's arcs would commence at new Comiskey Park on Thursday, August 25. (Interestingly enough, blueprints were sent to Comiskey in 1909 by a Cincinnati lighting firm, perhaps the Cahill-Herrmann combine, detailing how the new field could be illuminated.)

The first evening's action was lacrosse, featuring the Calumet and Illinois Athletic Club teams. Reaction was somewhat mixed. "Although the lamps were not in the best working condition," the Chicago *Tribune* noted, "the demonstration proved that in sports where the ball is not elevated more than fifteen to twenty feet in the air the lights will prove a success for night entertainments. Seven of the ten lights used last night threw their glare over a section from the batter's box to a point mid-way between second base and deep center. The remaining three lights stationed along the first base line spread their radiancy over the remaining section of the territory required for play."

Comiskey had hurried back from his cruise and was one of only 300 in attendance. Predictably, he pronounced himself pleased with the results. For the record, the I. A. C. trimmed Calumet 11-10.

The next evening highlighted soccer, featuring the local Hyde Park Blues and Campbell Rovers. The interminably-named *Electrical Review and Western Electrician* observed that the contest "was played without a hitch from lack of light; it was possible to observe all the details of the play even at the remote goal."

On Saturday evening, August 27 over 20,000 curious fans witnessed the Logan Square and Rogers Park semi-pros going full-tilt at our National Pastime. Semi-pro ball was then a significant part of the baseball firmament, drawing good crowds and employing players of real talent. Both squads belonged to the tough six-club Chicago Baseball League, which included the famed black Chicago Giants.

"Night Baseball A Success" proclaimed the *Tribune*, noting that unlike previous efforts—such as Al Lawson's—this event was performed with "exactly the same conditions as a contest in broad daylight.

A total of 137,000 candle power was available, the bulbs allegedly making "the diamond bright as day." Oddly enough, ten of the amps were installed in the traditional manner, facing down, while ten others were placed on the ground facing skywards. "By this manner," explained the *Reach Guide*, "'fly balls' and 'grounders' or 'liners' were equally discernible and could be seen plain at midnight as during any part of the day."

"This was the most severe test of the lighting system," judged the *Electrical Review and Western Electrician*, "but the ball was clearly observed at all times…. The players did not complain of glare from the lamps, some contending that it was not as

troublesome as facing the sun."

The Electrical Review and Western Electrician went on to explain the "Cahill flaming arc" in some detail:

Additional lights are provided for lighting the space above the field so that the ball can be clearly observed throughout its course. In the new installation at the 'Sox' Park these latter lamps were used for the first time, ten of them being placed in groups of two on the ground at the edges of the field, while ten similar lamps were mounted on top of the grand stand for the general illumination of the field.

These lamps were placed at a height of nearly eighty feet from the ground and were grouped as follows: four on the edge of the roof on the first-base side, two on a tower over the right wing of the grand stand, and two on a similar tower over the left wing.

Hinged screens were provided for the roof lamps and these were swung out in front of the lamps to shut off the brightest and most direct rays from the eyes of the baseball-players. The tower lamps, being more remote from the diamond, were not screened. Being placed over the roof line, the ten high lamps did not throw an objectionable direct glare into the eyes of the spectators.

The ten ground lamps were placed in groups of two, as follows: a group on each side of the home plate and close to the edge of the grand stand, a group near the edge of the center field, a group near the edges of the right and the left fields. A screen in the form of an arc was placed about ten feet in front of each of these groups to shield the players from the direct rays of the ground lamps.

Still only about 50 percent of the recommended voltage was employed. An "even better future" was in store, vowed the *Tribune*, "Of the nineteen operators…only seven were versed in their actual working. At times the lights would flicker, but when only two or three acted badly the change was not noticeable. The present voltage is below the amount wanted and promises of better current have been given."

Observers heralded the fielding as quite good (only four errors were made). Future big leaguer Al Wickland turned in an outstanding play in centerfield, converting a sure Rogers Parks extra-base hit into a spectacular double play. Logan Square won 3-0.

Ironically, while all this was going on, Comiskey's Pale Hose were at New York's Hilltop Park, playing to a 6-6 tie in the second game of a double-header—called on account of darkness.

Since all the comments seemed very favorable, it's somewhat mysterious why nothing further was done with Cahill's system. Yet it was his last attempt to light big league baseball. Not that Cahill abandoned the lighting business or even his interest in sporting events. In the late 1920's, he was even illuminating the Polo Grounds, Yankee Stadium and Forbes Field—not for baseball, but for other events such as football and boxing.

Part of the answer to the Cahills' abandonment of night ball was yet another futuristic venture they were pursuing. At about this same time Dr. Thaddeus Cahill was making startling advances on a device he dubbed the "Telharmonium." In 1911 the Cahills shifted their operation from Holyoke to New York City to facilitate progress on their new device, which certainly had promise and even today still sounds impressive—a combination of cable radio and the electric synthesizer.

Music would be produced at the West 56th Street studios of the New York Cahill Telharmonic Company (later Dr. Lee DeForest initiated one of the first wireless musical presentations from this site) and be transmitted to multiple "receiving telephones." This was not the only contemporary idea to utilize the telephone in methods other than what we know today. Proposals were advanced to place pay phones in every home, to have telephones transmit news and even to have them bill per word for messages like telegrams. The Cahill plan was simply the most sophisticated scheme advanced, and was considered much more significant than Thaddeus' electric typewriter.

The New International Encyclopedia described the Telharmonium thusly: "The keyboard is similar to that of an organ; the keys operate switches so as to bring the several alternators as required. The notes produced are of remarkable purity, being surpassed only by that of a good string. The performer has absolute control over the notes, both as to expression and timbre; he can produce at will the note of practically any instrument, and even notes of entirely new quality." The process aroused international interest, and representatives from the French, German and Austro-Hungarian governments travelled to the United States to inspect it.

The device was tested as early as March 1911 in Massachusetts, but 1912 saw a very successful Telharmonium concert taking place, with musicians playing their "electrical keyboards" at the studio which audiences in New York (at Carnegie Hall among other locations), Boston, Baltimore, Springfield, Washington and several other cities enjoyed.

New York's city fathers awarded a franchise to the Cahills to lay underground Telharmonium transmissions wires and even invested several hundred thousand dollars in the operation. It never flew, but it did help ground their night baseball adventures.

As a postscript, the relationship between George Cahill and Garry Herrmann continued, although in different forms. In February 1914 Cahill was sending Herrmann one of his newest inventions—an automobile braking signal, which "the natural forces of momentum and inertia" caused a "SLOW DOWN" sign constructed "of expensive materials" to flash out at following motorists.

But by year's end the two were at each other's throats, with Cahill suing Herrmann. At issue was "what was due us on the license fee" for Cahill's latest brainstorm. The inventor had given up on settling the matter amicably and turned it over to an attorney.

Perhaps yet another reason why Mr. Cahill shied away from the baseball powers of the day....

Post-season Palmer

Jim Palmer has appeared in the lineup in every World Series (six) and League Championship Series (seven) in which the Baltimore Orioles have been involved. He pitched in, and had one (and only one) decision in, each of those World Series. The '83 playoffs were the first in which he did not pitch, but he appeared as a pinch runner in Game Three. His playoff record was 4-1, spread over five LCS, one decision in each of five.

—Don Nelson

John C. Tattersall

An early SABR member with a passion for homers

Eddie Gold

John C. Tattersall was the Babe Ruth of baseball statisticians. His specialty was the homerun and he rounded all the bases.

The Philly resident was vice-president of a steamship company. But John was more shipshape when it came to his homerun logs.

Tattersall first gained national attention in 1953 when *The Sporting News*, the *New York Times* and other newspapers ran his story on the correction of Nap Lajoie's 1901 batting average. It was his calculations that changed Lajoie's average from .405 to .422, the highest in American League history.

The year 1901 was the inaugural season of the American League. Lajoie, a second baseman with the Philadelphia Athletics, was credited with a spectacular .422 batting average. However, in 1918 a statistician found that 220 hits in 543 at bats produces "only" a .405 average.

Several decades later Tattersall went to bat for Lajoie. He went through all the Philadelphia boxscores for that season and found Lajoie had 229 hits, which restored his average to .422. The original error was in the hit column, not the average.

Tattersall's interest in homeruns developed from watching the New York Yankees and Babe Ruth. His homer log listed every four-bagger hit each season by player and club, with date, pitching victim, park, inning, men on base, by pinch-hitter, leadoff batter, etc.

But the maven of mammoth homers encountered difficulties convincing baseball brass that statistical inaccuracies existed. One such happening (or hoppening) occurred during a game in Philadelphia in 1897. A bunny rabbit appeared on the field and the players gave chase. The bunny rounded first, took second and third, and raced home before being nabbed. The official scorer then came up with a hare-brained idea. He listed "Home Run—Rabbit" in the box score.

Ever the perfectionist, Tattersall couldn't find Rabbit's record anywhere. After scanning miles of microfilm, J. C. realized the joker just pulled the rabbit out of a hat. Tattersall wrote to the baseball bigwigs and urged them to eliminate the rabbit homer. But they ignored J. C., thus laying a fat Easter egg. Tattersall was determined to make the rabbit disappear. He contacted Fred Lieb, and the long-time baseball writer persuaded the moguls to bid bye-bye to the bunny.

Then there was the case of the vanishing grand-slam homer. The Yankees were playing the Philadelphia Athletics at the Polo Grounds on May 31, 1916. The A's were leading 6-4 in the eighth inning. The Yankees loaded the bases off Bullet Joe Bush, bringing utility outfielder Frank Gilhooley to the plate. Gilhooley blasted a Bush bullet over the center fielder's head. Frank chugged around the bases, scoring behind Home Run Baker, Hugh High and Roy Hartzell to slam the A's 8-7.

But when the "official" 1916 averages were re-

Eddie Gold is a Chicago sportswriter.

leased, Gilhooley had a big fat zero under the home run column. (Incidentally, Gilhooley added a homer in 1918 for a grand career total of two.) The record books "slammed" the door on Gilhooley and Tattersall, who argued it was a clean grand-slam homer.

Gilhooley was no household name and figured to get lost in the shuffle. But what about Hall of Fame first baseman George Sisler? The St. Louis Browns' immortal was refused admission to the 100-homer club after the record books credited him with 99. The factual evidence is that Sisler slugged 102 homers.

Tattersall discovered Sisler to be the victim of three baseball blunders. The first was on opening day, April 12, 1916. Sisler homered off southpaw Willie Mitchell of the Cleveland Indians in the third inning with the bases empty. The ball landed outside the ballpark for a legitimate homer. But the official scorer, who was probably battling John Barleycorn, erroneously listed the blow as a single in the boxscore.

Sisler again was robbed on September 22, 1921 against the A's at Shibe Park. He teed off against Rollie Naylor, sending the ball over the right-field wall in the eighth inning to give the Browns a 4-3 victory. The boxscore of that game lists Sisler with two hits and Jimmie Dykes of the A's with one hit, a sixth-inning single. But somehow the agate line lists: HR—Dykes. Chalk up another phantom error.

Sisler made it a three-peat on June 29, 1929 at Ebbets Field against the Brooklyn Dodgers. By now he was nearing the end of his career as a member of the Boston Braves. In the eighth inning, Sisler jumped on a Jughandle Johnny Morrison jughandle curveball with two on base, the ball going over the right-field screen. He again homered on October 5 at Braves Field. But when the "official" averages were released that winter, Sisler was left out in the cold with one homer.

Tattersall went to bat for Sisler with printed proof. He struck out. The baseball rules committee convenes every season, but it seems they're more interested in sipping martinis than sifting through documented material. (However, *Total Baseball* now shows Sisler with 102 homers and Gilhooley with two. *The Baseball Encyclopedia*, oddly, credits him with an even 100.)

As an early member of the Society for American Baseball Research in 1971, Tattersall organized his homerun material for that group. He died in Boca Raton, Florida, on May 29, 1981, at age 80. Subsequently, SABR purchased his large volume of homerun data, updated his listings and put it on computer for use by members.

John dreamed of publishing a large scale official Home Run Register, which would treat, in different ways, every one of the 130,000-plus major league homers hit from 1876 through today. His dream may become reality. A major publishing house is discussing just such a book with SABR officials.

The Bonham Connection

On August 5, 1940, Ernie "Tiny" Bonham made his major league debut, a 4-1 loss to Fritz Ostermueller in Fenway Park.

On that same day, a washed-up 31-year-old righthander named Johnny Whitehead of St. Louis pitched a 4-0 no-hitter against Detroit in a game called after six innings because of rain.

Whitehead's alleged fondness for alcoholic beverages shortened his career. This was the only game he won in 1940 and it was his last ever.

The irony: Whitehead died in 1964 at age 55 in Bonham, Texas.

Joe Marchetto

The Exemption of Baseball from Federal Antitrust Laws

A legal history

Stephen D. Guschov, Esq.

As major league baseball continues to deliver self-inflicted wounds to itself in the form of a players strike, the issue of baseball's long-standing exemption from federal antitrust laws has resurfaced.

While today's ballplayers and owners recently scrapped in conference rooms and hurled accusations instead of fastballs, Congress held hearings and heard testimony about the history of this curious anomaly, and why it may be time to repeal, either in whole or in part, the unprecedented antitrust exemption that baseball now enjoys.

The cornerstone of any examination of baseball's exemption from federal antitrust laws is the *Federal Baseball Club of Baltimore, Inc. v. National League of Professional Baseball Clubs* case of 1922. In it, the United States Supreme Court dealt for the first time with the issue of whether organized baseball was interstate commerce, or more accurately, whether the monopoly that organized baseball had established was a monopoly of any part of interstate commerce.

The plaintiff in this case was the Baltimore Terrapins Baseball Club, incorporated in Maryland, which with seven other teams was a member of the Federal League of Professional Baseball Clubs, which competed with the defendant American and National Leagues in 1914 and 1915. The Baltimore club alleged that the defendants had conspired to monopolize the business of baseball, and had attempted to destroy the Federal League by buying up some of the constituent clubs and inducing those clubs to leave the league. The plaintiff further alleged that even the President of the Federal League took part in this conspiracy, and he joined the American League of Professional Baseball Clubs and the National League of Professional Baseball Clubs as defendants in the case.

The Baltimore club initially won a judgment for treble damages under the Anti-Trust Acts in the Supreme Court of the District of Columbia, but a judgment of the Court of Appeals of the District of Columbia reversed that verdict.

The United States Supreme Court took the case on appeal, and noted that it was not concerned with whether the mere playing of baseball, that is the act of the individual player, was by itself interstate commerce. The Court added that "that act, it is true, is related to the business of the defendants, but it can no more be said to be the business than can any other single act in any other business forming a part of interstate commerce." The Court indicated that "at the foundation of the business of one of these leagues…is a circuit embracing seven different States. No single club in that circuit could operate without the other members of the circuit, and accordingly…the matter of interstate relationship is not only important but predominant and indispensable."

The Court also examined the business end of professional baseball, and observed that the defendants were not engaged in a sport; they were engaged in a money-making business enterprise in which all of the

Stephen D. Guschov, Esq. is an attorney in Danvers, Massachusetts.

features of any large commercial undertaking were found. The Court added that "when the profit-making aspect of the business is examined, it will be found that the interstate element is still further magnified...Every club in the league earns its profit not only by the drawing capacity of its team at home, but also by that of the teams of the clubs which its team visits in the various cities in the league. The continuous interstate activity of each club is essential to all the others. The clubs of each league constitute a business unit embracing territorially a number of different States."

Despite the overwhelming evidence of interstate activity by the defendants, the Supreme Court affirmed the judgment of the Court of Appeals of the District of Columbia, and held that Organized Baseball was not interstate commerce and did not constitute an attempt to monopolize within the Sherman Act. The Court reasoned that personal effort, not related to production, was not a subject of commerce, and the attempts by the defendants to sign players needed for baseball contests were not attempts to monopolize commerce or any part of it. The Court further noted that the doing of an act essentially local was not converted into an interstate act merely because people came from another State to do it. Justice Holmes, who delivered the opinion of the Court, observed that "the business is giving exhibitions of baseball, which are purely state affairs...and the fact that in order to give the exhibitions the Leagues must induce free persons to cross state lines and must arrange and pay for their doing so is not enough to change the character of the business." The Court concluded by repeating an illustration given by a lower court, that a law firm which sent out a member to argue a case did not engage in commerce because the lawyer travelled to another State. Thus, the conduct charged by the Baltimore club against the defendants was deemed not an interference with commerce among the States.

Gardella—The *Federal Baseball Club* decision met its first challenge in 1949 in the case of *Gardella v. Chandler*. Danny Gardella was an outfielder for the New York Giants, and a fairly talented player at that. In 1945, Gardella played in 121 games for New York, and batted .272 with 18 home runs and 71 runs batted in. In 1946, Gardella signed to play with Vera Cruz of the Mexican League. Major league club owners had heard that the Mexican League would become a legitimate third league and would steal away players, and as a result in June, 1946, Commissioner Chandler

announced that any American player who jumped to the Mexican League would be barred from American baseball for five years. Gardella consequently was barred from organized baseball upon his return from Mexico to the U.S. in 1947, and was therefore essentially deprived of his means of livelihood. Gardella brought suit against Albert B. Chandler, individually and as the Commissioner of Baseball; Ford C. Frick, individually and as President of the National League of Professional Baseball Clubs; William Harridge, individually and as President of the American League of Professional Baseball Clubs; George M. Trautman, individually and as President of The National Association of Professional Baseball Leagues; and the National Exhibition Company, which owned the New York Giants.

Gardella alleged that the leagues and the clubs comprising them had entered into agreements, designed to control the manner in which organized baseball was conducted, and which required players to be bound to their respective clubs by a standard contract. Gardella further alleged that the standard player contract included a reserve clause which required a player who was under contract to play with any club to refrain, at the expiration of the period of his employment, from contracting to play for, or playing for, any other club other than the one to which he had been under contract or its assignee. Gardella also argued that the club owners sold the right to broadcast play-by-play descriptions of the games on the radio and thus across state lines, and some were beginning to sell the right to broadcast the games on television. Some of those to whom the broadcast rights were sold used the opportunity to advertise goods which were sold and distributed nationally and internationally. The combination of operating baseball teams which travelled between states for the purpose of playing baseball games, and making contracts with radio broadcasting and television companies to send across state lines play-by-play narratives or moving pictures of the games, were alleged by Gardella to be sufficient to charge the defendants with being engaged in interstate commerce within the meaning of the Anti-Trust Acts.

In the initial trial, the United States District Court for the Southern District of New York ruled for the defendants in a judgment dismissing Gardella's complaint because the court lacked the proper jurisdiction to hear the case.

On appeal to the United States Court of Appeals, Second Circuit, Gardella found a more sympathetic forum. The court held that it would be necessary to determine whether all the interstate activities of the defendants, in conjunction with broadcasting and television, together formed a large enough part of the business to impress upon it an interstate character. The court suggested that the traveling involved was but a means to the end of playing games which, because of radio and television, essentially were played interstate as well as intrastate. This, the court remarked, was substantial interstate commerce of a sort not considered by the United States Supreme Court in the *Federal Baseball Club* case.

The court called the reserve clause "something resembling peonage of the baseball players...all players in organized baseball must 'accept' it...and severe...penalties are imposed for violation. The most extreme of these penalties is the blacklisting of the player so that no club in organized baseball will hire him. In effect, this clause prevents a player from ever playing with any team other than his original employer, unless that employer consents." The court further noted that such contracts were so opposed to the public policy of the United States that, if possible, they should be deemed within the prohibitions of the Sherman Act. Brooklyn Dodger executive Branch Rickey thundered back that anyone who opposed the reserve clause had "Communist tendencies".

In distinguishing *Gardella* from the *Federal Baseball Club* case, the Court of Appeals emphasized that in *Gardella* the defendants had lucratively contracted for the interstate broadcasts, by radio and television, of the playing of the games. In the *Federal Baseball Club* case, that Court had held that the travelling across state lines was an incidental means of enabling games to be played locally—i.e., within particular states—and therefore was insufficient to constitute interstate commerce. Here in *Gardella*, however, interstate radio and television broadcasts were not at all an incidental means of performing the intrastate activities—i.e., the local playings of the games. Thus, the *Gardella* Court reasoned that the *Federal Baseball Club* decision should have been deemed to hold no more than that the travelling of teams and their paraphernalia between states, as a means to the local playing of games, did not give rise to interstate commerce for Sherman Act purposes.

The court also rejected organized baseball's argument that it supplied millions of Americans with "desirable diversion", and would be unable to exist without the reserve clause. The court remarked that it could not predict whether that was true, but that in any event, the public's pleasure did not authorize the courts to condone illegality, and that no court should

strive to legalize a private (even if benevolent) dictatorship. As a result, the court reversed and remanded for trial.

Thus, it appeared that baseball was in dire jeopardy of losing its exemption from federal antitrust laws. Danny Gardella signed to play baseball for a semipro ballclub, the Gulf Oilers. Commissioner Chandler, sensing that baseball's exemption hold was weakening, announced on June 5, 1949, that he would offer amnesty to any player who had defected to the Mexican League. Gardella at first resisted the amnesty offer, and his suit commenced pre-trial hearings, as Commissioner Chandler testified concerning players' eligibility and radio fees. Gardella, however, was not financially secure enough to withstand a long trial and large legal fees, and on October 7, 1949, just two days before the New York Yankees won the World Series over the Brooklyn Dodgers, Danny Gardella dropped his suit when he reached a $60,000 settlement with organized baseball and was assured that he would be reinstated into the game. Gardella signed with the St. Louis Cardinals for the 1950 baseball season, but only batted once for them (unsuccessfully) that year. It marked the end of Gardella's playing career in organized baseball, and the major leagues avoided what could have been a damaging reversal of its exemption from federal antitrust laws.

Toolson—Baseball's continued exemption from federal antitrust laws next was upheld by the United States Supreme Court in 1953 in the case of *Toolson v. New York Yankees, Inc.* George Earl Toolson was a minor league player in the New York Yankees farm system. While playing for the Newark Bears, his contract was assigned to Binghamton. Toolson refused to report to Binghamton, and he was placed on that club's "ineligible list." The Yankees refused to reassign him, trade him, or let him play professional ball for any other club, organization, or league.

Toolson alleged damages due to the reserve clause, pursuant to nationwide agreements by the Yankees. Toolson charged organized baseball, through its illegal monopoly and unreasonable restraints of trade, had exploited the players who attracted the profits for the benefit of its member clubs and leagues. Toolson also alleged that the Yankees and other clubs had entered into a conspiracy and monopoly of professional baseball in the United States to his substantial damage.

The Court, however, held that if there were any evils in this field which warranted application of the antitrust laws, it should be by Congress, not the Supreme Court that rectified them. The Court affirmed the judgment against Toolson, on the authority of *Federal Baseball Club of Baltimore v. National League of Professional Baseball Clubs*, so far as those decisions determined that Congress had no intention of including baseball within the scope of the federal antitrust laws.

The Court's vote was 7-2 against Toolson. The dissent, as authored by Justices Burton and Reed, was vigorous. It emphasized that in light of baseball's capital investments used in conducting competitions between teams constantly travelling between states, its receipts and expenditures of large sums transmitted between states, its numerous purchases of materials in interstate commerce, the attendance at local exhibitions of large audiences often travelling across state lines, its radio and television activities which expand its audiences beyond state lines, its sponsorship of interstate advertising, its farm system of minor league baseball clubs, coupled with restrictive contracts and understandings between individuals and among clubs or leagues playing for profit throughout the United States, Canada, Mexico, and Cuba, it would be a contradiction in terms to say that the defendants were not engaged in interstate trade or commerce as the terms were used in the United States Constitution and in the Sherman Act.

The dissent in *Toolson* added that in 1952 the Subcommittee on Study of Monopoly Power, of the House of Representatives Committee on the Judiciary, issued a report dealing with organized baseball in relation to the Sherman Act. The report stated that organized baseball at that time was a combination of approximately 380 separate baseball clubs, operating in 42 different states, the District of Columbia, Canada, Cuba, and Mexico, so as to make organized baseball inherently intercity, intersectional, and interstate. The report further noted that of the 42 leagues associated within organized baseball in 1951, 39 were interstate in nature.

The dissent used the 1952 report findings to stress that exemption from federal antitrust laws was a matter within the discretion of Congress and Congress had enacted no express exemption of organized baseball from the Sherman Act. In the absence of such an exemption, the popularity of organized baseball increased, rather than diminished, the importance of its compliance with standards of reasonableness comparable with those required by law of interstate trade or commerce. Thus, the dissent concluded, organized baseball was interstate trade or commerce and, as such, it was subject to the Sherman Act until exempted. In spite of this forceful dissent, baseball retained its exemption from federal antitrust laws.

Flood—Nineteen years after the *Toolson* decision, the United States Supreme Court once again considered the issue of whether baseball was within reach of the federal antitrust laws, in the case of *Flood v. Kuhn*. One of the most remarkable items about the *Flood* opinion, as delivered by Justice Blackmun, was the Court's lengthy and romantic portrayal of the history of the game. For more than four pages, the Court waxed nostalgic about the game's early days and bygone heroes. The Court noted the New York Nine's defeat of the Knickerbockers, 23-1, in Hoboken, New Jersey, on June 19, 1846, as being a significant date in baseball's dawn. The Court also hailed the 1871 establishment of the National Association of Professional Baseball Players; the formation of the National League in 1876; the formation of the American Association and the Union Association in the 1880's; the introduction of Sunday baseball; interleague warfare with cut-rate admission prices and player raiding; the 1885 emergence of the Brotherhood of Professional Baseball Players; the appearance of the American League in 1901; the first World Series in 1903; the short-lived Federal League during the World War I years; the 1919 Black Sox scandal; major league expansion; and the 1966 formation of the Major League Baseball Players Association. The Court then proceeded to list a rollcall of "names, celebrated for one reason or another, that have sparked the diamond and its environs and that have provided tinder for recaptured thrills, for reminiscence and comparisons, and for conversation and anticipation in-season and off-season..." The Court included the likes of such legends as Ty Cobb, Babe Ruth, Walter Johnson, Lou Gehrig, Jackie Robinson, Honus Wagner, Christy Mathewson, Satchel Paige, Three-Finger Brown, Connie Mack, Cy Young, and Dizzy Dean in its list of 88 baseball greats worthy of inclusion in the *Flood* decision.

Not done yet, the Court also included references to the baseball poems "Casey At The Bat" by Ernest L. Thayer and "Tinker to Evers to Chance" by Franklin Pierce Adams, the latter of which was deemed worth to be printed in its entirely in the opinion.

The Court eventually arrived at the facts inherent to the dispute at hand: the petitioner, Curtis Charles (Curt) Flood, had begun his major league career in 1956 when he signed a contract with the Cincinnati Reds for a salary of $4,000 for the season. Flood was traded to the St. Louis Cardinals before the 1958 season, and he rose to fame as a center fielder with the Cardinals between 1958 and 1969. During those twelve seasons Flood hit .293, with his single best offensive campaign being 1967, when he hit .335. Flood played in the 1964, 1967, and 1968 World Series. He was awarded seven Gold Gloves. He was co-captain of the Cardinals from 1965 to 1969, and he ranked among the ten major league outfielders possessing the highest lifetime fielding averages. Flood's St. Louis compensation in 1961 was $13,500; in 1962, it was $16,000; in 1963, $17,500; in 1964, 23,000; in 1965, $35,000; in 1966, $45,000; in 1967, $50,000; in 1968, $72,500; in 1969, $90,000. These figures did not include any fringe benefits or World Series shares.

In October, 1969, at age thirty-one, Flood was traded by the Cardinals to the Philadelphia Phillies in a multi-player transaction. Flood was not consulted about the trade, but was informed of it by telephone and received formal notice only after the deal was consummated. In December, 1969, Flood complained to the Commissioner of Baseball and asked that he be made a free agent, and that he be placed at liberty to strike his own deal with any other major league club. His request was denied. Flood declined to play for Philadelphia in 1970, despite a salary offer of $100,000. He sat out the season and sued Commissioner Kuhn and the Presidents and clubs of the American and National Leagues. After the 1970 campaign concluded, Philadelphia sold its rights to Flood to the Washington Senators, and Washington and Flood were able to come to terms for 1971 at a salary of $110,000. Flood started with the Senators, but apparently dissatisfied with his performance and his outlaw status in the game, he left the Washington club on April 27—less than a month into the season—and never played major league baseball again.

Flood's suit charged professional baseball with violations of the federal antitrust laws and civil rights statutes; violation of state statutes and the common law; and the imposition of a form of peonage and involuntary servitude contrary to the Thirteenth Amendment.

The U.S. District Court for the Southern District of New York rendered judgment in favor of the defendants on August 12, 1970, holding the *Federal Baseball Club* and *Toolson* were controlling law. On appeal, the Court of Appeals for the Second Circuit upheld the District Court decision on April 4, 1971.

On further appeal by Flood, the United States Supreme Court heard the case and affirmed the judgment of the Court of Appeals on June 19, 1972. The Supreme Court acknowledged that professional baseball was a business and was engaged in interstate commerce, but stated that baseball was an exception and an anomaly. The Court reasoned that the aberration was an established one that had been recognized for half a century, and was an exception fully entitled to the recognition of legally-binding precedent.

The Court noted that the advent of radio and television, with their consequent increased coverage and additional revenues, had not occasioned an overruling of *Federal Baseball Club* and *Toolson*. The Court also emphasized that Congress as yet had not subjected baseball's reserve system to the reach of the antitrust statutes and, as a result, if any change were to be made, it should come by legislative action. The remedy, if any were to be indicated, was for congressional, and not judicial, action.

Chief Justice Burger remarked that "courts are not the forum in which this tangled web ought to be unsnarled...it is time the Congress acted to solve this problem."

Justice Douglas dissented from the Court's majority decision, and observed that "this Court's decision in *Federal Baseball Club*...is a derelict in the stream of the law that we, its creator, should remove. Only a romantic view of a rather dismal business account over the last fifty years would keep that derelict in midstream." Justice Douglas noted that he had joined the Court's opinion in *Toolson*, but had lived to regret it, and would now correct what he believed to be its fundamental error. Justice Douglas added that "the unbroken silence of Congress should not prevent us from correcting our own mistakes."

Justice Marshall also vigorously dissented, and stressed that baseball should be covered by antitrust laws beginning with the *Flood* case, unless Congress decided otherwise. Nevertheless, the vigorous opposition of Justices Douglas and Marshall could not displace the decision of the majority of the Supreme Court.

The exemption—In 1993, Florida Senator Connie Mack—grandson of the legendary Philadelphia Athletics manager—and Ohio Senator Howard Metzenbaum forged an alliance and introduced into the United States Senate the "Professional Baseball Antitrust Reform Act of 1993." The bill was intended to rescind baseball's exemption from federal antitrust laws, and the authors stated that "the business of organized professional baseball is in, or affects, interstate commerce; and the antitrust laws should be amended to reverse the result of the decisions of the Supreme Court...which exempted baseball from coverage under the antitrust laws."

Senator Metzenbaum has stated:

". . . [W]hile the game of baseball remains a simple pleasure, the business of baseball has become complicated and, at times, cut-throat. Major league baseball is not just a sport. It is also a billion-dollar big business. And, it is a big business which enjoys unique treatment under the law.

"Unlike any other big business in America, Major League Baseball is a legally-sanctioned unregulated cartel. The Supreme Court conferred that extraordinary privilege upon baseball seventy years ago, when it granted (baseball) a complete exemption from the antitrust laws…Although the soundness of this ruling has often been questioned—even by the Court itself—it has never been overturned. Instead, the Court has tossed the ball to Congress, which is why we are here today.

"Baseball's antitrust exemption is a privilege that the baseball owners may be abusing. I am particularly concerned that their ouster of Fay Vincent and their plans to weaken the Commissioner's powers invites more abuse of that privilege.

"Jerry Reinsdorf, the owner of the Chicago White Sox and one of the key participants in Vincent's ouster has stated that the job of the next baseball commissioner will be to 'run the business for the owners, not the players or the umpires or the fans.'

"It appears that the owners don't want a strong and independent commissioner who can act in the best interests of the sport or act as a potential check against abuse of their monopoly power. Instead, they want a commissioner who will function as the cruise director for their cartel. If decisions about the direction and future of Major League Baseball are going to be dictated by the business interests of teams' owners, then the owners should be required to play by the same antitrust rules that apply to any other business."

At about the same time that Senators Mack and Metzenbaum introduced their bill, Vincent Piazza— father of Los Angeles Dodgersw catcher Mike Piazza— and business partner Vincent Tirendi filed suit in federal court seeking to overturn Major League Baseball's antitrust exemption and force the sale of the San Francisco Giants to investors in St. Petersburg, Florida. Piazza and Tirendi, partners in a computer company, were prepared to invest $27 million as part of a $115 million deal to purchase the Giants and move the club to St. Petersburg, before major League Baseball quashed the deal and maneu-

vered to keep the Giants in San Francisco.

The reaction of baseball's owners to the Senate bill and the federal suit, however, appeared to be less than panic-stricken. Peter Gammons of the Boston Globe commented that "most baseball people aren't overly concerned about threats to take away the antitrust exemption…[T]here are too many members of Congress from key states like Washington, Wisconsin, Pennsylvania, Ohio, Missouri and California who realize that if such a bill resulted in one of their teams walking to Florida, it would cost them their jobs. Second, Congress has a few more urgent items on the agenda…than giving Howard Metzenbaum and Connie Mack publicity. Finally, the reality is that for more than 40 states, the real result of such a bill would be the end of the minor leagues as they are now constituted."

On August 5, 1993, U.S. District Court Judge John R. Padova rejected a motion by Major League Baseball to dismiss the suit of Vincent Piazza and Vincent Tirendi. Padova noted in his decision that baseball's antitrust exemption applied only to its now-defunct reserve system, wherein a club held a player's contract in perpetuity. The reserve system essentially has been replaced by the system of limited free agency. As a result, the Padova decision stripped away much of baseball's protection from adherence to federal antitrust rules.

On the heels of this decision, it was reported that Vincent Piazza and Vincent Tirendi received feelers from Major League Baseball regarding whether they would be willing to drop their suit if they were awarded a Tampa Bay-St. Petersburg franchise the next time that baseball expands.

Just over a year later, on September 28, 1994, it was announced that Piazza and Tirendi had settled their case with Major League Baseball out of court, and would receive a $6 million settlement as compensation.

In Congress, even though Major League Baseball once again held onto its coveted antitrust exemption, the sentiment in Washington was that if the players and owners have not reached an agreement to end the strike by early 1995, the legislation will be re-introduced in the next session of Congress.

"The real message should be a wake-up call to baseball," Utah Senator Orrin Hatch commented. "If you do not want Congress to be involved, then settle this dispute yourself."

Baseball, Bluegrass and Suicide

A cluster of Kentucky tragedies

Bob Bailey

Suicide is a particularly tragic means of death. With or without a note, it is often impossible to comprehend why someone would take their own life. There have been five active players and one league president who have committed suicide in major league history. There have been others who took this way out of their existence subsequent to their major league careers.

In one 10-year period from 1907 to 1916 four Kentuckians—three former players and the previously mentioned league president—took their own lives. There is no connection among the events but geography.

The first was Bob Lankswert, who played under the name Bob Lankford (some sources list him as Langsford). He was a shortstop who played a single game for the Louisville Colonels in their final National League season, 1899. But from 1890 to 1905 he had a 15-year professional career with Memphis, New Orleans, Mobile, Indianapolis, Milwaukee, and several other clubs.

It was a freak accident while he was with the Mobile team that is thought to have contributed to his later suicide. In 1894 or 1895, Mobile pitcher Pat Daniels, another Louisville native, was warming up before a game. One of Daniels' tosses got away and struck his teammate on the left temple. Lankswert was disabled for several weeks, and when he returned

he found that he had sustained a severe hearing loss which would worsen over the years. Through the rest of his baseball career, he was also reported to display brief periods of irrational behavior.

Returning to Louisville at the end of his playing days, he took a job at a tannery across the river in New Albany, Indiana. The head injury caused him to be hospitalized several times over the next year. He had just been released from a four-week stay at City Hospital and was being prepared by his brother and sister to be admitted to St. Anthony Hospital when he was found unconscious in his boarding house room on January 10, 1907.

The former player had complained that the head injury would not allow him to sleep more than twenty minutes at a time. He would occasionally go into a "daze," during which he would not comprehend anything going on about him or understand anything said to him.

His family felt sure that it was during one of these periods of irrationality that the 41-year-old former shortstop swallowed some carbolic acid in his room. Still alive when found by a fellow roomer, he was rushed to City Hospital, but died as he entered the hospital. He was buried in Cave Hill Cemetery, where he lies in an unmarked grave.

Harry Clay Pulliam had risen rapidly through baseball's executive ranks to the position of President of the National League in 1903, when he was only 34. He was born in Scottsville in south central Kentucky, but early in his life his father moved the family to

Bob Bailey is a frequent contributor to SABR publications. He lives in Goshen, Kentucky.

Louisville to enter the tobacco business.

In the late 1880s, Pulliam joined the *Louisville Commercial* as a reporter after several years of working on newspapers in California. At the same time he studied law at the Louisville Law School and there met Zach Phelps, prominent local attorney and President of the Louisville ball club. Phelps and Pulliam developed a close friendship, and in 1890 Pulliam left the *Commercial*, where he had risen to become City Editor, and joined the ball club as secretary.

In 1897, Pulliam became club President and was elected to the Kentucky legislature. In 1899, Barney Dreyfuss raised his stake in the ball club and assumed the title of President. Late that year, knowing that Louisville was a leading candidate to be dropped from the National League, Dreyfuss purchased a controlling interest in the Pittsburgh franchise. Pulliam went with him as club secretary. Four years later, he was elected league president.

Pulliam, who never married, was apparently a quiet, moody, but likable person. He was given to periods of depression. Friends never knew what was the cause of this depression but speculated that it somehow related to his family.

Early in 1909 he suffered what was described as a nervous breakdown during a league meeting in Chicago. He took a leave and returned to his office in early June.

On the evening of July 28 he left his office and went to his apartment at the New York Athletic Club. After having dinner at the Club, he returned to his room. At 9:30, a light on the club switchboard flashed, indicating that Pulliam wished to place a call. The operator was unable to get any response when he answered the light and sent up a porter with a pass key to investigate. He found a

Harry Pulliam

blood-spattered room with the President of the National League slumped on the divan, a bullet hole in his temple and a revolver next to him. Pulliam had apparently staggered about the room after the shot and knocked over the telephone.

A doctor was summoned. Pulliam was still alive, but was given no chance of survival. He died in his room the next morning.

No note was left, but Pulliam had posted several letters before retiring that evening. One of the letters is presumed to have been his resignation. Only speculations about the weight of his duties and the effects of his earlier breakdown were given as reasons for the suicide. The pressures had certainly increased in the previous year. Pulliam had long been on the wrong side of Giants owner John Brush. This enmity manifested itself in Brush's consistently annually voting against Pulliam's reelection as league president. On top of this was the ongoing feud between Brush's manager, John McGraw, and Pulliam's mentor, Barney Dreyfuss. With these battle line drawn, when Pulliam upheld umpire Hank O'Day's decision in the Merkle affair that ultimately led to the Giants losing the 1908 pennant, it is not difficult to imagine the fury that fell on Harry from Brush, McGraw and the New York press.

The shocked family made arrangements to have the body brought to Louisville, where an estimated 1,300 people attended the burial services at Cave Hill Cemetery.

Dan McGann, a native of Shelbyville, Kentucky, had a 13-year major league career, starting with Louisville in 1895. In 1898, he joined the Baltimore squad as a teammate of John McGraw. He shifted to Brooklyn in 1899, when the Baltimore-Brooklyn syndicate franchise loaded up the

Brooklyn roster with the best of the two teams. In 1900, he rejoined McGraw on the St. Louis National League team, then followed McGraw to Baltimore of the American League and finally the New York Giants in 1903. McGann played six seasons in New York, and participated in the 1905 World Series. He was traded to the Boston Braves in 1908, was released after the season, and played the next two years with Milwaukee of the American Association.

Following the 1910 season McGann had taken up residence at the Bosler Hotel at Second and Jefferson in Louisville. It was reported that arrangements were in progress to secure his services for the Louisville club for 1911.

McGann was well known around Louisville from his earlier playing days and the fact that his hometown was just 30 miles east of the city. The day before his death, he was seen around town by several acquaintances who reported that he was in good spirits and looking forward to playing for Louisville in the upcoming season. Guests at his hotel agreed.

Nevertheless, on the afternoon of December 13, 1910, the hotel maid had to call the manager when she was unable to get into McGann's room. A hotel employee crawled through the transom and found McGann's lifeless body in a pool of blood on his bed. He had been shot through the chest. A .32 calibre Smith & Wesson revolver was nearby.

The coroner determined that the 39-year-old ballplayer had died of a gunshot through the heart, and declared the death a suicide. While a ring was missing from the player's room, other pieces of jewelry and a small amount of cash remained.

There was no note and no one, family or friend, could provide a reason for the act. McGann was the second brother in the family to commit suicide that year. During the summer, his brother Dan (the ballplayer's given name was Dennis, but he always played under his brother's given name, Dan), a railroad agent for the L & N Railroad at Midway, Kentucky, had also shot himself to death for no apparent reason.

McGann's body was taken by train to Shelbyville where he was buried next to his brother in Grove Hill Cemetery.

The fourth of the Kentucky suicides occurred in Covington, Kentucky, on March 28, 1916. Eddie Hohnhorst had been a slugging first baseman for many local teams before he spent two seasons with Cleveland in 1910 and 1912. Most recently he had played for the Covington Federals in 1913.

In 1914, he had ended his baseball career and joined the Covington police force as a patrolman. During 1915, he was involved in a shoot-out in the discharge of his responsibilities. As a result, Hohnhorst had killed one of the suspects involved in the gun battle. Apparently this event weighed heavily on his mind. On March 27, 1916, he was working the late shift out of the South Covington station. At midnight, he tendered his badge and club to his lieutenant and announced he was quitting. The lieutenant told him to go home, think things over and come back the next day.

A fellow patrolman walked out of the station with Hohnhorst and offered to take him home. Hohnhorst refused and started walking down the street. He was wearing his patrolman's helmet and still had his revolver. The friend returned to the station where the lieutenant told him to stay with his depressed colleague. The officer caught up with Hohnhorst at the corner of Park and South Avenue. He found the 31-year-old Hohnhorst with a bullet wound in his right temple.

The victim was rushed to St. Elizabeth's Hospital, where he soon died. He is buried in Highland Cemetery, Fort Mitchell, Kentucky.

To these four major league suicide was added one from the minor leagues in 1921. Despondent over not making the Louisville club, 25-year-old pitcher Clay Daily of Frankfort went to Pepper's Cave outside the city and shot himself with a revolver.

The Bill James Historical Abstract notes that there appeared to be more suicides in the baseball world in the first 25 years of the twentieth century. Twenty suicides are catalogued there in a list that is acknowledged to be incomplete. James speculates that the reason for this might have been rooted in the growth and expansion of American society. Men had great ambitions and lofty hopes of hard work and true grit providing a platform upon which they might rise above their stations in life. When this expectation collapsed, a certain number of the disappointed took the seemingly easy way out via suicide. Maybe. In the end, though, all we can do is speculate about such tragedies—and also about why a relatively small place like Kentucky would have such a disproportionately large number of occurrences. We can only speculate, and sense the terrible pain that must lie behind such a tragic step.

Correlating Fielding and Batting Position

A careful study

Randy Klipstein

Thought of the batting order brings to mind many stereotypes: the centerfielder or second baseman bats lead-off; the cleanup hitter is usually the first baseman or an outfielder; the shortstop bats at the bottom of the order.

To better understand the relationship between fielding position and batting position, I undertook the following study. For every regular season major league game played in 1990, I recorded the fielding position for each batting position in each starting lineup. I then summed the data by league. The result is a matrix for each league, with rows for each spot in the batting order and columns for each fielding position. Each cell represents the total appearances where a fielding position coincides with a batting position.

For the National League, this meant the first eight batting order spots. For the American League, all nine batting order positions were used. I assumed that pitchers always hit ninth in the NL, and treated the DH as a 'null' fielding position. Thus batters hitting eighth in the NL and ninth in the AL are considered to be batting last.

There are two basic questions which this study attempts to answer:

1. Where do fielders bat?
2. Where do hitters field?

The same data, analyzed from different perspectives, is used to answer each of the questions.

American League by Total Appearances

	C	1B	2B	SS	3B	LF	CF	RF	DH
1	0	38	547	140	291	464	503	193	90
2	33	137	595	334	359	180	392	177	59
3	37	481	113	188	332	306	389	159	261
4	81	450	1	19	58	340	150	453	714
5	266	495	39	33	156	332	216	261	468
6	403	361	44	32	244	278	164	356	384
7	585	213	123	61	320	227	153	362	222
8	688	79	389	299	387	80	91	201	52
9	173	12	415	1160	119	59	208	104	16

American League by Percentages

	C	1B	2B	SS	3B	LF	CF	RF	DH
1	0	2	24	6	13	20	22	9	4
2	1	6	26	15	16	8	17	8	3
3	2	21	5	8	15	14	17	7	12
4	4	20	0	1	3	15	7	20	32
5	12	22	2	1	7	15	10	12	21
6	18	16	2	1	11	12	7	16	17
7	26	9	5	3	14	10	7	16	10
8	30	3	17	13	17	4	4	9	2
9	8	1	18	51	5	3	9	5	1

American League shortstops batted last 51 percent of the time. No catcher in the American League led off. These were the extremes. More surprising was that the designated hitter batted last in 16 lineups!

Randy Klipstein is a systems analyst who lives in Tarrytown, New York.

National League by Total Appearances

	C	1B	2B	SS	3B	LF	CF	RF
1	4	38	255	97	285	388	846	31
2	70	99	711	427	67	71	333	166
3	51	394	172	97	190	430	346	264
4	16	675	8	5	266	277	109	588
5	121	301	14	22	398	519	87	482
6	376	355	97	159	441	130	86	300
7	706	73	333	355	212	97	79	89
8	600	9	354	782	85	32	58	24

National League by Percentages

	C	1B	2B	SS	3B	LF	CF	RF
1	0	2	13	5	15	20	44	2
2	4	5	37	22	3	4	17	9
3	3	20	9	5	10	22	18	14
4	1	35	0	0	14	14	6	30
5	6	15	1	1	20	27	4	25
6	19	18	5	8	23	7	4	15
7	36	4	17	18	11	5	4	5
8	31	0	18	40	4	2	3	1

Similarity—One would expect that second basemen and shortstops would show similar characteristics in terms of where in the order they bat. Also, one would expect that the fourth and fifth spots in the batting order would be manned by fielders playing the same set of positions most of the time. To measure the degree of similarity between two fielding or batting positions, I summed the absolute differences of the total appearances of the positions being compared. The lower the difference, the more similar the positions.

What fielding positions are most similar? Dissimilar?

In the National League, the two most similar pairs were first base/right field, and third base/left field. In the American League, this right and left similarity was not evident; the most similar pairs were first base/designated hitter and the outfield corners.

In the NL, catchers and centerfielders were the most dissimilar.

In the AL, it was designated hitters and middle infielders.

American League Defensive Similarity

	C	1B	2B	SS	3B	LF	CF	RF	DH
C		2368	2854	3158	1824	2410	2636	1662	2350
1B			3360	3334	1994	1062	1856	1122	704
2B				1676	1580	2326	1504	2542	3458
SS					2082	2948	2320	2680	3432
3B						1330	1086	1308	2216
LF							988	984	1232
CF								1718	2210
RF									1196

National League Defensive Similarity

	C	1B	2B	SS	3B	LF	CF	RF
C		2490	2026	1356	2024	2846	2986	2538
1B			2868	2884	1290	1302	2194	558
2B				1040	2068	2396	1878	2686
SS					2400	2786	2334	2702
3B						958	1966	1158
LF							1492	1152
CF								2196

What batting positions are most similar / dissimilar?

In both leagues, the middle batting order spots, particularly consecutive pairs, were generally the most similar.

The last two spots were very similar in the NL, but not in the AL. American League catchers rarely bat last in the order.

The first two positions were much more similar in the American League. In the NL, an outfielder was twice as likely to bat lead-off than an infielder; and an infielder was twice as likely to bat second than an outfielder. In the AL, the pattern is there, but to a much lesser degree. Here is an explanation:

In the AL, the two weakest hitters will generally bat at the bottom of the order. In the NL, a manager might be reluctant to do the same, as that would mean there would be three weak hitters in a row (with the pitcher batting ninth). A National League manager may choose to bat one of the weak hitters second, using that spot to advance the base runners; thus avoiding three consecutive weak hitters. The weak hitters are likely to be a catcher or middle infielders. The middle infielder is the more likely choice to bat second, as catchers frequently ground into double plays, the last thing one wants from a number two hitter.

Cleanup and the last spot were the most dissimilar, in both leagues.

American League Offensive Similarity

	1	2	3	4	5	6	7	8	9
1		884	1480	2754	2338	2366	2180	1984	2386
2			1352	2904	2472	2392	2046	1414	1932
3				1650	1156	1372	1522	2270	2820
4					892	1156	1866	3208	3532
5						650	1392	2538	3006
6							744	2080	3086

7	1348	2892
8		2008

National League Offensive Similarity

	1	2	3	4	5	6	7	8
1		2096	1356	2412	2150	2352	2262	2760
2			1776	2806	2696	2258	1614	1806
3				1362	1170	1348	2192	2832
4					1004	1556	2730	3414
5						1144	2474	3158
6							1524	2208
7								896

Standard Deviation—I derived the standard deviation for each fielding and batting position, in each league; and used it an indication of how strong the tendency is for a fielder to bat in a certain position, or a batter to field in a certain position. The higher the standard deviation, the stronger the tendency.

What is the standard deviation of each fielding position?

In other words, which fielders have somewhat set batting order positions and which are more likely to bat anywhere in the order? The ranking was similar for each league. Catchers and middle infielders showed the least diversification. They were followed by designated hitters and first basemen. Outfielders and third basemen were relatively ubiquitous, reflecting the variety of offensive roles expected from these players.

Standard Deviation of Fielding Positions

	C	1B	2B	SS	3B	LF	CF	RF	DH
AL	240	186	221	339	209	123	133	108	221
NL	242	216	216	248	125	174	253	194	

What is the standard deviation of each batting position?

Or, which spots in the lineup are generally associated with one or a few fielding positions, and which are not? In each league, the spots that were most constant were: first, cleanup, and the bottom of the order. This indicates that managers conform to ideas about which fielders should bat in these positions. The most variation is at the third position in the batting order, in each league. This reflects the variety of offensive skills required to be a number three hitter. There is no dominant characteristic for these hitters. Speed, power, and the ability to reach base are all valued attributes for the third spot in the order.

Standard Deviation of Batting Positions

	1	2	3	4	5	6	7	8	9
AL	197	171	133	235	155	135	147	199	341
NL	263	217	130	247	194	132	205	282	

How do the leagues differ?

Excluding random chance, all of the differences between the American and National Leagues can be attributed to the former's use of the Designated Hitter Rule. The standard deviation of each fielding position and batting order spot are generally lower in the American League. This is expected, as another hitter increases the number of permutations. It is particularly true among first basemen and outfielders; and the middle batting positions that designated hitters typically occupy. The rule adds not simply another hitter, but usually another good hitter to the lineup.

The last position in the batting order is affected in several ways.

1. In the NL, catchers generally bat in the last two spots (67 percent of the time in seventh or eighth). In the AL, the catcher seldom bats last (8 percent in ninth), as managers are reluctant to have a slow-footed runner bat immediately ahead of the top of the order.

2. Shortstops are more likely to bat last in the AL (51 percent vs 40 percent). This can be attributed to the infrequency of catchers batting last.

3. Center fielders are three times more likely to bat last in the AL.

American League managers, freed of the burden of placing the pitcher in the batting order, view the lineup as a cycle. An AL center fielder who is a weak hitter will often bat last, where his speed can be utilized as a 'secondary' lead-off hitter.

Spectrums—This refers to rankings of defensive and offensive positions according to the level of offensive production that is expected. Certainly a DH is expected to produce more offense than a middle infielder; but a complete ranking requires a more quantitative approach. One method is to rank each fielding position based on where the fielders bat (or don't bat) in the order. For instance, one could rank the defensive positions by how often each fielder bats cleanup or how infrequently each fielder bats last.

Similarly, a ranking of offensive positions could be constructed based on how often certain fielders occupy that spot. For instance, one could rank batting order positions by how often an outfielder bats in that spot.

The dilemma is that to generate an offensive spectrum using this type of method, one needs to have some idea of the defensive spectrum (and vice versa). Therefore, a starting assumption must be made.

The approach that I chose was to assume that for catchers and middle infielders, offense is a secondary consideration; for first basemen, corner outfielders, and designated hitters, it is of primary importance. Each time a catcher or middle infielder batted in a given spot, I subtracted a point from a total for that place in the order; when a fielder from the latter group batted in that spot, I added a point. Summing the resulting totals for each batting order position yielded a ranking of the batting order in terms of offensive importance. The offensive spectrums are:

Offensive Spectrums

AL	4	5	3	6	7	1	2	8	9
NL	4	5	3	6	1	2	7	8

I used the offensive spectrums to establish the defensive spectrums. Multiplying the number of appearances by the corresponding offensive ranking, and then summing the resulting totals for each fielding position, yielded a ranking of defensive positions, again in terms of offensive importance. For instance, in the AL, the total appearances for each fielding position in the first spot in the batting order was multiplied by four, as lead-off was fourth from the bottom in the offensive spectrum. I then summed the totals for each fielding position. The defensive spectrums are:

Defensive Spectrums

AL	DH	1B	LF	RF	CF	3B	C	2B	SS
NL	1B	RF	LF	3B	CF	2B	C	SS

Defensive Spectrums are similar to what one would have predicted. They simply offer objective evidence.

Conclusion—Every fan knows that the relationship between where a player bats and fields is not a random pairing. Using quantitative methods, I have tried to bring this relationship into a clearer view.

I believe that there are two rules that shape these relationships:

1. The more demanding the defensive position, the less demanding the offensive roll. Shortstops bat last more often than outfielders. Since much of a shortstop's value is defense, a poor hitting shortstop can remain on the team and in the lineup.

2. There are certain physical attributes that are associated with skills that are valued (or avoided) at offensive and defensive positions. A fast player is likely to play centerfield and bat at the top of the order. A big, muscle-bound player will generally bat fourth or fifth, and not play a middle infield position. Offensive and defensive positions are linked by skills.

These rules imply that managers share perceptions of what are the key batting order positions and what type of offensive production is required from each. This evidence suggests that managers are in general agreement on how to construct a lineup.

Finally an observation: it will not come as a surprise that those who field in the middle generally bat at the beginning or the end; and those that bat in the middle generally field on the left or the right. Did you know however, that players who field on the left are likely to bat in odd positions in the batting order and players who field on the right are likely to bat in even numbered spots?

1894!

The modern game's greatest hitting explosion

David Q. Voigt

Over the long river of human time, some years jut out like sentinel rocks with their numerals vividly recalling the great events that transpired during their days. Certainly that part of the river we call American history demonstrates this effect as one need merely utter such dates as 1776, 1812, 1865, 1918 or 1963 to summon up the memories of associated events. And in like manner the peak events of major league baseball history can readily be recalled by invoking such salient dates as 1869, 1876, 1919, 1941 or 1969. But if most devout fans can recount the diamond dramas associated with these years, how many can invoke the stirring events associated with the touchstone date of 1894?

Indeed, that forgotten season of a century ago marked the onslaught of the greatest hitting explosion in the modern history of the major league game. The great batting eruption of '94 occurred at a time when batters were taking full advantage of the modern 60' 6" pitching distance that was introduced only the year before. Coupled with the rule confining pitchers to a 12" by 4" slab mounted atop a pitching mound, the extra five foot pitching distance had already boosted National League batting averages from a puny .245 overall mark in 1892 to .280 in 1893. It was an astonishing increase, and one astute observer, veteran outfielder Jim O'Rourke, rightly cited the confining slab rather than the extra distance for robbing pitchers of the deceptive mobility that they had

long enjoyed while hurling from the now discarded pitching boxes.

For harried pitchers, the 1893 season was a brutal experience, but if hurlers expected some relief from the 1894 rule that counted foul bunts as strikes (except with two strikes), they were grasping at straws. Instead, what followed was the worst pounding that pitchers suffered in the modern history of the game.

With the NL batting averages soaring 29 points over the previous year's mark, it was not surprising that the great hitting eruption of '94 produced a record fallout of batting achievements. For openers, NL hitters set a modern record by *averaging* .309 at the plate. And by leading that onslaught with a .349 average, the hard-hitting Phillies set the enduring seasonal record for team batting. What's more, the Phillies mounted another team record (since broken) by scoring at least one run a game over a skein of games; when the streak ended in 1895, their mark stood at 194 consecutive games.

The Phillies' lusty hitting only carried that pitching-poor team to a fourth place finish. Championship honors went to the more versatile Baltimore Orioles, whose .343 hitting (still the second highest team average in modern history) and gritty pitching enabled them to dethrone the three-time champion Boston Beaneaters. And if playing manager John Ward's runner-up New York Giants soured the Oriole victory by thrashing the birds in the first of four post-season Temple Cup playoffs, the Orioles extended their dynastic sway by winning the next two NL pennants.

Historian **David Q. Voigt** *is a professor at Albright College.*

Meanwhile, eight of the 12 NL teams of 1894 batted above .300. Even the worst hitting team, the Louisville Colonels, who finished dead last, 54 games behind the winners, managed to bat .269.

Equally impressive were the individual batting feats of '94. Topping all hitters that year was outfielder Hugh Duffy of the Beaneaters. The little right-handed batter's .438 average still stands as the seasonal record at the new distance, and his 18 homers and 145 RBIs also led the pack in 1894. By modern standards it was a Triple Crown performance, but statisticians of the time took little notice of RBIs, and any notion of a triple batting crown was beyond their ken. Indeed, Duffy was hard pressed to beat out rival hitters in each category. His closest rivals for the batting title were the four Phillies' outfielders; Tuck Turner swatted .416, Sam Thompson .404, Ed Delahanty .400, and Billy Hamilton .399. In RBIs, Sam Thompson finished four behind the Boston star. In the

Sam Thompson

Billy Hamilton

homer-hitting derby Duffy's output barely topped the 17 blasts poled by Bill Joyce and Bobby Lowe.

However, at this time neither fans nor statisticians were much impressed by homer hitting. In fact, throughout the nineteenth century and as late as 1920, the triple was the big blow of choice. And in 1894, Heinie Reitz of the Orioles led the way with 31 three-baggers, which was not a record. Most hits during this explosive year were singles; indeed, during the 'nineties only Dan Brouthers, Sam Thompson and Ed Delahanty managed to top the .500 mark in slugging percentage.

Nevertheless, hitters of 1894 used their heavy bats to drive in runs at a record setting pace. Over the course of the 132-game playing season Big Sam Thompson of the Phillies averaged 1.39 RBIs *per game*, a feat that stands second to his 1895 mark of 1.42 a game. What's more, in 1894 Pop Anson, Duffy, and Delahanty each averaged better than an RBI a game to rank among the top 20 all-time leaders in this category.

Such prodigious hitting also produced run scoring records. Despite the short season, outfielder Billy Hamilton plated an unsurpassed 196 runs. And he set another all time mark by scoring at least one run a game over 24 consecutive contests. His closest rival in this department is Red Rolfe of the 1939 Yankees, who managed a skein of 18 games. What's more, "Sliding Billy" Hamilton burnished his reputation as the nineteenth century's base stealing king by swiping a league-leading 99 sacks. Although that was no record performance, Hamilton's seven steals during a single 1894 game is unsurpassed.

The record fallout of 1894 also included a consecutive game hitting streak by Chicago infielder Bill Dahlen. Before going hitless during an August 7 slugfest, Dahlen had hit safely in 42 straight games. But like Duffy's unsung "Triple Crown" performance, Dahlen's feat was unheralded by the more innocent statisticians of the day. Besides, Dahlen's achievement was fleeting. In 1897, Willie Keeler hit in 44 consecutive games, which also passed unnoticed until Joe DiMaggio approached the mark on his way to his record 56 in 1941.

What happened to pitching standards in 1894, to yield such awesome hitting? Not since the 1887 season, when the rules allowed batters a fourth strike and when bases on balls officially counted as hits, was the pitching-batting equation so tilted in favor of the batters. But unlike the 1887 "explosion" with its "phantom" base on balls hits, there was nothing artificial about the battering pitchers absorbed in '94.

Obviously, pitchers had a devilish time adapting to the modern distance and the confining pitching slabs. As a result overall pitching ERA rose to a horrendous 5.32, and bases on balls exceeded strikeouts by nearly 2,500. Only the Giants' pitching corps managed to compile an ERA in the 3.00 range. In 1894, Amos Rusie and Jouette Meekin each won 36 games, with the doughty Rusie posting what would now be called a Triple Crown performance by leading the NL in victories (36), strikeouts (195), and ERA (2.78).

But there were few such standouts among the harried pitchers of '94. Indeed, all were overworked and it would take a few more seasons before managers realized that hurlers could no longer shoulder the workloads of the pre-1893 years. Mercifully, some relief came in 1895, with a rule that increased the size of the pitching slab to 24" by 6". That made for more mobility, and another ruling that counted foul tips as strikes afforded some slight relief. But not until 1901, when the NL adopted the modern foul strike system, did the pitching-batting equation tilt in favor of the

hurlers. By then clubs also deployed more pitchers who learned to use more varied deliveries, including

Hugh Duffy

such doctored pitches as the spitter and the cut ball. And above all, NL pitchers had learned to control their deliveries. Thus, after eight seasons during which NL hurlers annually walked far more batters than they fanned, beginning in 1901, 21 seasons would pass before walks would again exceed strikeouts.

By 1901, the hitting explosion of the 1890s was over. Thereafter, seasonal batting averages in both majors seldom rose above the .270 mark. The single exception, of course, was the 1930 season when NL hitters averaged .303. But if short-sighted fans are inclined to fix on that date as the epitome of seasonal hitting, they should peer further down the river of baseball history. For the touchstone date of 1894 was the year when batters staged the greatest eruption in the modern history of the major league game.

Waiting for the Hall to Call

Charting the years between retirement and induction

Nat Rosenberg

I was 15 years old when my parents and I arrived at Cooperstown, New York on August 6, 1973. It was Hall Of Fame Game Day. The Texas Rangers beat the Pittsburgh Pirates 6-4. We sat next to Rich Hebner's mother at the game (a wonderful woman).

A few hours later at the lobby of the Hotel Otsego, my father was sitting and talking with Buck Leonard and Satchel Paige. My grandfather took my father to many of the old Negro League baseball games in Chicago and Dad knew many friends of the recently-honored Negro Leaguers.

I was content to spend the day running from one ribboned elderly gentleman to the next asking them to sign my scorecard or any other piece of paper. There were probably only about 200 people in the lobby at any one time. Most of the fans just wanted to speak to the Pirates and Rangers.

My mother, however, had the conversation that led to the writing of this paper. She sat with Mrs. Casey Stengel and Mrs. Stanley Coveleski for most of the afternoon.

In their conversation, Mrs. Coveleski elegantly told my mother and Mrs. Stengel that had Stanley not been inducted into the Hall Of Fame while he was alive, she would not have accepted the honor once he had died. They felt he deserved the honor and had earned it as one of the greats of the early days.

Stan Coveleski retired in 1928. He was inducted into the Hall in 1969, 33 years after voting for the Hall began in 1936. Coveleski was born in 1890. He was 79 when he got the call from Cooperstown. He died in 1984, one of baseball's immortals.

Like most baseball fans, I wonder what made Hal Newhouser better in 1992 (year of induction) than he was in 1982, 1972, or 1962. I also am thrilled that the likes of Enos Slaughter, Bobby Doerr, Tony Lazzeri, and Hal Newhouser have been honored. I know others disagree, but I feel empty inside when the Veterans Committee does not give me even one golden player to reminisce about, as occurred in 1993 and other years.

The purpose of this paper is not to compare inductees to deserving players. It is also not to build a case for those trying to crack the magic list. It is not even to comment on the commercialization of the Hall Of Fame (no 15-year-old will ever again experience the joy I did spending the afternoon just talking to the greats and their families).

The purpose of this paper is to share my research on a subject I have found quite interesting. Just how long does it take for a player to get into the Hall Of Fame? How old will the players be once they get there? Why it takes so long from player to player is an issue to be left for another time.

Lou Gehrig and Roberto Clemente were honored early because of their tragic early deaths. Besides them, only Hubbell (4), Ott (4), DiMaggio (4), and Hornsby (5) sneak in under the 6 year barrier. It was

Nat Rosenberg, *36 and happily married to wife Kathy, lives in Woodridge, Illinois. He is a fulltime sales manager and a nearly fulltime baseball archeologist and collector.*

possible to induct a person into the Hall before a 5-year waiting period before 1954. In 1954, the 5-year grace period became the accepted law.

The average age at induction is just under 65 years (64.7), but Ed Walsh is the only player to actually be inducted at age 65. The average waiting time for a player is 15.5 years. Don Drysdale fits the bill at 15 years. Lou Gehrig was the youngest player (36 years old) inducted. If he had lived, Roger Connor would have been 119 years old when he got the call.

Key to column headings:

Player: No managers or executives.

Retire: The year the player retired according to *The Baseball Encyclopedia* and *Only The Ball Was White*. Years of experience in the major leagues are not counted for Negro Leaguers.

HOF: Year of induction.

YRS: The number of years it took to be voted into the Hall Of Fame. 1936 is ground zero for white major leaguers (this is why Babe Ruth, for example, shows 0 instead of 1). Time begins for the Negro Leaguers in 1971.

Born: The year the player was born.

Ind Age: Induction Age of the player. This is the difference between the year of the player's birth and the year of his induction, even in the case of posthumous induction.

Sources:

National Baseball Hall Of Fame Yearbook, 1994. National Baseball Hall Of Fame and Museum.

Spalding's Official Baseball Guide, 1938. American Sports Publishing Company.

Daguerreotypes 8th Edition, 1990. The Sporting News.

Players Of Cooperstown, 1992. Publications International Ltd.

The Baseball Encyclopedia 8th Edition, 1990. Macmillan.

Baseball's Hall Of Fame, 1973. Smith.

Reach Baseball Guide, 1939. American Sports Publishing Company.

National Baseball Hall Of Fame And Museum Yearbook, 1973. National Baseball Hall Of Fame and Museum.

Only The Ball Was White, 1970. Peterson
Historical Baseball Abstract, 1988. James
Bernard Rosenberg (my father).

Player	Retire	HoF	Yrs	Born	Age
Gehrig	1939	1939	0	1903	36
Koufax	1966	1972	6	1935	37
Clemente	1972	1973	1	1934	39
Ruth	1935	1936	0	1895	41
DiMaggio	1951	1955	4	1914	41
Hunter	1979	1987	8	1946	41
Ott	1947	1951	4	1909	42
Bench	1983	1989	6	1947	42
Dean	1947	1953	6	1911	42
J Robinson	1956	1962	6	1919	43
Mantle	1968	1974	6	1931	43
Hubbell	1943	1947	4	1903	44
Feller	1956	1962	6	1918	44
Foxx	1945	1951	6	1907	44
Cochrane	1937	1947	10	1903	44
Palmer	1984	1990	6	1945	45
Marichal	1975	1983	8	1938	45
Greenberg	1947	1956	9	1911	45
Sisler	1930	1939	3	1893	46
Hornsby	1937	1942	5	1896	46
Aaron	1976	1982	6	1934	46
B Gibson	1975	1981	6	1935	46
B Robinson	1977	1983	6	1937	46
Banks	1971	1977	6	1931	46
Brock	1979	1985	6	1939	46
Carew	1985	1991	6	1945	46
Kaline	1974	1980	6	1934	46
Fingers	1985	1992	7	1946	46
Ford	1967	1974	7	1928	46
Gehringer	1942	1949	7	1903	46
F Robinson	1976	1982	6	1935	47
Grove	1941	1947	6	1900	47
Morgan	1984	1990	6	1943	47
R Jackson	1987	1993	6	1946	47
Stargell	1982	1988	6	1941	47
Berra	1965	1972	7	1925	47
Dickey	1946	1954	8	1907	47
Mathews	1968	1978	10	1931	47
Mays	1973	1979	6	1931	48
McCovey	1980	1986	6	1938	48
Seaver	1986	1992	6	1944	48
T Williams	1960	1966	6	1918	48
Jenkins	1983	1991	8	1943	48
Killebrew	1975	1984	9	1936	48
Campanella	1957	1969	12	1921	48
Drysdale	1969	1984	15	1936	48
W Johnson	1927	1936	0	1887	49
Speaker	1928	1937	1	1888	49
Musial	1963	1969	6	1920	49
P Waner	1945	1952	7	1903	49
B Williams	1976	1987	11	1938	49
Frisch	1937	1947	11	1898	49
Traynor	1937	1948	11	1899	49
Carlton	1988	1994	6	1944	50
Cobb	1928	1936	0	1886	50
Yastrzemski	1983	1989	6	1939	50
Roberts	1966	1976	10	1926	50
Aparicio	1973	1984	11	1934	50
Cronin	1945	1956	11	1906	50
Alexander	1930	1938	2	1887	51

Name						Name					
Simmons	1944	1953	9	1902	51	J Collins	1908	1945	9	1873	72
E Collins	1930	1939	3	1887	52	Chesbro	1909	1946	10	1874	72
Spahn	1965	1973	8	1921	52	Rixey	1933	1963	27	1891	72
Wynn	1963	1972	9	1920	52	M Brown	1916	1949	13	1876	73
Perry	1983	1991	8	1938	53	Rice	1935	1963	27	1890	73
Boudreau	1952	1970	18	1917	53	Averill	1941	1975	34	1902	73
Kiner	1955	1975	20	1922	53	Vaughan	1948	1985	37	1912	73
Irvin	1948	1973	2	1919	54	Dandridge	1949	1987	16	1913	74
Pennock	1934	1948	12	1894	54	Bottomley	1937	1974	38	1900	74
Snider	1964	1980	16	1926	54	Jennings	1918	1945	9	1870	75
Lyons	1946	1955	9	1900	55	McGinnity	1908	1946	10	1871	75
Hartnett	1941	1955	14	1900	55	Klein	1944	1980	36	1905	75
Mathewson	1916	1936	0	1880	56	Youngs	1926	1972	36	1897	75
Lemon	1958	1976	18	1920	56	J Johnson	1938	1975	4	1899	76
Terry	1936	1954	18	1898	56	Bresnahan	1915	1945	9	1879	76
Appling	1950	1964	14	1907	57	Burkett	1905	1946	10	1870	76
Medwick	1948	1968	20	1911	57	Faber	1933	1964	28	1888	76
Evers	1929	1939	3	1881	58	Crawford	1917	1957	21	1880	77
Heilmann	1932	1952	16	1894	58	Haines	1937	1970	33	1893	77
J Gibson	1946	1972	1	1911	61	G Kelly	1932	1973	37	1896	77
L Waner	1945	1967	22	1906	61	Rizzuto	1956	1994	38	1917	77
Kell	1957	1983	26	1922	61	Delahanty	1903	1945	9	1867	78
Wagner	1917	1936	0	1874	62	Lombardi	1947	1986	39	1908	78
Lajoie	1916	1937	1	1875	62	Duffy	1906	1945	9	1866	79
Wilhelm	1972	1985	13	1923	62	Wallace	1918	1953	17	1874	79
Ruffing	1947	1967	20	1905	62	Coveleski	1928	1969	33	1890	79
Maranville	1935	1954	19	1891	63	Bancroft	1930	1971	35	1892	79
Schalk	1929	1955	19	1892	63	Ferrell	1947	1984	37	1905	79
Manush	1939	1964	25	1901	63	Sewell	1933	1977	41	1898	79
Vance	1935	1955	19	1891	64	Wilson	1934	1979	43	1900	79
Gomez	1943	1972	29	1908	64	T Jackson	1936	1982	46	1903	79
Paige	1950	1971	0	1906	65	Charleston	1950	1976	5	1896	80
Leonard	1950	1972	1	1907	65	Nichols	1906	1949	13	1869	80
Walsh	1917	1946	10	1881	65	Marquard	1925	1971	35	1889	82
Tinker	1916	1946	10	1880	66	Hooper	1925	1971	35	1887	84
Reese	1958	1984	26	1918	66	Radbourn	1891	1939	3	1853	86
Schoendienst	1963	1989	26	1923	66	T McCarthy	1896	1946	10	1864	86
Herman	1947	1975	28	1909	66	Anson	1897	1939	3	1852	87
Keeler	1910	1939	3	1872	67	Brouthers	1904	1945	9	1858	87
Hafey	1937	1971	34	1904	67	Ewing	1897	1946	10	1859	87
Mize	1953	1981	28	1913	68	Flick	1910	1963	27	1876	87
Goslin	1938	1968	30	1900	68	K Kelly	1893	1945	9	1857	88
Doerr	1951	1986	35	1918	68	Lazzeri	1939	1991	52	1903	88
Chance	1914	1946	10	1877	69	Spalding	1878	1939	3	1850	89
Bender	1925	1953	17	1884	69	Cummings	1877	1939	3	1848	91
Baker	1922	1955	19	1886	69	Lloyd	1931	1977	6	1884	93
Roush	1931	1962	26	1893	69	O'Rourke	1904	1945	9	1852	93
Slaughter	1959	1985	26	1916	69	Hamilton	1901	1961	25	1866	95
Cuyler	1938	1968	30	1899	69	Joss	1910	1978	42	1880	98
Young	1911	1937	1	1867	70	Kelley	1908	1971	35	1871	100
Waddell	1910	1946	10	1876	70	Foster	1926	1981	10	1879	102
Hoyt	1938	1969	31	1899	70	Clarkson	1894	1963	27	1861	102
Bell	1946	1974	3	1903	71	Ward	1894	1964	28	1860	104
Plank	1917	1946	10	1875	71	Beckley	1907	1971	35	1867	104
Wheat	1927	1959	23	1888	71	Rusie	1901	1977	41	1871	106
Carey	1929	1961	25	1890	71	Keefe	1893	1964	28	1857	107
Grimes	1934	1964	30	1893	71	Galvin	1892	1965	29	1856	109
Coombs	1935	1970	34	1899	71	Welch	1892	1973	37	1859	114
Lindstrom	1936	1976	40	1905	71	Thompson	1906	1974	38	1860	114
Dihigo	1945	1977	6	1905	72	Connor	1897	1976	40	1857	119

Do Lefties Mature Late?

An examination of the "Koufax Phenomenon"

Perry Sailor

The conventional wisdom in baseball has long held that lefthanded pitchers are an essentially different breed from their "normal" righthanded counterparts. Read widely about the game, and I'll guarantee you'll find plenty of statements like these:

"Lefties think screwy."

"Typical wild lefty."

"Lefties' pitches have better movement."

"Lefties have more stuff."

"Little lefties can sometimes be successful; little righties can't."

To my knowledge nobody has come up with a single credible explanation for *why* any of these might be true—for that matter, I've never seen hard evidence that any of them *are* true. But among baseball men, "everybody knows" they're true.

One statement which I have read—most recently in *USA Today* on the day this is being written—has particularly intrigued me: "Lefties mature late." Now this is something which, if widely believed, could have a profound influence on certain pitchers' careers. Say a team has two 27-year-old pitchers, one lefthanded, the other righthanded. These two pitchers have each spent time in the majors, have good arms and a lot of ability, but neither of them has managed to get command of his stuff and turn into a real pitcher. Which one will be released or traded, and which will get another year to try to turn it around?

My guess is that the lefthander will get that extra year, because of the belief that lefties are late developers. I call this belief the "Koufax phenomenon," because I think that Sandy Koufax's incredible success, after years of struggling to put it together, has created a powerful archetype in the minds of baseball people, which continues today to benefit young—and not so young—lefties still trying to get over the hump. Is the Koufax phenomenon simply a vivid example of what is in fact a common pattern? Is the conventional wisdom true? Is there still hope for David West? This study is a report of my attempt to study the question objectively and systematically.

Definitions—There are two major issues to be resolved before we can begin a study of when pitchers reach maturity. First, we must come up with an objective measure of pitching performance, preferably a single number that will let us rate a pitcher's performance and rank the seasons of his career. Second, we must define "maturity."

I used ERA as the measure of performance, with one small adjustment: I divided the pitcher's ERA for each season by the league ERA (LERA) for that league in that season. For example, if a pitcher's ERA for a given season was 3.75, while the league ERA for the same season was 4.03, the pitcher's adjusted ERA (AERA) would be 3.75/4.03 = 0.93. This was done so that pitchers seasons could be ranked even though hitting conditions may have changed over time. For example, here are two seasons in the career of a ficti-

Perry Sailor a lefty, is a data analyst at the Early Intervention Research Institute at Utah State University in Logan, Utah.

tious pitcher:

Season	ERA	LERA	AERA
A	3.75	4.20	0.89
B	3.65	3.50	1.04

Clearly, Season A was better *in its context*, even though the pitcher's ERA was lower in Season B. AERA reflects this. (This is similar in concept to Thorn and Palmer's Normalized ERA (NERA), as presented in *The Hidden Game of Baseball*. The difference is that they use LERA divided by ERA, rather than the reverse, so a higher number reflects a better performance. They also remove the decimal. With AERA, as with ERA, a lower number is better.)

The second issue to be resolved is to define what constitutes maturity. What might it mean to say "Lefties mature late"? Does it mean that they tend to reach their peak ability at a later age? That they tend to reach the majors at a later age? That the time *between* reaching the majors and reaching peak ability is longer? I chose to study the issue using each of the above definitions in turn, reasoning that if all three pointed to the same conclusion, we could be very confident that it was correct. I defined each pitcher's "age at peak ability" as follows. First, I listed his AERAs by season, along with his age that year. Then I found his best three seasons (with a minimum of 30 innings). The age of his peak ability was the age at which he had the *first* of his three best seasons, or his first "peak season." This was the age at which he was essentially "as good as he ever got." For example, here's Sandy Koufax's career:

Age	AERA
19	0.75
20	1.30
21	1.00
22	1.13
23	1.03
24	1.04
25	0.87
26	0.64
27	0.57
28	0.49
29	0.58
30	0.48

Atypically, Sandy's best season was his last, at age 30, closely followed by the three previous seasons. His best three were at ages 30, 28, and 27, so I define 27 as his age at peak ability. In the remainder of this study, this will be called the "first peak season."

This method is not perfect. Although it pretty much confirms what we know about Koufax, we can see that if he'd had a little more luck at age 19, the re-

sult would have been very misleading. This can easily happen with any one individual, but over a large group, flukes tend to cancel out. All in all, I think this method is an accurate indicator of when a pitcher has developed to the limits of his ability.

The second definition of time to mature was the age at which the pitcher first reached the majors for a minimum of 30 innings. This defines maturity in terms of a fixed standard, rather than the pitcher's own eventual ability level.

The third definition of time to mature is the number of years between reaching the majors and the first peak season. I derived this for each pitcher by simply subtracting his age during his first season from his age during his first peak season.

The sample in this study was all pitchers born in the 1930s who had at least three seasons of 30 or more innings pitched. This included 201 pitchers—142 righthanders and 59 lefthanders. I chose this group because all of them have completed their careers. Results are show in Tables 1-3 below.

Table 1. Age at First Peak Season

	No.	Average
Righthanders	142	25.2
Lefthanders	59	25.4

Table 2. Age at Pitcher's First 30-Inning Season

	No.	Average
Righthanders	142	23.6
Lefthanders	59	23.8

Table 3. Number of Years Between Pitcher's First Season and His First Peak Season

	No.	Average
Righthanders	142	1.56
Lefthanders	59	1.54

For each definition of time to mature, the differences between righthanders and lefthanders are trivial and quite likely to occur by chance, according to a conventional statistical test called a "Student's *t* test."

Rather than focusing on averages, another way to study the issue is to focus on those pitchers who *did* mature late. Are they more likely to be lefthanded? No, they are not. Twenty-nine percent of these pitchers (27 percent of righties, 34 percent of lefties) had their first peak season at age 27 or later. Again, the difference between right- and lefthanders is very likely to occur by chance. Only five, and only one lefty (Koufax himself), peaked after eight or more years in the majors.

The conclusion seems quite clear. This study found no evidence for differences between lefthanded and righthanded pitchers in average time to mature.

Individual Cases— How common is it for pitchers, right- *or* lefthanded, to show the Koufax pattern? How many pitchers reach maturity, as defined by the "first peak season" method, after eight years in the big leagues? Very few— in fact, only five of the 201 in this study. Besides Koufax, the others were righthanders Ted Abernathy, Dave Giusti, Mudcat Grant, and Ron Kline, all of whom posted peak AERA years as relievers after long careers as starters.

Abernathy was in the majors at 22, making 14 starts and 26 relief appearances

Ted Abernathy

for the Senators, and getting hammered for a 5.96 ERA. He got 20 more starts and 11 relief appearances the next two years, and was even worse. He then basically disappeared for five years, but came back at 30 as a submarining relief ace and had his best years at 34, 37, and 39. Giusti, Grant, and Kline show very similar patterns, except they were better as starters than Abernathy. Grant, in fact, led the AL in victories and shutouts for the pennant-winning Twins at age 29. But all three posted their best AERAs after becoming relief aces in their 30's.

If we relax the criterion a little and look at the five

pitchers who took *seven* seasons to mature, rather than eight, we see the same career pattern with two of the five. Dick Hall and Pete Richert had their best years in relief, after many years as starters. The other three, however, remained starters and still had their best years relatively late: Vern Law, Bob Gibson, and Gaylord Perry. These three are the only seeming parallels to Koufax in this group of 201 pitchers.

Upon closer examination, however, none made quite the leap that Koufax did. Perry's and Gibson's peak years—except Gibson's 1968—were not *dramatically* better than several seasons early in their careers.

They were already fine pitchers who just got a bit better. Gibson reached the majors at 23 and won 28 games with low ERAs at 25 and 26. Perry also reached the bigs at 23, and was a 21-game winner in his fifth season. And Law makes the list only because he spent 1950 and 1951 (age 20 and 21) getting shelled for those awful Pirate teams, when he probably should have been in the minors. He didn't come back to the majors until 1954, when he was 24, and had his first peak year at 27, although by far his best year was at 35. Interestingly, Gibson, Perry, and Law were all righthanded.

How Long Does it Take Most Pitchers to Peak?— Based on this sample, pitchers—right- *and* lefthanded—peak earlier than is commonly believed. Fully half of the 201 pitchers in this study had what turned out to be one of their three best AERAs *in their first season.* Of course, this finding may simply be an artifact of the fact that a lot of marginal pitchers have short careers. To check this possibility, I analyzed the careers of the 83 pitchers in this group who had at least 10 years between their first and last seasons in the majors. This eliminated anyone who could be considered a marginal talent. Even among this group of pitchers who had long careers, 49 percent (52 percent of the righties, 44 percent of the lefties) had a peak season in one of their first three years.

I also examined this subsample of pitchers with long careers for evidence of the Koufax phenomenon. There still appeared to be no average tendency for lefties to mature late, by any of the three definitions of time to mature (Tables 4-6). Thirty-nine percent of the 83 pitchers with long careers matured at 27 or older—36 percent of the righties, and 44 percent of the lefties. The small difference in favor of lefties is likely to occur by chance, as determined by a statistical (chi-square) test. Only five pitchers in the subsample—Koufax and the four righties described above in the analysis of the full sample of 201—matured after eight or more big league seasons.

Table 4. Age at First Peak Season, Among Pitchers With Long Careers

	No.	Average
Righthanders	56	25.7
Lefthanders	27	25.6

Table 5. Age at Pitcher's First 30-Inning Season, Pitchers With Long Careers.

	No.	Average
Righthanders	56	22.6
Lefthanders	27	22.6

Table 6. Number of Years Between Pitcher's First Season and His First Peak Season, Pitchers With Long Careers.

	No.	Average
Righthanders	56	3.05
Lefthanders	27	2.93

Summary—For this sample of 201 pitchers, and for the subgroup of 83 pitchers with long careers, there was no evidence that the average time to mature was any different for lefthanders than righthanders. Furthermore, the Koufax phenomenon—a big leap forward in ability after many years at a lower level—was not especially characteristic of lefthanders, and was in fact pretty much limited to Koufax. The very few other pitchers having their best ERA years late in their careers were quality starters who converted to relief, much as Dennis Eckersley has done in recent seasons; or pitchers who were already quite good, but were still able to improve somewhat. I wouldn't bet on David West to make a breakthrough.

Baseball's Amateur Draft

An abstract analysis

David C. Thomas

Amajor league team's amateur draft has always been judged by how many of its signed picks make it to the majors. This abstract analysis focuses, not necessarily on a team's signed draft choices, but on all the players that a given team drafts, signed or unsigned, and ranks the team's drafting performance based on all the players' cumulative lifetime major league results in key statistical categories. I've broken down the rankings by draft years, decades, and for the overall draft period of 1965 through 1989. I've then compared the statistical rankings to post season performance to determine how each team's drafting capabilities compares with its actual post-season results.

If the total number of draft signings is not the primary criterion for evaluating a given team's draft, how can we determine the success of baseball drafts? This analysis provided a balanced statistical weighting between career major league batting and pitching statistics that combines longevity (at bats and innings pitched) with performance (homeruns, RBIs, batting average and wins, won-loss percentage, ERA). Each team's draft year player statistics are added together by year, decade, and overall (1965 through 1989). Each of the eight statistical categories (four batting and four pitching) are then ranked based on the number of teams in the majors during that given draft period. These eight categorical rankings are then added together, by team, to determine a final ranking point total. Last, this point total is ranked to determine each team's statistical performance for a given period. These rankings are detailed in this analysis.

Having determined the statistical rankings, we now want to analyze actual team post-season performances. Let's assume a team's post season participation, based on a point system, is a more accurate measure of a team's performance than a cumulative won-loss record. Given that the draft began in 1965 and that it usually takes a few years for players to develop before advancing to the majors, we can conveniently track drafted players' performances from the beginning of divisional playoffs in 1969 through the 1992 playoffs. By setting up a point system that awards one point for divisional champions, three points for league champions, and five points for World Series winners, we are able to calculate and rank a team's post season performance that can then be compared against the previously determined statistical rankings.

Reviewing the results of this analysis, we find that the best drafting teams of the 1960s, 1970s, and 1980s were the Dodgers, the Expos, and the Mets, respectively, with the Dodgers holding the best overall results during the entire draft period despite a significant fall-off in the 1980s. It is interesting to point out only one American League team is listed in the top seven overall. Even more significant, with the exception of the batting rankings of the 1970s when players such as Brett, Yount, Molitor, Boggs, Murray, Rice,

David C. Thomas is a product manager for AMP Incorporated in Greensboro, North Carolina.

Lynn, Baines, Henderson, and Willie Wilson were drafted by American League teams, the National League has dominated statistically, based on the career results of their draftees. This is clearly indicated by the overall (1965-1989) average rankings by league, even when factoring out the two 1977 American League expansion teams. With the exclusion of these two teams, the statistical average ranking of the remaining 24 teams is 12.5, providing there are no ties at a given ranking. In comparing the overall rankings, we find the National League to have a 10.83 average ranking and the American League a 13.75 ranking. This difference is so impressive that we would naturally assume the actual post-season results to favor the National League. In fact, though, the American League has won 14 of the 25 World Series since divisional playoffs began in 1969.

Other interesting findings also stand out when comparing overall team statistical draft rankings and actual post-season performance rankings. The Pirates, Reds, Royals, Mariners, White Sox, and Dodgers were very close to their statistical versus actual rankings. The A's, Blue Jays, Orioles, and Phillies, significantly outperformed their statistical rankings, while the Angels, Expos, Red Sox, Giants, Rangers, Cubs, and Cardinals were clearly underperformers.

Other highlights of this draft research study:

The Blue Jays, who only started drafting in 1977, had the fifth best draftee pitching results in the 1980s.

The Pirates have made the most draft selections (1628) in the history of the amateur draft. Rounding out the top five are the Mets (1598), the Orioles and

	1965-1969 TEAM RANKINGS			1970-1979 TEAM RANKINGS				1980-1989 TEAM RANKINGS			OVERALL 1965-1989 TEAM RANKINGS		
Team	Bat	Pitch	Comb.	Bat	Pitch	Comb.	Team	Bat	Pitch	Comb.	Bat	Pitch	Comb.
Angels	19	4	13	7	9	4	Angels	16	8	13	12	6	8
Athletics	3	18	10	3	24	17	Athletics	6	21	10	2	25	15
Blue Jays	-	-	-	-	-	-	Blue Jays	21	5	17	26	14	24
Brewers	-	-	-	10	22	18	Brewers	12	13	12	18	24	22
Indians	17	9	17	22	21	24	Indians	17	17	18	22	16	21
Mariners	-	-	-	-	-	-	Mariners	4	16	6	25	26	26
Orioles	3	17	9	16	17	18	Orioles	25	23	25	7	20	14
Rangers	10	16	15	11	16	15	Rangers	19	7	19	16	18	16
Red Sox	2	11	4	4	19	11	Red Sox	10	8	9	1	14	5
Royals	-	-	-	9	4	2	Royals	6	2	2	15	4	8
Tigers	20	13	18	5	14	6	Tigers	24	26	26	19	13	17
Twins	6	7	5	20	20	23	Twins	8	8	5	9	12	11
White Sox	16	19	20	11	8	10	White Sox	22	18	22	21	19	20
Yankees	13	11	13	7	12	6	Yankees	9	15	11	8	9	8
AVE.	10.9	12.5	12.4	10.4	15.5	12.8	AVE.	14.2	13.4	13.9	14.4	15.7	15.4*
Astros	15	15	16	21	18	21	Astros	18	25	24	22	23	25
Braves	14	5	7	15	23	22	Braves	22	11	20	17	17	17
Cardinals	9	8	7	1	13	3	Cardinals	12	3	6	3	8	2
Cubs	18	3	11	24	2	14	Cubs	2	20	8	24	3	13
Dodgers	1	1	1	18	1	4	Dodgers	20	22	22	4	1	1
Expos	-	-	-	1	3	1	Expos	14	12	15	12	11	12
Giants	7	10	6	13	6	9	Giants	3	24	13	6	10	7
Mets	8	2	3	22	7	20	Mets	1	1	1	10	2	4
Padres	-	-	-	14	11	13	Padres	14	18	16	20	22	23
Phillies	12	20	19	5	15	8	Phillies	26	13	21	10	21	19
Pirates	10	13	11	17	5	12	Pirates	11	4	4	12	4	6
Reds	5	6	2	19	10	16	Reds	4	6	3	5	7	2
AVE.	9.9	8.3	8.3	14.2	9.5	11.9	AVE.	12.3	13.3	12.8	12.1	10.8	10.9*

*Overall rankings without expansion teams; AL-13.75, NL-10.83

	OVERALL STATISTICAL 1965-1989 RANKINGS	ACTUAL 1965-1992 POST-SEASON RANKINGS	OVERALL VS. ACTUAL RANKING
Angels	8	19	-11
Athletics	15	1	+14
Blue Jays	24	12	+12
Brewers	22	17	+5
Indians	21	24	-3
Mariners	26	24	+2
Orioles	14	3	+11
Rangers	16	24	-8
Red Sox	5	14	-9
Royals	8	9	-1
Tigers	17	13	+4
Twins	11	7	+4
White Sox	20	22	-2
Yankees	8	5	+3
Astros	25	20	+5
Braves	17	14	+3
Cardinals	2	9	-7
Cubs	13	20	-7
Dodgers	1	3	-2
Expos	12	22	-10
Giants	7	16	-9
Mets	4	6	-2
Padres	23	17	+6
Phillies	19	11	+8
Pirates	6	7	-1
Reds	2	2	0

Yankees (1597), and the Indians (1573).

The Mets have had the most signed and unsigned draft picks make it to the majors (197) followed by the Rangers (196), the Angels (193), the Giants (191), and the Cardinals (176). With the exception of the Mets, the other top five teams sending drafted players to the majors happen to also be the underperforming teams mentioned earlier. Draw your own conclusions.

Of the non-expansion teams, the Cubs sent the least number of drafted players (148) to the majors.

The highest percentages of total signed and unsigned drafted players making it to the majors versus total players drafted were the Padres and Red Sox with 16.37 percent and 16.1 percent, respectively. The lowest percentages were the Pirates (10.09 percent) and the Orioles (10.54 percent). Given these teams' better than average post-season performances, it could be suggested that drafting in quantity may have its benefits.

The Rangers have had the most overall higher than 20th round draft picks (38 selections over 28 years of drafting) that made it to the majors.

The next table shows team statistical bests and worsts by decade and the overall period of 1965 through 1989

The Expos high team batting average in the 1970s was a result of drafting the likes of Andre Dawson, Gary Carter, Warren Cromartie, Tim Wallach, Hubie Brooks, and Tim Raines in the same decade.

The Red Sox had the highest percentage (12.41 percent) of signed players only, versus total players drafted to make it to the majors. The Padres were second (11.81 percent) and the Rangers third (10.12 percent). The Pirates and Orioles had the lowest percentages with 5.21 percent and 6.27 percent respectively. As mentioned previously, the Pirates and Orioles were in the top five of total players drafted and actually had more players make it to the majors than the Red Sox despite having a "signed" player percentage of roughly half that of the Red Sox.

Twenty-nine last round draft choices have made it to the majors. Some of the better known players, and the teams that drafted them in which year and round:

Doug Griffin	Angels	1965	21
Dick Billings	Senators	1965	25
Steve Hovley	Angels	1966	35
John Wockenfuss	Senators	1967	42
Andy McGaffigan	Reds	1974	36

STAT. CATEG.	1965-1969		1970-1979		1980-1989		NON-EXPANSION TEAMS 1965-1989	
	BEST	WORST	BEST	WORST	BEST	WORST	BEST	WORST
AB	Dodgers	Tigers	Angels	Cubs	Mets	Braves	A's	Cubs
Totals	68,807	14,208	82,982	20.045	42,618	12,134	158,955	79,121
HR	A's	WhtSox	Expos	Cubs	Mets	Phils	A's	Astros
Totals	2,227	273	2,153	336	1,127	215	4,991	1,673
RBI	A's	Tigers	Expos	Cubs	Mets	Tigers	A's	Cubs
Totals	8,289	1,800	9,848	2,193	4,566	1,469	20,719	8,963
BA	RedSox	Angels	Cards	Giants	Padres	Or'les	RedSox*	Indians*
Totals	.275	.246	.273	.249	.287	.244	.272	.256
IP	Mets	Phils	Dodgers	Brewrs	Rangrs	Astros	Mets	A's
Totals	18,338	4,852	24,688	10,120	12,002	4,049	49,648	26,001
WINS	Mets	Phils	Dodgers	A's	Mets	Astros	Mets	A's
Totals	1,004	207	1,487	510	706	236	2,765	1,327
W/L PCT	Dodgers	Phils	Dodgers	A's	BluJays	Marnrs	BluJay*	Mariners*
Totals	.554	.412	.533	.436	.547	.460	.542	.467
ERA	Braves	Phils	Dodgers	A's	Mets	Tigers	Dodgrs*	A's*
Totals	3.44	4.11	3.64	4.12	3.47	4.18	3.58	4.05

*Expansion teams are included in these categories since they are percentages and not cumulative totals.

David Palmer	Expos	1976	21
Howard Johnson	Yankees	1978	23
Rick Aguilera	Cardinals	1980	37
Jeff M. Robinson	Padres	1980	40
Jeff Hamilton	Dodgers	1982	29
Mike Piazza	Dodgers	1988	62

*June-Regular Phase

As for the top statistical team draft years, the final rankings are based solely on statistics, with those teams balanced with good hitting and pitching in the same year faring better than a team loaded with only hitters or pitchers. If even some subjectivity was used here, there would most certainly be a rearranging of the rankings. However, there is absolutely no doubt of the top two team draft years; the 1968 Dodgers and the 1976 Tigers draft classes, in that order, clearly stand out from the rest of the top 25 teams.

Although there are some of the 1976 Tigers' draft class still active in the majors, it is doubtful they would surpass the performance of the 1968 Dodgers. The fifth ranked 1982 Mets are clearly the best draft class of the 1980s and, barring career ending injuries to Gooden and/or Palmeiro, will certainly move up in the rankings, as will the 1983 Red Sox draft class.

The table on the facing page is a list of the Top 25 Statistical Team Draft Years.

What about the worst team drafts since 1965? The following are the nominees:

1968 Expos
1971 Mets
1973 Indians
1980 Blue Jays
1981 Braves
1982 Indians
1983 Astros
1984 White Sox

The 1968 Expos and the 1981 Braves are noteworthy since not one player from those teams' draft picks made it to the majors. The Expos situation is somewhat understandable since it was their first draft as an expansion team. In the case of the Braves, they lost their second and third picks to free agent compensation; however, their first pick never made it out of Class A ball.

The subject of "Draft Analysis" is practically endless. One could rate the overall draft by year (1965, by the way, was a good year), focus, statistically, on just signed players, or even analyze the performances of first round draft choices. Baseball, though, has been bombarded by too many statistics in recent years so doing too much of a good thing takes the fun out of, not only the reading of the material, but also the research. So we will end here and hope what has been presented in this study gives one a better feel of the draft performance of each major league team since the inception of the draft in 1965.

TOP 25 STATISTICAL TEAM DRAFT YEARS

RANK	TEAM	YEAR	PLAYERS TO MAJORS	KEY PLAYERS
1	Dodgers	1968	15	Garvey, Cey, Buckner, Lopes, Zahn
2	Tigers	1976	13	Morris, Kemp, Trammell, Petry, O. Smith
3	Reds	1969	9	Grimsley, Gullet, Griffey, Grubb
4	Red Sox	1968	5	Cooper, Ogilvie, Curtis, Lee, McGlothen
5	Mets	1982	17	Gooden, Palmeiro, Daniels, R. Myers
5	Pirates	1972	10	Candelaria, W. Randolph, J. Morrison
7	Royals	1971	10	Brett, Wathan, Littell, Busby
8	Athletics	1967	8	Blue, Soderholm, Dar. Evans
9	Cardinals	1971	9	K. Hernandez, Herndon, Mumphrey, Langford
9	Dodgers	1977	7	Welch, M. Hatcher
11	Twins	1969	5	Blyleven, Burleson
12	Red Sox	1971	10	Smalley, Rice, E. Rasmussen, Kuiper
12	Orioles	1967	7	Grich, Baylor, Oates, Rau, Montague
12	Red Sox	1983	9	Clemens, Burks, Manwaring, M. Brumley
15	Reds	1965	5	Bench, Carbo, McRae, P. Reuschel
16	Braves	1966	6	Seaver, F. Duffy, G. Ross
17	Indians	1972	10	Kuiper, Manning, Eckersley, Dauer
18	Giants	1968	6	G. Maddox, G. Foster, G. Matthews, Goodson
19	Dodgers	1979	5	Howe, G. Brock, Welch
20	Reds	1967	9	W. Simpson, Kendall, Chambliss
21	Dodgers	1981	8	Bream, S. Fernandez, D. Anderson
22	Angels	1966	12	K. Forsch, Messersmith, Barr, Hovley
23	Athletics	1965	10	Monday, Bando, Tenace
24	Mets	1965	10	N. Ryan, K. Boswell, Renko, McAndrew
25	Dodgers	1965	5	Seaver, A. Foster

The Buck Stops Here

Phillies pitcher Bucky Walters lost both ends of a doubleheader to the Cardinals in 1937, 10-3 and 18-10. Si Johnson won both games. Walters and Johnson were the starters in the opener, relievers in the 10-inning nightcap.

A Gone Goose

Goose Goslin of the Tigers hit into four straight double plays in a game with the Indians in 1934.

It's Lonesome at First

Phillies first baseman Dolph Camilli tied a major league record by playing a nine-inning game in 1937 without a putout. The Phils lost to the Reds, 1-0.

Doubles Yes, Double Plays No

Augie Galan of the Cubs hit 41 doubles in 1935, but didn't hit into a single double play. He played all 154 games.

—Don Nelson

A Brief History of the Complete Game

An endangered species

Dennis Stegmann

Numbers. Some are memorable, some aren't. Some astound us, some amuse us, and some do both. I can't tell you what I paid for my first new car but I can recall other numbers with razorlike precision. Certain historical dates, for example, or family birthdates. It's all a matter of priorities. To almost any baseball fan, numbers are not just a priority, they are the heart and soul and measuring stick of the game. Certain numbers have a nearly magical quality about them—.367, 511, 61, 56, 714—or 755 to fans of more recent vintage—,190, 749.

The 749, of course, refers to Cy Young's lifetime complete games total. And if there are unbreakable baseball records, this must be at or near the top of the list. This is an astonishing record. Pitchers of today probably get arm cramps simply on hearing of it.

Before taking a closer look at complete games, their decline, and its consequent affect on the game I must make two disclaimers: first of all, the old complete game records may look unbreakable at the present time, but there may come a time, in future centuries, when human evolution will have created super-athletes capable of pitching all day every day—my tongue is firmly in my cheek—or when player delays—coffee breaks for batters between pitches, homerun trots that last longer than some South American governments, pitchers who reason that if they don't throw the ball the batter can't possibly hit it, among others—will have created the necessity for three inning games. Secondly, I recognize that all of Cy Young's complete games were thrown in the pitcher-friendly dead-ball days, the days when entire teams hit fewer homeruns in a season than some reserve infielders do today. But dead ball or not, 749 complete games is still a lot of pitches.

Why the decline?—Let us step back in time and examine some numbers. In professional baseball's earliest days complete games were the rule, rather than the exception. Many pitchers—good ones and bad—completed 90 to 95 percent of their starts, and completing 50, 60, even 70 or more games in a season was not rare.

There are many reasons for the large number of complete games—short schedules, shorter pitching distances, small rosters with room for only one, two, or three pitchers, and rules that regulated and discouraged substitution. As time went on, schedules lengthened, rosters were expanded, and the pitching distance stretched out. After 1893, we find teams using three or four regular starters. There were still nearly as many complete games, percentage-wise—they were just spread among more pitchers. No longer would one pitcher throw 74 complete games in a season as Will White did in 1879 (only a handful of pitchers since 1900 have thrown 40 complete games in a season, none since 1920), but some amazing totals were compiled in the first decade of the twentieth century, with 1904 being the year when the complete game cup truly ran over. The Boston Pilgrims (Red

Dennis Stegmann lives in St. Louis.

Sox) set the all-time record that year with 148 complete games out of a total of 157, while the St. Louis Cardinals set the National League record with 146 out of 155. The New York Highlanders (Yankees), despite 48 complete games from Jack Chesbro—the most in this century—and 38 from Jack Powell, finished last in the major leagues with 123 complete games in 155 chances. The two leagues combined for—hold on, now—2,187 complete games, both leagues establishing records that, not surprisingly, still stand. The 16 Major League teams averaged 137 complete games per team. Chesbro led the majors with 48 while Jack Taylor of the Cardinals completed 39 straight starts between April 15 and October 6. Actually, this was not much more than a normal season for Taylor, who holds the modern record for percentage of complete games in a career and who completed all of his starts in 1898, 1899, 1902, 1903, 1904, and 1905. No doubt suffering from a tired arm, he slipped badly in 1906, completing only 32 of 33 starts.

The complete game mentality of those days also carried over to World Series play with nine complete games being pitched in the five-game Series of 1905, and with Deacon Phillippe tossing five in the 1903 series alone.

The team leader in both the National and American Leagues averaged 129 complete games per season between 1901 and 1910. Surprisingly, we see a huge drop-off, percentage-wise, in complete games between the first and second decades of this century. The American League team leader dropped from an average of 129 complete games from 1901-1910 to 103 per year from 1911-1920, while the National League leader dropped from 129 to 99. In 1905, American League teams averaged 122 complete games and National League teams averaged 125, but by 1915, AL teams averaged 83 and NL teams averaged 85.

There are a few apparent reasons for the drop-off. For one thing, increases in roster size meant there were more pitchers around. In 1906, the average pitchers used per team in the majors was just over nine, while in 1915 the average was 14. In 1905, there were 67 major league pitchers with 20 or more decisions, in 1915 the total falls to 56. With more pitchers around—in 1905 there were 146 pitchers in the majors, as opposed to 224 in 1915—pitchers didn't have to complete games simply because there was no one else available to pitch.

Another important factor was the increased use of relief pitchers in what we would now call save situations. Applying our modern stat retroactively, in 1905, there were 44 saves in the majors. By 1915 the

figure had more than tripled to 155. A third influencing factor may be that pitchers threw more pitches in 1915 than in 1905. There were, for example, 1289 more walks issued in 1915 than in 1905. Before leaving the decade that saw the beginning of the decline of the complete game, we should also note Cy Young's last complete game, in 1911.

After seeing such a drop in complete games between the first and second decades of the century, we would expect to see a drastic drop in the heavy-hitting 1920s. But a look at the numbers fails to confirm this. There was a drop-off, yes, but a less drastic one than that in the previous decade. The AL team leader averaged 90 complete games per year from 1921-1930, a drop of 13 per year from the 'teens, while the NL leader averaged 89, a drop of 10 games from the previous decade. In again taking a random year for comparison, in 1925 all AL teams averaged 72 complete games vs. 83 in 1915 and the NL average dropped to 79 from 85.

1920 saw Grover Cleveland Alexander and Burleigh Grimes each complete 33 starts, the most—along with Robin Roberts' 33 in 1953—for a National League pitcher since then. There were three other significant complete game achievements in the 1920s, two of them occurring in World Series play. In the 1928 Series, a ho-hum four game sweep of the Cardinals by the mighty Ruth-Gehrig Yankees, three Yankee pitchers—Pipgras and Zachary with one apiece, Hoyt with two—combined for four complete games. In Game Six of the 1926 Series, Grover Cleveland Alexander became, and remains, the oldest (39) pitcher to throw a World Series complete game. Finally, in a game that neatly wrapped up the whole dead-ball era, on May 1, 1920, pitchers Joe Oeschger of Boston and Leon Cadore of Brooklyn each nearly pitched the equivalent of three complete games in one in the course of their epic 26-inning duel. (As an aside, not only would one more inning have given both pitchers the equivalent of three complete games each, but it would have given Oeschger 300 innings pitched for the season and, perhaps, a bargaining chip for his 1921 contract. As it is, he remains forever perched at 299. Too bad all around.)

The 1930s and '40s show a general, gradual, decrease in complete games, with the AL team leader dropping from 90 in the 1920s to 86 the '30s and 87 '40s and the NL team leader falling off from 89 to 85 to 82 over the same time. The only significant complete game record to come out of those years was the 36 complete games tossed in 1946 by Bob Feller, still the best in baseball since Grover Cleveland

Alexander had 38 and Walter Johnson had 36 in 1916.

The 1950s continue the decline of complete games, but in a more dramatic fashion. We see a decrease in the American League team leader average of 19 between the 1940s and '50s, and a National League decrease of 13 between the decades. An obvious reason is the greater use of a relief pitcher to close out victories, with an increase in saves from 218 in 1945 to 356 in 1955. The number of pitchers with ten or more saves was three times greater in 1955, and it is obvious that more and more managers no longer expected nine innings out of their starters. Old habits die hard, and it is also obvious from the complete game totals that many tired pitchers were still being allowed to stagger through nine innings, but we can see the idea of using more than one

Cy Young and Bob Feller

NBL

pitcher, no matter the score, beginning to take hold in this decade, an idea that continued to germinate in the 1960s and '70s, and then explode in the 1980s.

The 1960s saw another drop in complete games, the team leader average falling in the American League from 67 in the 1950s to 55 in the 1960s and from 69 to 61 in the NL over the same period. In 1955 the American League teams averaged 45 complete games; in 1965 the average fell to 32. In the NL the fall was not as great: from 48 in 1955 to 42 in 1965. Again,

the most obvious reason for the drop is the greater and greater use of relief pitchers in close game save situations. Major league save totals increased from 1955's 356 to 678 in 1965. The save was here to stay.

A couple of new factors enter the picture in the 1960s; expansion—in the AL in 1961 and the NL in 1962—which may have contributed to surges in complete game totals in those years; and a decade long decrease in batting averages which surely contributed to a late '60s revival of the complete game. For example, in 1968, the San Francisco Giants set the modern—post 162-game schedule—NL record of 77 complete games. Another factor which probably contributed to the complete game surge in the NL—which was to continue until 1973—was an abundance of power pitchers who—along with knuckleballers—seem to contribute a large share of complete games in any given season. Pitchers such as Bob Gibson, Juan Marichal, Fergie Jenkins, Tom Seaver, Steve Carlton regularly threw 20 to 30 complete games per season. In the World Series between 1965 and 1968, the winning pitcher pitched a complete game in 22 of the 25 games played.

As noted above, the complete game resurgence continued in the National League until 1973, at which point it leveled off to an average of nearly 50 per year for the rest of the decade. The American League in the 1970s saw one dramatic rule change which, on the surface, would seem to have been a major factor in the AL's team leader average increasing from 55 in the 1960s to 70 in the 1970s. (In the NL the leader average dropped from 61 in the '60s to 52 in the '70s.) The rule change, of course, was the Designated Hitter rule, and in its first year the AL leader, the California Angels, had 72 complete games—the most for an AL team since 1954.

For the rest of the '70s the AL leader averaged 67 complete games per season. Yet in the three seasons preceding the DH, 1970-1972, the leader averaged 64 complete games per season. Strangely, the DH seems to have had less effect on AL hurlers than NL pitchers—or, perhaps, on NL managers, who may have felt pressured to resort to all manner of measures in order to contrast with their AL counterparts. Whatever the case, in the five years prior to 1973 the NL league leader averaged 69 complete games per season, and from 1973-1977 the leader averaged 48 complete games per season. However, there is no doubt that overall the DH did increase complete games in the AL. In 1975, for example, AL teams averaged 52 complete games, in contrast to the 1965 average of 32 per team, and in contrast also to the 1975 NL average of 36 per team.

The complete game numbers for the seasons of 1980 and '81 are skewed. In 1980, Billy Martin's apparent attempt to destroy the young arms on his Oakland A's pitching staff resulted in their tossing the modern (162 game schedule) record total of 94 complete games. In 1981, the strike played havoc with the complete game totals, though percentage-wise they were above normal thanks to Martin and his Oakland rubber-arms.

The rest of the '80s showed another great decrease in complete games, with AL seasonal leaders down 27 per season from the '70s and the NL leader down 19 per year. And, DH or no DH, by 1990 a National League team led the majors for the first time since 1972. In 1985, AL teams averaged 26 complete games each as opposed to 52 in 1975 and the NL was down to 22 from 36 in 1975. Also, in the '80s we begin to see entire teams with fewer than 10 per season. No doubt the increase use of "stoppers" to finish close games played a part in this, but a more important reason for the near disappearance of complete games in the '80s was—and remains—free agency, which began in the mid-'70s and which resulted in salaries in the stratosphere by the '80s.

It is quite possible that complete game totals would have fallen more drastically 10, 20, even 30 years earlier except that pitchers needed complete games as part of their salary argument, something not as necessary today. In fact the opposite may be true today—why risk a sore arm and the loss of a fortune for a higher complete game total? Economics, in baseball as elsewhere in our society, is often the determining factor.

In the '90s we continue to see a decrease in complete games, to the point where in 1991 the NL leaders (Glavine, Martinez) fell below 10 for the first time, and the 1991 New York Yankees established a new team low with three. We may soon see a team complete a season without a complete game.

Will we see a change, a resurgence of complete games? I think not. Few power pitchers even throw them now, and there are only a couple of knuckleballers. Complete games are a rarity even in Little League, high school, Legion, college or minor league ball today, and a number of those are six- or seven-inning games, hardly preparation for a nine-inning major league game. If pitchers are not throwing complete games at lower levels they are not likely to begin throwing them at the major league level. Additionally, many coaches and managers establish pitch limits for pitchers, which virtually assure that they will not pitch nine innings. So while more complete games might mean some positive things for baseball observers—quicker games, cleaner scorecards and increased offense—Cy Young's 749 seems safe for the foreseeable future.

On Batting Order

The Monte Carlo approach

Steven Seifert, M.D.

The 1992 BRJ article by Mark Pankin proposed the Markov model (MM) as the way to determine a better batting order. This model uses matrix algebra on "transition probabilities" based on assumptions made regarding batters' baseline performance. For a particular team, he computed the expected runs per game for 1800 randomly generated batting orders which allowed him to evaluate each player batting in each position 200 times. He then determined the optimal lineup from the results by extrapolating optimal offensive values and characteristics for each batting position. He gave two examples, the 1991 Minnesota Twins and the 1991 Toronto Blue Jays and compared their conventional wisdom (CW) order with that determined by the MM. The mathematical basis of the Markov model is logical and elegant, but because there is no way to actually test the resultant order, the Markov model is incomplete and, as I will show, its results fall somewhat short of the goal of an optimal batting order.

I have developed a Monte Carlo Simulation (MCS)which can evaluate the run production of any proposed batting order. With this model I can demonstrate first, that the conventional wisdom (CW) is definitely not the optimal batting order (OBO); second, that the Markov model, as described for the

1991 Minnesota Twins and Toronto Blue Jays, is better than the CW but it does not yield the optimal order for those teams; third, that the Monte Carlo Simulation model allows a determination of the OBO for any collection of nine players, although no one simple rule applies, and fourth, that such an approach has other implications for the analysis of offensive strategy in general.

Computer Model—How does a Monte Carlo Simulation work? For our example, let's use the 1991 Minnesota Twins cited by Pankin. We specify all of the relevant offensive statistics for each batter in the lineup (based on his full season data, which we will call his baseline performance) and then enter the players into the simulation in the conventional wisdom order (Gladden, Knoblauch, Puckett, Hrbek, Davis, Harper, Mack, Pagliarulo, Gagne). As with the Markov model, base advancement occurs according to major league average probabilities. We assume that batters will perform similarly to their baseline performance and use that performance to determine their results at the plate as follows.

The leadoff batter, Gladden, comes to bat. The game simulation generates a random number between 0 and 1 and compares it with his on-base percentage (OBP) of 0.303. Since the number generated is random, there is a 0.303 chance that the number will be equal to or less than that number. If the random number generated is less than or equal to 0.303, then Gladden is assumed to have gotten on base. If we

Steven Seifert, M.D. lives in Tucson, Arizona, is a lifelong baseball fan, and coaches Little League. He has been interested in the question of batting order since 1966, and developed this model in 1990 using an IBM-compatible 80486 computer and programming in BASIC. He encourages comments via CompuServe (ID# 73237,100).

have determined that Gladden has gotten on base (that is, the random number was less than or equal to .303), we next look to see what portion of Gladden's on-base at-bats have resulted in walks, singles, double, triples, home runs, and so forth. A new random number would be generated and compared with these various probabilities to determine the result of this plate appearance.

Likewise, if the original random number had been greater than 0.303, this plate appearance would be determined to have resulted in an out. Further random numbers would tell us whether this was a simple out, a sacrifice or a ground-into-double-play (GIDP). If Gladden reached first base, further random number generations compared with actual performance would determine if he attempted a stolen base and whether he was successful. Strict percentages, corresponding to major league averages, would govern the advancement of runners and the occurrence of fielding errors. The game would continue thus until nine innings were over and the total number of runs scored would be recorded.

One structural aspect of the Monte Carlo Simulation program, which, I believe, corrects a flaw in the Markov model, needs to be addressed here. A batter will face a different proportion of offensive opportunities if he is placed in a different batting slot than his usual one—different frequencies of finding men on base ahead of him, for example.

Strict adherence to a batter's baseline performance would require you to allow a GIDP (when the random numbers generated indicated this result) regardless of whether there was a man on-base. This would result in a final performance of this batter identical to his baseline performance. A more flexible (and realistic) approach allows the program to have him, at the expense of strict statistical results, hit into a double play only when there is another man on base. Thus, if we allow the program to accept the situations created by a new batting order and to react in a realistic manner, a batter's performance may vary slightly from his baseline performance. The elements affected include sacrifices, steals, intentional walks and GIDP's This context-sensitive approach seems to more accurately reflect how changing the batting order would alter offensive performance, which is a great advantage.

Remember, there is no other team against which our hypothetical team is playing. There is no provision for what sort of pitcher it is facing or how the pitcher is performing. No strategy is employed in game situations either offensively or defensively. Every event is otherwise rigidly determined by these pre-set rules and the probabilities of the actual players. The result is the score that this particular team produced under those rules batting in that particular order.

In any single game under these circumstances, the number of runs scored can be 0 or 20. Gladden who had a batting average of 0.247, can go 0-for-4 or he can go 4-for-4 because, in any one game, the nature of using random numbers results in performances which may be significantly different from an individual's average performance.

But let us not stop at one game. Let us use this same hypothetical team batting in the same batting order and play another game. In fact, let us have this team play one million games just like this (it takes this many games to achieve statistically significant results). At this point, Gladden is batting very close to 0.247, because over time the random numbers generated to determine his performance average out to this value. Likewise, all of the other batters will perform very close to their real-life probabilities. Now if we look at the average number of runs scored for such a team we discover that, batting in this order, it averages 5.1468 runs per game.

Now we have a tool by which we can test hypotheses about batting order. If we change the batting order of our hypothetical team, we can see what effect that has on the run production. By varying the batting order we can try to find orderings that produce more runs per game, on average, than the conventional wisdom.

What about the Markov model order proposed by Pankin (Hrbek, Davis, Mack, Puckett, Harper, Gagne, Gladden, Pagliarulo, Knoblauch)? If we run the MCS in this order we find an average of 5.1952 runs per game (a season increase of 8 runs over the CW—exactly what Pankin predicted). Is this, then, the optimal batting order?

Basic principles of the Optimal Batting Order (OBO)—From analysis of the MCS model using many different teams in a variety of batting orders, the primary principle that emerges is that if the stronger batters (let's call it run producing ability) get up to bat more times than the weaker batters, the team will produce more runs. We can demonstrate this by looking at our team batting in the exact opposite of the Markov model order. Knoblauch, whom the MM chooses to bat ninth, instead now leads off, followed by Pagliarulo, Gladden, etc. If we now play one million games with this lineup we discover that this team only scores 5.115 runs per game on average, resulting in 13 fewer runs over the course of the season. We should not be surprised. We have our weaker hitters getting up to bat more often, and our best run producers are near the end of the batting order, where they get up to bat the least. The seasonal difference in number of at-bats is not trivial. In fact, from many runnings of various lineups, the computer model can predict the percentage that each batting slot gets of the total number of plate appearances. Over the course of a 162 game season, the first hitter gets about 140 more plate appearances than the ninth hitter, or about 17.5 extra at bats for each notch up in the batting order. So the overriding basic principle is this: If we have our better run producers getting up to bat more frequently over the year we will produce more runs.

A baseball game is limited by the number of outs in an inning and the number of innings in a game. Increased plate appearances increase run scoring opportunities. So there is an advantage to having players with high on-base percentages higher in the lineup when possible. The trick is determining when the increase in runs produced by this move exceeds the decrease in runs caused by moving a weaker run producer (a table setter) ahead of a stronger one (a power hitter).

Finally, we need to look at specific batting slots. The one characteristic that the Monte Carlo Simulation identifies as important is the percentage of times that each batting slot leads off an inning, since the simulation verifies the principle that having runners on base at the beginning of an inning is a desirable occurrence. The first batting slot has the distinction of leading off an inning more than twice as often as any other batting slot. In fact, about 40 percent of the leadoff batter's plate appearances will lead off an inning. Batting slots four and five also have a slightly higher than average rate of leading off innings but this is much less significant.

Specific batting attributes other than run producing ability and OBP do not appear to be of significance in matching a batter to a slot.

What determines the relative run producing potency of a batter? Bill James, in his *Baseball Historical Abstract*, has developed a formula that he uses to compare the relative offensive worth of two players or two teams. This is his Runs Created formula.

In this formula (Table 1), each of a player's offensive parameters contributes a weighted amount to the number of runs he "creates" at the plate. By limiting a player to one at bat, we can see the effect of each possible result at the plate in terms of runs created

(RC). If our batter hits a home run, for example, he "creates" 4 runs. Every time he draws a walk he "creates" 1.26 runs, and so on. Hitting home runs is the easiest way to increase RC.

Table 1. Runs Created Formula.

$$RC = \frac{(H+W-CS+HBP-GIDP) \times (TB+(.26 \times (TBB-IBB+HBP)+ (.55 \times (SF+SH+SB)))}{(AB+W+HBP+SF+SH)}$$

Where: H=Hits, W=Walks, CS=Caught Stealing, HBP=Hit By Pitch, TB=Total Bases, TBB=Total Walks, IBB=Intentional Walks, SF=Sacrifice Flies, SH=Sacrifice Bunts, SB=Stolen Bases

Now, if we divide the number of "runs created" by the total number of plate appearances we have the ratio "runs created per plate appearance" (RCPPA). The RCPPA formula takes all offensive actions into account and tells you who creates more runs per trip to the plate. (James argues that we should look at "runs created per out" [RCPO], but the Monte Carlo Simulation model demonstrates that RCPPA is more powerful.)

Power hitters, in general, have the highest RCPPA's. To find our optimal batting order, batters should initially be ordered by descending RCPPA. This rule works best when there is a clear and consistent decrease in offensive production from one player to the next. We make adjustments to this rule by placing (if possible without trading off RCPPA) batters with higher OBP's in the batting slots with high liklihoods of leading off innings. The leadoff slot is the most important, and can tolerate a lower RCPPA for a sufficiently high OBP. The leadoff batter's OBP need not be higher than the number two batter's—just high enough to increase run production in those innings that he leads off more than he decreases run production (relative to a batter with a higher RCPPA) in those innings that he doesn't. Because a batter's actual performance in the simulation will change slightly from his baseline performance (because we have allowed the simulation to take context into account) we actually have to run the simulation and experiment with orders to find the optimal order for any given team.

Discussion—The 1991 Minnesota Twins was a fairly typical team in terms of distribution of batting talent and conventional wisdom ordering. In the Monte Carlo Simulation we find the conventional wisdom produces 5.1468 runs per game, the MM produces 5.1952 runs per game and the OBO (straight descending RCPPA) produces 5.2219 runs per game, an improvement with the OBO over the course of the season of 12 runs over the CW and 4 runs over the MM.

Notice that the OBO leads off with Davis, the team's homerun leader. When there is nothing to be gained by placing a high OBP/lower RCPPA player in the number one slot, (because the highest RCPPA

ment of Alomar and White ahead of Carter in the OBO requires explanation. Because of context-sensitive changes in performance in that order, the RCPPA's of those players change to produce the ordering used. The difference between this ordering and using a straight descending RCPPA (from slots

Table 2. Conventional v. Markov Model v. Optimal Batting Order and player RCPPA's and OBP's, 1991 Minnesota Twins

Conventional Wisdom 5.1468 r/g, 834 r/seas.	Markov Model 5.1952 r/g, 842 r/seas.	Optimal Batting Order 5.2219 r/g, 846 r/seas.	Optimal Batting Order	
			RCPPA	OBP
1. Gladden	1. Hrbek	1. Davis	.1694	.3849
2. Knoblauch	2. Davis	2. Mack	.1671	.3620
3. Puckett	3. Mack	3. Hrbek	.1469	.3708
4. Hrbek	4. Puckett	4. Puckett	.1371	.3480
5. Davis	5. Harper	5. Harper	.1321	.3348
6. Harper	6. Gagne	6. Knoblauch	.1167	.3502
7. Mack	7. Gladden	7. Pagliarulo	.1102	.3206
8 Pagliarulo	8. Pagliarulo	8. Gagne	.1015	.3065
9 Gagne	9. Knoblauch	9. Gladden	.0952	.3033

player also has the highest OBP), you don't need to modify a straight descending RCPPA. You may lament a Davis solo leadoff homer in the first inning, but he'll get up to bat 70 more times over the course of the season than in his CW slot. In the end, it results in more runs being scored.

On the other hand, the 1991 Blue Jays are an example of a team with a very narrow range of offensive ability, with the top six or seven players being very closely bunched. Also, the CW order used by the Blue Jays was much closer to the OBO than is typical. Using a modified descending RCPPA and comparing its results with the CW and MM in the Monte Carlo Simulation, we find that the OBO produces three ad-

two to nine) is one run per season. The Markov model uses three players with lower RCPPA's in the first three slots, but note that they have high OBP's. This partially compensates for the loss of RCPPA but not enough. I believe that the difference of only one run between the CW order and the MM order (instead of the nine runs predicted by Pankin) is explained by the closeness of the CW order to the OBO and the fact that the Monte Carlo Simulation model takes into account offensive context rather than just strict adherence to baseline performance.

Although the 1991 Blue Jays had uncommon uniformity of performance from their top six or seven batters, which results in a very small benefit for the

Table 3. Conventional v. Markov Model v. Optimal Batting Order and player RCPPA's, OBP's, 1991 Toronto Blue Jays.

Conventional Wisdom 4.7517 r/g, 770 r/seas.	Markov Model 4.7594 r/g, 771 r/seas.	Optimal Batting Order 4.7747 r/g, 774 r/seas.	Optimal Batting Order	
			RCPPA	OBP
1. White	1. Mulliniks	1. Mulliniks	.1068	.3636
2. Alomar	2. Olerud	2. Alomar	.1494	.3463
3. Carter	3. Maldonado	3. White	.1462	.3399
4. Olerud	4. White	4. Carter	.1523	.33
5. Gruber	5. Alomar	5. Olerud	.1339	.3512
6. Maldonado	6. Carter	6. Maldonado	.1305	.3423
7. Mulliniks	7. Gruber	7. Gruber	.1217	.3059
8 Borders	8. Borders	8. Borders	.0852	.266
9 Lee	9. Lee	9. Lee	.0725	.268

ditional runs per year over the MM and four runs over the CW model.

Notice the placement of Mulliniks at the top of the order in both the MM and the OBO. This is because of his high OBP despite a low RCPPA. The place-

OBO, the use of the OBO for the 1990 Blue Jays would have resulted in eight additional runs. I don't think I need to remind Blue Jays fans that that team finished only two games out of first place. The teams which would benefit the most from adoption of the

OBO are those with one or two particularly potent batters with high RCPPA's who are not batting early in the lineup (the 1991 Minnesota Twins, 1990 Detroit Tigers and 1989 Mets). The teams which would benefit least from this approach are those with relative uniformity of RCPPA's among its batters or who are already using their high RCPPA batters in the early batting slots (the 1991 Dodgers and Toronto Blue Jays). When tested against real team lineups over the course of the last three seasons, the difference between the OBO and the conventional wisdom is usually projected to be between six and 12 runs per season.

Pankin's achievement in analyzing offensive strategy through the Markov model is impressive. The Monte Carlo Simulation model verifies most of his findings: Stolen base ability in the leadoff batter is not relevant; putting a weak hitter in the second slot is indeed "a prescription for a lower-scoring batting order," and most of the difference in expected runs between batting orders shows in the first inning.

Other findings suggested by the Monte Carlo Simulation model are that (1) base running speed adds only about one run per season per exceptional runner; (2) RBIs and runs scored are more a function of where in the order a batter hits than as an indicator of batting proficiency; and (3) that intentional walks in almost any context result in additional runs. (Using the computer's game simulation, if we increase the number of walks various batters receive in different degrees and game situations—to reflect both intentional walks and more cautious pitching—we always see an increase in the average number of runs per game. This implies that pitchers can't "pitch around" the stronger hitters to defeat a descending RCPPA approach.)

Pankin also raises the question of loss of "protection" that the CW leadoff and second batters now get from batting ahead of the power hitters in the third, fourth and fifth slots. However, it seems as likely as not that any changes in performance produced by changes in batting order protection will cancel out with some batters having decreased run creating productivity because of the loss of protection while other batters will improve their run creating productivity because of new-found protection.

Finally, we have been talking only of using year-to-date (or full-year), averaged data. In actual practice, an OBO would use performance against right/left-handed pitching, a moving average RCPPA (this takes into account players who are on streaks and slumps) and have a few other enhancements. I estimate that these modifications could increase the actual efficiency of the OBO by another 50 percent to 100 percent, up to 25 runs per year over current conventional wisdom. This level of increased run production would: (1) maximize offensive output; (2) be statistically demonstrable in a relatively short time (we could also use predicted changes in runs per inning to validate the model); (3) provide a significant increase in victories (if adopted by only a few teams), and (4) would lend some scientific precision to what is currently a collection of generally erroneous beliefs and archaic practices. As Pankin suggests, "mathematical and statistical techniques can be useful tools for designing higher-scoring batting orders."

56, 511....

Don't forget Whitey Ford and his World Series achievements when you think of records that may just last forever. Ford is No. 1 in:

Decisions: 18
Wins: 10
Games: 22
Starts: 22
Innings pitched: 146
Strikeouts: 94.

On the flip side, he also leads in:

Losses: 8
Hits: 132
Bases on Balls: 34.

—Jim Murphy

The True Triple Crown

A better measurement?

Mark Simon

In the aborted season just past, Frank Thomas and Jeff Bagwell were making exciting runs at the Triple Crown. While the Triple Crown is a measure of great hitting ability in its own right, a more accurate way to measure hitting greatness is available. It is what I call "The True Triple Crown".

The True Triple Crown (henceforth referred to as the TTC), like its counterpart, requires winning three prestigious titles. To win this crown, though, a hitter must lead the league in Batting Average, On-Base Percentage and Slugging Percentage. As opposed to the Triple Crown, which relies too much on luck (RBIs) and power hitting (HRs), the true crown shows all three assets that demonstrate outstanding hitting ability. Batting Average demonstrates the ability to hit the ball, on-base percentage shows that the hitter was selective in what he chose to swing at, while slugging percentage shows a hitter's ability to hit for power. Since 1900, the TTC has been won 39 times, including once in the Federal League. However, it has only been taken five times in the past 40 seasons, and no one has come remotely close to winning it since George Brett's incredible season in 1980.

The first post-1900 TTC was accomplished in 1901 by Hall-of-Famer Napoleon Lajoie of the Philadelphia Athletics. Lajoie went on to win it again in 1904 with the Cleveland Indians. The 1900s was the most prosperous decade for TTC winners, producing 10. By

contrast, during the the 70s no hitter was able to win the TTC.

The two hitters who dominated the TTC in their eras were Rogers Hornsby and Ted Williams. Hornsby won the crown an amazing six years in a row and seven times overall, while winning the real Triple Crown twice. Williams, who also won two Triple Crowns, not only won the TTC six times, he was also the oldest to win it, taking it in 1957 at the age of 38.

Several TTC's have been denied by the slimmest of margins. Ty Cobb lost the award twice by .001—in batting average in 1910 (although he was mistakenly credited with this title for many years, and many still think he deserves it because of the way Napoleon Lajoie was "given" hits by the Browns on the last day of the season), and in slugging percentage in 1911. Ted Williams was denied a tying seventh crown by .00016 in the batting race of 1949. (Williams would have won in 1954, too, if his bases on balls had counted as official at bats for purposes of the batting title. But in those days, they didn't.) In 1970, Carl Yastrzemski lost a chance at a second TTC by .00037 to Alex Johnson in the batting race.

Strangely enough, players who have won the TTC have had a tough time getting into the World Series the year in which they won. Of the 36 times since 1903 that the award has been won, only seven of their teams made it to the World Series, while only two of them won it. Of the four years in which the honor was achieved in both leagues, only once, in 1909, did the two winners meet in the World Series. In that fall

Mark Simon, son of SABR member Richard Simon, is a sophomore journalism major at Trenton State College. He is currently sports editor of his college paper, The Signal.

classic Honus Wagner's Pirates bested Ty Cobb's Tigers four games to three with Wagner falling one hit shy of winning the World Series TTC.

George Brett opened the 80s by winning the American League TTC with a .390 BA a .461 SA and a .664 OBA. This broke baseball's longest TTC drought—13 years. Brett's TTC gave the American League a 20-17 edge in TTC winners over the National League, which has not had a TTC winner since Stan Musial in 1948.

Why is the TTC so rare today? Over the last 20 years, batting titles have been soaked up by singles hitters like Rod Carew, Wade Boggs, and Tony Gwynn, while the slugging title generally goes to .250-.280 hitters like Cecil Fielder, Mark McGwire and Fred McGriff.

TTC Winners

Yr	Player	Team	BA	OBA	SA
1901	Nap Lajoie	Phi (AL)	.426	.451	.643
1902	Ed Delahanty	Was	.376	.449	.590
1904	Honus Wagner	Pit	.349	.419	.520
1905	Cy Seymour	Cin	.377	.427	.559
1906	George Stone	StL (AL)	.358	.411	.501
1907	Honus Wagner	Pit	.350	.403	.513
1908	Honus Wagner	Pit	.354	.410	.542
1909	Honus Wagner	Pit	.339	.420	.489
1909	Ty Cobb	Det	.377	.431	.517
1910	Sherry Magee*	Phi (NL)	.331	.445	.507
1915	Benny Kauff	Bkl (Fe)	.342	.440	.509
1916	Tris Speaker	Cle	.386	.470	.502
1917	Ty Cobb	Det	.383	.444	.571
1918	Ty Cobb	Det	.382	.440	.515
1920	Rogers Hornsby	Stl	.370	.431	.559
1921	Rogers Hornsby	Stl	.397	.458	.639
1922	Rogers Hornsby	Stl	.401	.459	.722
1923	Rogers Hornsby	Stl	.384	.459	.627
1924	Rogers Hornsby	Stl	.424	.507	.696
1924	Babe Ruth	NY	.378	.513	.739
1925	Rogers Hornsby	Stl	.403	.489	.756
1928	Rogers Hornsby	Bos (NL)	.387	.498	.632
1933	Chuck Klein	Phi	.368	.422	.602
1934	Lou Gehrig	NY	.363	.465	.706
1935	Arky Vaughan	Pit	.385	.491	.607
1938	Jimmie Foxx	Bos	.349	.462	.704
1941	Ted Williams	Bos	.406	.551	.735
1942	Ted Williams	Bos	.356	.499	.648
1943	Stan Musial	Stl	.357	.425	.562
1947	Ted Williams	Bos	.343	.499	.634
1948	Stan Musial	Stl	.376	.450	.702
1948	Ted Williams	Bos	.369	.497	.615
1957	Ted Williams	Bos	.388	.528	.731
1966	Frank Robinson	Bal	.316	.415	.637
1967	Carl Yasztremski	Bos	.326	.421	.622
1980	George Brett	KC	.390	.461	.664

From A Researcher's Notebook

Al Kermisch

Jim Corbett almost an Oriole in 1894

In January 1894, Ned Hanlon, manager and president of the Baltimore club of the National League, made an effort to sign Heavyweight Champion James J. Corbett as a member of the Orioles. After Corbett had successfully defended his title by knocking out Englishman Charley Mitchell at Jacksonville, Florida on January 25, 1894, Hanlon offered Corbett the then exorbitant sum of $10,000 for the season or $1,000 a week for the months of July and August. Corbett, who had theatrical commitments, expressed interest in the two month deal.

Following is an excerpt from an article that appeared in the *Baltimore Sun* on January 31, 1894:

"A special dispatch to THE SUN from Boston last night says that champion 'Jim' Corbett will probably play ball with the Baltimore Base-Ball Club during July and August of 1894. He said yesterday to THE SUN's correspondent: 'If manager Hanlon wants me during those two months I shall seriously consider the offer of $1,000 a week which he made me. I shall be disengaged for that period. My company will be idle and you may say I will come very near accepting.'

"Mr. Hanlon, who returned from New York yesterday, said when asked about his offer to Corbett: 'I first offered Corbett $10,000 for the season, which he re-

---

Al Kermisch is an original member of SABR.

fused. I then telegraphed him I would pay him $1,000 a week during July and August. The offer was made in good faith, and I shall be glad to sign him at these terms. Although the public doesn't seem to know it, Corbett is an excellent ball-player. He was noted for his heavy batting, and both Van Haltren and "Fred" Carroll, who have played with him in the California League, say he is a good outfielder and a fair pitcher. I hope he is in earnest about becoming an Oriole. My offer is still open to him and will remain so.'"

The next day Hanlon's offer to Corbett was denounced in New York by the directors and stockholders of the New York and Brooklyn clubs. They declared that if the Baltimore club insisted on it, the affair would be taken before the National League at the convention to be held in New York on February 26. Since the league frowned on it, the offer was quietly withdrawn.

As things turned out the Orioles got along very well without Corbett and surprised the baseball world by winning the first of their three successive pennants. In 1893 they had finished eighth in the 12-club league.

While Corbett did not get a chance to play in the majors, he did play a lot of minor league baseball, starting in 1895. He travelled from city to city, playing first base for the home team. He continued to play in the bushes for five years and showed a handsome profit for his barnstorming.

As Joe Murphy detailed on page 102 of last year's *Baseball Research Journal*, Jim's younger brother, Joe, was a pitcher with the Orioles for two years. In 1897, his only full season in the big leagues, he won 24 games and lost only eight. He was a holdout in 1898 and never pitched for the Orioles again. Ironically, it was Jim Corbett who urged Joe to hold out. He did not like the way Hanlon had treated his brother as far as salary was concerned.

Big swing by Pete Gray cost him a hit

Hits were hard to come by for one-armed Pete Gray in 1945—his only big league season for the St. Louis Browns. He wound up with 51 hits in 234 times at bat for a .218 average. Gray made his only visit to Griffith Stadium in Washington on May 30, 1945, when the Browns met the Senators in a Memorial Day double header.

In the second game little Marino Pieretti blanked St. Louis 5-0 on five hits. In the sixth inning, Gray was sent up to bat for Nelson Potter, and the crowd of 22,021 greeted him with a thunderous ovation. Gray swung lustily at the first pitch and hit a drive toward second base. First baseman Joe Kuhel knocked the ball down but apparently had no play. But fate was against Gray. He had swung so hard at the pitch the bat hit him in the knee and pained him so much that he could not run to first base. Kuhel was able to make the play and Gray had to be satisfied with more cheers as he limped back to the dugout. That one hit could have raised his season (and major league career) average to .222.

Waddell once touted for Lt. Governor of PA

George Edward "Rube" Waddell was a great major league pitcher, but the southpaw was one of the most eccentric players in history. Considering Waddell's reputation, imagine the surprise when the *Philadelphia North American*, in a front page story on June 20, 1910, stated that a boom had been started to name Waddell for the position of lieutenant governor of Pennsylvania. What probably inspired the announcement was that it was almost a certainty that another former major league pitcher, John Tener, then a congressman, would receive the Republican nomination for governor. The *North American* commented: "It is pointed out that the two would make most harmonious running mates. Both have won fame as baseball players, and both are popular with the liquor interests. How Rube has distinguished himself at times by acting as a bar tender is a matter of history."

Efforts to contact Waddell proved unsuccessful. At the time he was under suspension by the St. Louis Browns for breaking training rules. But the Rube was

heard from the next day and said: "Sure, I'll take it." When certain factions made accusations that the boom for Waddell was not sincere, the *North American* offered to put up $10,000 that if Waddell got the nomination for lieutenant governor he would be elected.

Several days later the Republicans did pick Tener for governor, but a veteran politician, John W. Reynolds, was picked for the other spot. Officially, it was announced that Waddell's acceptance was received after the slate had already been picked. When Waddell heard of his rejection he went berserk and took it out on Mrs. Waddell. He said his wife had put him under a spell and that he was only playing crack-the-whip with her when the landlady interrupted and called the police. A charge of cruelty was entered against Waddell and he was released on bail. At the time of his arrest, Rube's capital consisted of 25 cents, four pairs of cuff buttons, two letters, and a can opener.

On June 27, Waddell appeared in Police Court and was fined $150, but when he said he had no money the judge allowed him to sign a pledge promising to abstain from the use of liquor for one year and, if he broke the pledge, he would spend a year in the workhouse. Waddell signed the papers while his wife maintained a chilly and ominous silence. By August Waddell had drifted to the minors and never pitched in the majors again. In November, Tener was elected governor of Pennsylvania.

Eddie Cicotte had sore arm in 1919

In recent years there has been much speculation as to why Eddie Cicotte, White Sox pitching ace, pitched only several times after September 5, 1919. One theory, highly publicized, was that White Sox owner Charley Comiskey kept him out of games so that he would not qualify for a bonus for winning 30 games. Probably a better answer is that Cicotte had a sore arm and was rested so that he would be at his best for the World Series. The Cleveland *Plain Dealer* expanded on that theory in the following story on September 17, 1919:

"Philadelphia, September 16—The mystery has been solved. The Indians have discovered why it is that Eddie Cicotte, the star pitcher of the White Sox, has not worked since Sept. 5, when he beat the Indians. His arm, which bothered him in that game, causing him to pass six batsmen, an unusually large number for him, has troubled him ever since.

"He thought yesterday that it was nearly right and planned to pitch against the Athletics, but after

THE BASEBALL RESEARCH JOURNAL

warming up he declared it did not feel good enough to warrant his going in.

"He told friends it was not lame, but very tired. Gleason is confident his big winner will be rested enough when the World Series starts."

On September 19, Cicotte defeated the Red Sox 3-2 on seven hits at Boston. After the game, he was allowed to go to his home in Detroit for five days. He came back to Chicago on September 24 and started the game in which the White Sox clinched the pennant by defeating the St. Louis Browns 8-5. Cicotte gave up ten hits and five runs in seven innings, and the Browns led 5-4 when he departed. Chicago rallied to win the game and little Dickie Kerr was the winning pitcher.

On Sunday, September 28, the final day of the season, Cicotte started against Detroit and gave up three hits and one run in two innings, and was ahead 2-1 when he left the game. The Tigers won the game 10-9, with Roy Wilkinson taking the loss. It is likely that if there had been a big bonus riding on Cicotte's winning one more game to give him 30 victories, he would have continued pitching in the games of September 24 and 28, since he was only one run behind in the first and had a 2-1 lead in the second.

Pitcher George Cobb walked five times in game

George W. Cobb pitched just one year in the majors and posted a mediocre 10-37 record with the last place Baltimore Orioles of the National League in 1892. One of Cobb's infrequent victories came on August 10, 1892, when he defeated Washington 7-2 on seven hits in a game in Baltimore. But Cobb accomplished something that afternoon that should have won him a spot in the record book for most bases on balls in a game by a pitcher. Cobb came to bat five times and walked all five times. He was passed once by Alex Jones and four times by Frank Killen.

Not much is known about Cobb. His record in the baseball encyclopedias doesn't show much personal information other than to state that he was born in San Francisco. Cobb pitched for San Francisco and Oakland before he joined the Orioles, and later settled in California. It's more likely, however, that he was born in Iowa, where he graduated from college. He died in Pomona, California on August 2, 1926, at age 63. At the time of his death he was secretary of the Los Angeles County Fair Association.

Walter Johnson worked overtime in 1918

In 1918 there were no long relievers, short relievers, set-up men or closers in major league baseball.

Pitchers usually were expected to finish what they started. For Walter Johnson, Washington's great hurler, it also meant working a great deal of overtime.

Johnson started 29 games and finished them all, winning 20 and losing nine. No fewer than nine of his 29 games went into extra innings, Johnson winning six and losing three. He won games of 18, 15, 14, 13, 11, and 10 innings. He lost games of 18, 11, and 10 innings. Walter won three of four extra-inning games at home and three of five on the road. His only Washington loss in overtime came when Boston's Babe Ruth hit a two-run home run in the 10th inning to beat him 3-1.

Johnson's extra inning games as starting pitcher in 1918:

May 15—At Washington. Defeated White Sox 1-0 in 18 innings.

June 2—At Cleveland. Lost to Indians 1-0 in 11 innings.

June 21—At New York. Defeated Yankees 3-2 in 13 innings.

June 30—At Washington. Lost to Red Sox 3-1 in 10 innings.

July 16—At Washington. Defeated Indians 4-3 in 11 innings.

July 25—At St. Louis. Defeated Browns 1-0 in 15 innings.

July 31—At Chicago. Defeated White Sox 3-2 in 10 innings.

August 4—At Detroit. Lost to Tigers 7-6 in 18 innings.

August 19—At Washington. Defeated Browns 3-2 in 14 innings.

Orioles' Lefty Grove sparkled against big leaguers

During his four and a half years with Jack Dunn's International League Orioles, Robert Moses (Lefty) Grove won 109 games against only 36 defeats for a percentage of .752. Baltimore won seven straight pennants from 1919 through 1925, and Dunn was able to keep his star players because he successfully fought the major league draft and satisfied his players with top salaries. After the 1924 season, Dunn finally sold Grove to Connie Mack's Athletics for $100,600. No doubt, Grove's performance in exhibition games against major league opposition during his last three seasons with the Orioles convinced Mack that Lefty had the stuff to eventually become a big winner in the majors.

On September 28, 1922, Grove was impressive in losing to the New York Giants 4-3 at Oriole Park. He gave up seven hits and fanned 12. Then on Septem-

110

ber 27, 1923, the Giants again visited Oriole Park and Lefty defeated them 4-3 in 10 innings, allowing nine hits while fanning nine. Four days later, the Yankees visited Baltimore and were blanked by the Orioles 4-0. Grove pitched the first three innings and held the Yanks hitless, striking out six while walking only one. Two days later at the Polo Grounds, New York, the Giants caught up with Grove as they defeated the Orioles 9-3 in a benefit game for John B. Day and Jim Mutrie, owner and manager of the first team in New York bearing the name Giants. Lefty gave up five runs, four hits and three bases on balls in the three innings he worked, including home runs to Emil Meusel and George Kelly. The Oriole defense was shaky as Dick Porter, playing short in place of Joe Boley, committed three errors. The Giants were augmented for this game by Babe Ruth, Aaron Ward, and Elmer Smith of the Yankees. After Grove left the game, Ruth homered off Jack Ogden. In the Giant lineup were eight players who made the Hall of Fame as players or managers—Ruth, Dave Bancroft, Travis Jackson, Frank Frisch, Hack Wilson, Casey Stengel, Kelly and Bill Terry. Grove faced Ruth eleven times in exhibitions and fanned the home run king nine times.

In 1924, Grove had two great games against the big leaguers in Baltimore. On August 19, he defeated the Chicago White Sox 9-3 on eight hits and 14 strikeouts. And on September 3, he shut out the Athletics 5-0 on two hits, fanning 13 and not walking a batter. After the game, Mack stated that Grove was one of the best southpaws he had ever seen.

For his entire minor league career and also his first major league season Lefty was "Groves" in all box scores and league records. It was not until the spring training session of 1926 that James C. Isaminger, baseball writer for the *Philadelphia Inquirer*, discovered that the "s" in Lefty's name was superfluous and in his story of February 22, 1926, he included the following:

"Fans, proof readers and copy readers, lend me your ears! A great injustice has been inflicted on a nation-ally known southpaw by misspelling his name. The correct moniker is Robert Moses Grove and "s" is superfluous and incorrect. Grove not Groves. Let this sink in. Grove is meeting with the same experience of Mathewson, Dolan, Harriss and several others who were in the game a long time before their names were printed the way it is spelled in the family bible."

Louisville's Long of 1888 was not Danny

Danny Long, a fleet-footed outfielder in his playing days, mostly on the Pacific Coast, played briefly in the majors with the Baltimore American Association club in 1890. Long's record in the baseball encyclopedias also includes one game for Louisville, American Association, on August 29, 1888. On that day, however, Long was playing for Oakland in the California League.

Then who was the player named Long in the Louisville lineup in the first game of a double header against the Athletics at Philadelphia that afternoon? The *Philadelphia Press* noted that "Long, late of the Athletic Reserves, guarded left field for Louisville." On March 15, 1889, the *Philadelphia Inquirer*, commenting on the strong team that the Chester Base Ball Association had put together, included among the players signed "Tom and Harry Long, late of the Athletic Reserves, who played with the team last season." Since Harry was an outfielder he could have been the Long who played with Louisville on August 29, 1888.

Getting back to Danny Long, he became an outstanding scout after his days as player and minor league manager were over. He scouted for the Chicago White Sox for many years. He discovered Frank Chance on the sandlots of Fresno. Among the others he recommended to the majors were Hal Chase, Ping Bodie, Buck Weaver, Duffy Lewis, Oscar Vitt, Swede Risberg, Gavvy Cravath and Willie Kamm. Long was crushed to death by a commuter train at Sausalito, California on the evening of April 30, 1929. He was 61 years old when he died.

For more than 20 years, the Society for American Baseball Research has published unique, insightful, entertaining literature. In addition to SABR's annual publications, *Baseball Research Journal* and *The National Pastime*, special issues have focused on specific aspects of baseball history. For further reading enjoyment, consider obtaining other SABR publications.

Baseball Research Journals

____	1975 (112 pp)	$3.00
____	1976 (128 pp)	$4.00
____	1977 (144 pp)	$4.00
____	1978 (160 pp)	$4.00
____	1979 (160 pp)	$5.00
____	1980 (180 pp)	$5.00
____	1981 (180 pp)	$5.00
*	1982 (184 pp)	
*	1983 (188 pp)	

larger format

____	1984 (88 pp)	$6.00
____	1985 (88 pp)	$6.00
____	1986 (88 pp)	$6.00
____	1987 (88 pp)	$6.00
____	1988 (88 pp)	$7.00
____	1989 (88 pp)	$8.00
____	1990 (88 pp)	$8.00
____	1991 (88 pp)	$8.00
____	1992 (96 pp)	$7.95
____	1993 (112 pp)	$9.95

Baseball Historical Review

____ 1981; Best of '72-'74
Baseball Research Journals.......$6.00

Index to SABR Publications

____ 1987 (58 pp).............$3.00
The National Pastime, BRJ &
SABR Review of Books I

The Negro Leagues Book

____ 1994 (382 pp, softcover).......$29.95
The most extensive research published
on the Negro Leagues, illustrated with
many never before published photos.

____ 1994 (382 pp, hardcover).......$49.95

The National Pastime

____	#1 Fall, 1982 (88 pp)	$5.00
*	#2 Fall, 1983 (88 pp)	
____	#3 Spring 1984 (88 pp)	
	19th Century Pictorial	$7.00
____	#4 Spring 1985 (88 pp)	$6.00
____	#5 Winter, 1985 (88 pp)	$6.00
____	#6 Spring, 1986 (88 pp)	
	Dead Ball Era Pictorial	$8.00
____	#7 Winter, 1987 (88 pp)	$6.00
____	#8 Spring, 1988 (80 pp)	
	Nap Lajoie Biography	$8.00
*	#9 1989 (88 pp)	
____	#10 Fall, 1990 (88 pp)	$8.00
____	#11 Fall, 1991 (88 pp)	$7.95
____	#12 Summer, 1992 (96 pp)	
	The International Pastime	$7.95
____	#13 Summer, 1993 (96 pp)	$7.95
____	#14 Summer, 1994 (112 pp)	$9.95

Nineteenth Century Stars

____ 1988 (144 pp)...............$10.00
Bios of America's First Heroes
(Non-Hall of Fame players)

Baseball in the Nineteenth Century

____ 1986 (26 pp) An Overview......$2.00

The Federal League of 1914-15

____ 1989 (64 pp).................$12.00
Baseball's Third Major League

SABR Review of Books

Articles of Baseball Literary Criticism

____	Volume 1, 1986	$6.00
____	Volume 2, 1987	$6.00
____	Volume 3, 1988	$6.00
____	Volume 4, 1989	$7.00
*	Volume 5, 1990	

Baseball Records Update 1993

____ 1993 ....$4.95

Minor League Baseball Stars

____ Volume I, 1978 (132 pp).......$5
*Year-by-year record of 170 minor
league greats*
____ Volume II, 1984 (158 pp).......$5
20 managers and 180 players
____ Volume III, 1992 (184 pp).....$9.
250 players

Minor League History Journal

a publication of SABR's Minor League Commi

____	Volume 1 (40 pp)	$6
____	Volume 2 (54 pp)	$6
____	Volume 3 (72 pp)	$7

Saint Louis's Favorite Sport

____ 1992 Convention Publication
(64 pp)...............$7.

A History of San Diego Baseball

____ 1993 Convention Publication
(40 pp)...............$7.

Texas is Baseball Country

____ 1994 Convention Publication
(48 pp)...............$5.

Award Voting

____ 1988 (72 pp).............$7.
History & listing of MVP, Rookie
of the Year & Cy Young Awards

Cooperstown Corner

Columns From The Sporting News by Lee Alle
____ 1990 (181 pp).............$10.

Run, Rabbit, Run

Tales of Walter "Rabbit" Maranville
____ 1991 (96 pp).............$9.

Baseball: How to Become a Player

by John Montgomery Ward (reprint of 1889)
____ 1993 (149pp).............$9.

* - out of print